CAMBRIDGE

EMPOWER
SECOND EDITION
STUDENT'S BOOK
WITH EBOOK

"You had better hurry up"
↳ = you better

overcast day - cloudy

C1
ADVANCED

Adrian Doff, Craig Thaine
Herbert Puchta, Jeff Stranks, Peter Lewis-Jones
with Mark Hancock and Wayne Rimmer

CAMBRIDGE

EMPOWER SECOND EDITION is a six-level general English course for adult and young adult learners, taking students from beginner to advanced level (CEFR A1 to C1). *Empower* combines course content from Cambridge University Press with validated assessment from the experts at Cambridge Assessment English.

Empower's unique mix of engaging classroom materials and reliable assessment enables learners to make consistent and measurable progress.

Content you love.

Assessment you can trust.

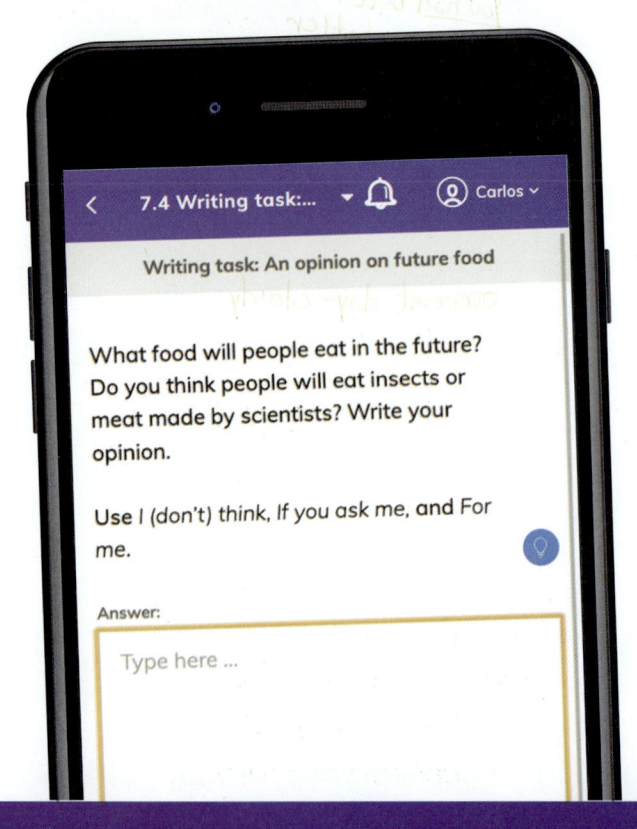

Better Learning with *Empower*

Better Learning is our simple approach where insights we've gained from research have helped shape content that drives results.

Learner engagement

1 Content that informs and motivates

Insights
Sustained motivation is key to successful language learning and skills development.

Content
Clear learning goals, thought-provoking images, texts and speaking activities, plus video content to arouse curiosity.

Results
Content that surprises, entertains and provokes an emotional response, helping teachers to deliver motivating and memorable lessons.

2 Personalised and relevant

Insights
Language learners benefit from frequent opportunities to personalise their responses.

Content
Personalisation tasks in every unit make the target language more meaningful to the individual learner.

Results
Personal responses make learning more memorable and inclusive, with all students participating in spontaneous spoken interaction.

> "There are so many adjectives to describe such a wonderful series, but in my opinion it's very reliable, practical and modern."
>
> Zenaide Brianez, Director of Studies, Instituto da Língua Inglesa, Brazil

Measurable progress

1 Assessment you can trust

Insights
Tests developed and validated by Cambridge Assessment English, the world leaders in language assessment, to ensure they are accurate and meaningful.

Content
End-of-unit tests, mid- and end-of-course competency tests and personalised CEFR test report forms provide reliable information on progress with language skills.

Results
Teachers can see learners' progress at a glance, and learners can see measurable progress, which leads to greater motivation.

Results of an impact study showing % improvement of Reading levels, based on global *Empower* students' scores over one year.

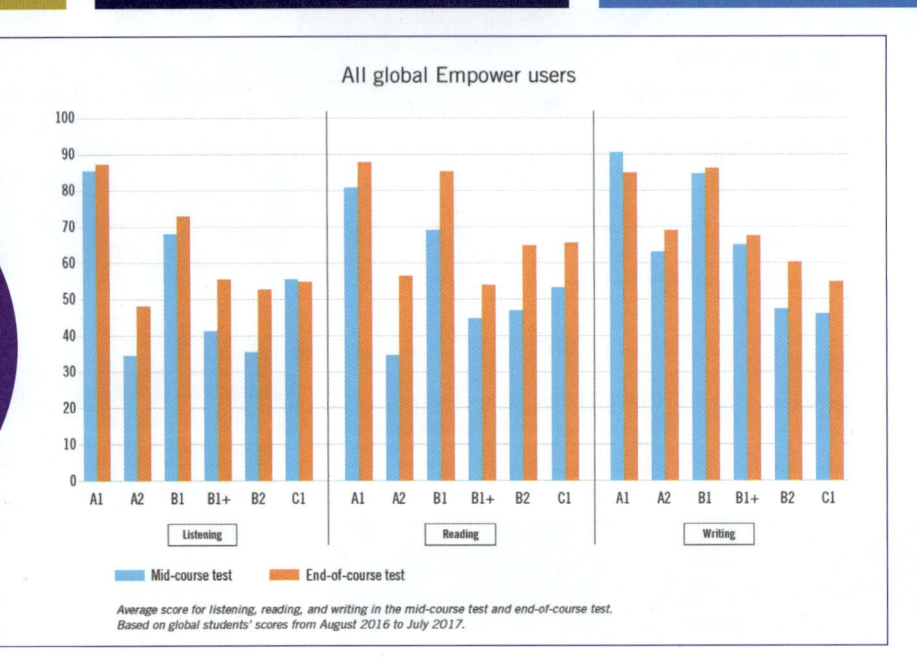

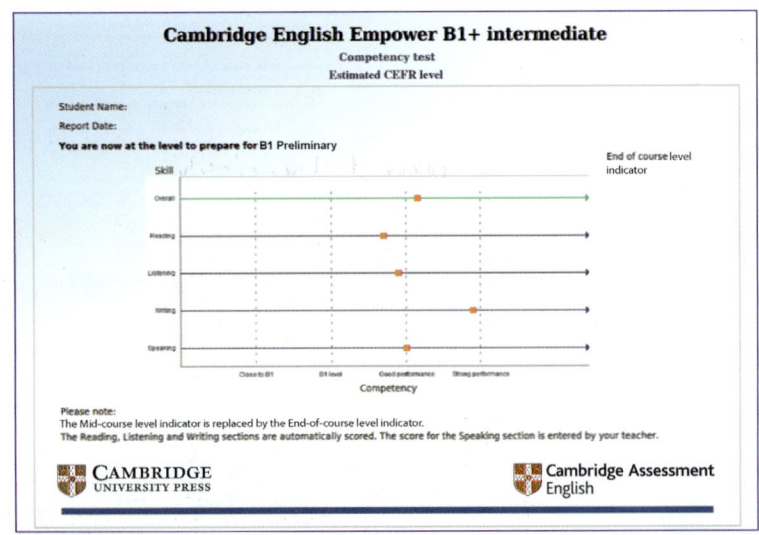

Average score for listening, reading, and writing in the mid-course test and end-of-course test. Based on global students' scores from August 2016 to July 2017.

> "We started using the tests provided with Empower and our students started showing better results from this point until now."
>
> **Kristina Ivanova, Director of Foreign Language Training Centre, ITMO University, Saint Petersburg, Russia**

2 Evidence of impact

Insights
Schools and universities need to show that they are evaluating the effectiveness of their language programmes.

Content
Empower (British English) impact studies have been carried out in various countries, including Russia, Brazil, Turkey and the UK, to provide evidence of positive impact and progress.

Results
Schools and universities have demonstrated a significant improvement in language level between the mid- and end-of-course tests, as well as a high level of teacher satisfaction with *Empower*.

Manageable learning

1 Mobile friendly

Insights
Learners expect online content to be mobile friendly but also flexible and easy to use on any digital device.

Content
Empower provides easy access to Digital Workbook content that works on any device and includes practice activities with audio.

Results
Digital Workbook content is easy to access anywhere, and produces meaningful and actionable data so teachers can track their students' progress and adapt their lesson accordingly.

> *I had been studying English for ten years before university, and I didn't succeed. But now with Empower I know my level of English has changed.*

Nikita, *Empower* Student, ITMO University, Saint Petersburg, Russia

2 Corpus-informed

Insights
Corpora can provide valuable information about the language items learners are able to learn successfully at each CEFR level.

Content
Two powerful resources – Cambridge Corpus and English Profile – informed the development of the *Empower* course syllabus and the writing of the materials.

Results
Learners are presented with the target language they are able to incorporate and use at the right point in their learning journey. They are not overwhelmed with unrealistic learning expectations.

Rich in practice

1 Language in use

Insights
It is essential that learners are offered frequent and manageable opportunities to practise the language they have been focusing on.

Content
Throughout the *Empower* Student's Book, learners are offered a wide variety of practice activities, plenty of controlled practice and frequent opportunities for communicative spoken practice.

Results
Meaningful practice makes new language more memorable and leads to more efficient progress in language acquisition.

2 Beyond the classroom

Insights
Progress with language learning often requires work outside the classroom, and different teaching models require different approaches.

Content
Empower is available with a print workbook, online practice, documentary-style videos that expose learners to real-world English, plus additional resources with extra ideas and fun activities.

Results
This choice of additional resources helps teachers to find the most effective ways to motivate their students both inside and outside the classroom.

> "There are plenty of opportunities for personalisation."
>
> Elena Pro, Teacher, EOI de San Fernando de Henares, Spain

Unit overview

Unit Opener
Getting started page – Clear learning objectives to give an immediate sense of purpose.

↓

Lessons A and B
Grammar and Vocabulary – Input and practice of core grammar and vocabulary, plus a mix of skills.

— **Digital Workbook (online, mobile):** Grammar and Vocabulary

↓

Lesson C
Everyday English – Functional language in common, everyday situations.

— **Digital Workbook (online, mobile):** Listening and Speaking

↓

Unit Progress Test

↓

Lesson D
Integrated Skills – Practice of all four skills, with a special emphasis on writing.

— **Digital Workbook (online, mobile):** Reading and Writing

↓

Review
Extra practice of grammar, vocabulary and pronunciation. Also a 'Review your progress' section for students to reflect on the unit.

↓

Mid- / End-of-course test

↓

Additional practice
Further practice is available for outside the classroom with these components:
Digital Workbook (online, mobile)
Workbook (print)

Components

Resources – Available on cambridgeone.org

- Audio
- Video
- Unit Progress Tests (print)
- Unit Progress Tests (online)
- Mid- and end-of-course assessment (print)
- Mid- and end-of-course assessment (online)
- Digital Workbook (online)
- Photocopiable Grammar, Vocabulary and Pronunciation worksheets

CONTENTS

Lesson and objective	Grammar	Vocabulary	Pronunciation	Everyday English
Unit 1 Language				
Getting started Talk about animals learning language				
1A Talk about learning a second language	Adverbs and adverbial phrases	Language learning; Noun forms	Word stress: noun forms with -tion and -ity	
1B Describe languages and how they change	The perfect aspect	Describing changes	Sentence stress	
1C Express yourself in an inexact way			Sound and spelling: ea, ee and ie	Expressing yourself in an inexact way
1D Write a web forum post				
Review and extension More practice		**WORDPOWER** Idioms: Body parts		
Unit 2 Going to extremes				
Getting started Talk about tolerance of extreme conditions				
2A Describe extreme sensory experiences	Comparison	Multi-word verbs: social interaction	Consonant–vowel linking	
2B Talk about plans, intentions and arrangements	Intentions and arrangements	Verbs of movement		
2C Give advice			Word groups and main stress; Emphatic stress	Giving advice
2D Write a report				
Review and extension More practice		**WORDPOWER** Idioms: Movement		
Unit 3 Travel and adventure				
Getting started Talk about a mishap on a road trip				
3A Emphasise positive and negative experiences	Inversion	Wealth and poverty	Intonation in inversion structures; Word stress	
3B Describe journeys and landscapes	Future in the past; Narrative tenses	Landscape features	Different pronunciations of t	
3C Paraphrase and summarise			Consonant clusters across two words	Paraphrasing and summarising
3D Write a travel review				
Review and extension More practice		**WORDPOWER** Idioms: Landscapes		
Unit 4 Consciousness				
Getting started Talk about manipulating the senses				
4A Talk about using instinct and reason	Noun phrases	Instinct and reason	Sound and spelling: /ʃəs/, /iəs/, /dʒəs/	
4B Talk about memories and remembering	Structures with have and get	Memory	Sentence stress	
4C Use tact in formal discussions			Homophones in words and connected speech	Being tactful in formal discussions
4D Write a profile article				
Review and extension More practice		**WORDPOWER** mind		
Unit 5 Fairness				
Getting started Talk about activities for prisoners				
5A Talk about crime and punishment	Relative clauses	Crime and justice	Sound and spelling: s and ss	
5B Talk about job requirements and fair pay	Obligation, necessity and permission	Employment	Word stress: nouns and verbs	
5C Recall and speculate			Main stress	Recalling and speculating
5D Write an opinion essay				
Review and extension More practice		**WORDPOWER** Idioms: Crime		

Contents

Listening	Reading	Speaking	Writing
Interview: A bilingual upbringing	Blog post: *Speaking Italian to cats*	Describing experiences of language learning Discussing language learning factors	Five pieces of advice for language learners
Monologue: The origins of words Four monologues about how languages change	Article: *How quickly is the English language changing?* Fact file: *How languages are special*	Speculating when English words originated Discussing interesting facts about your language and others	Changes in your world
Friends and rivals		Sharing rough details of an experience	✓ Unit Progress Test
Monologue: The dominance of English as a world language	Four web forum posts	Predicting the main points of a talk and discussing your predictions	Web forum post Expressing opinions
Monologue: My vow of silence	Article: *I've been to the quietest place on Earth*	Questionnaire: *How sensitive are you to sound?* Discussing different views on communication	
Interview with a base jumper	Article: *The wonder of weightlessness: A short history of zero-gravity flight*	Giving opinions on zero-gravity flights and extreme sports Discussing a blog post	Blog post: A new experience
A guest overstays his welcome		Advising a friend about a problem	✓ Unit Progress Test
Four monologues about university social programme activities	Report: Review and recommendations of a social programme committee	Discussing the merits of activities for a student social programme	Reports Linking: contrast and concession
BBC talk: The problem with volunteering, Daniela Papi	Two reviews: *Thinking of volunteering abroad?*	Discussing volunteer work abroad Describing new experiences	Blog post: An unusual travel or tourism experience
BBC audio blog: Journey of a lifetime, Will Millard	Narrative article: *Survival on the Mano River*	Telling the story of an adventurous journey	Article: An adventurous journey
A bad interview		Paraphrasing and summarising	✓ Unit Progress Test
Two monologues about Cusco	Traveller's review: *Cusco getaway*	Describing the best and worst places you have been to as a tourist Expressing an opinion about a place	Travel review Descriptive language; Writing briefly
BBC radio discussion: Gut instinct in medical diagnosis	Article: *Learn to trust your gut!*	Quiz: *Do you have a sixth sense?* Dilemmas: *Would you go with your gut instinct?*	
Three monologues about childhood memories	Article: *False childhood memories* Article: *How eyewitness evidence can be unreliable*	Talking about a childhood memory Giving an eyewitness account of a crime Discussing ways to improve memory	
Feedback and an unexpected opportunity		Giving opinions tactfully	✓ Unit Progress Test
Interview: musician Noni-K	Profile article: *Noni-K*	Asking and answering questions about being interviewed for a profile article Interviewing a classmate for a profile article	Profile article Organising information; Showing time relationships
Radio news: Bizarre crimes	Article: *Can we have a swimming pool? Life at Halden Prison*	Giving definitions of crime vocabulary Discussing punishments for crimes	
Four monologues about employment	Two job descriptions: *Bomb disposal diver* and *Pet food taster*	Discussing employment terms and conditions Exchanging information about different jobs Negotiating salaries for a range of jobs	
Opening up		Recalling and speculating	✓ Unit Progress Test
Two monologues about job applications and social media	Essay: *Social media and recruitment*	Discussing how an employer should respond to employee comments on social media	Opinion essay Essays; Linking: addition and reinforcement

3

Lesson and objective	Grammar	Vocabulary	Pronunciation	Everyday English
Unit 6 Perspectives				
Getting started Talk about the impact of 3D street art				
6A Describe photos and hobbies	Simple and continuous verbs	Adjectives: describing images		
6B Tell a descriptive narrative	Participle clauses	Emotions	Main stress and emphatic stress (adverbs and adjectives)	
6C Organise a presentation			Intonation in comment phrases	Organising a presentation
6D Write an application email				
Review and extension More practice		WORDPOWER Idioms: Feelings		
Unit 7 Connections				
Getting started Talk about technology in the classroom				
7A Speculate about inventions and technology	Speculation and deduction	Compound adjectives	Main stress: compound adjectives	
7B Emphasise opinions about the digital age	Cleft sentences	Nouns with suffixes: society and relationships	Intonation in cleft structures	
7C Apologise and admit fault			Sound and spelling: *ou* and *ough*	Apologising and admitting fault
7D Write a proposal				
Review and extension More practice		WORDPOWER *self-*		
Unit 8 Body and health				
Getting started Talk about physical activity in old age				
8A Describe sleeping habits and routines	Gerunds and infinitives	Sleep	Stress in fixed expressions	
8B Talk about lifestyles and life expectancy	Conditionals	Ageing and health	Pitch: extra information	
8C Negotiate the price of a product or service			Intonation in implied questions	Negotiating
8D Write promotional material				
Review and extension More practice		WORDPOWER *and*		
Unit 9 Cities				
Getting started Talk about an obstacle to urban development				
9A Talk about city life and urban space	Reflexive and reciprocal pronouns	Verbs with *re-*	Sound and spelling: *re-*	
9B Describe architecture and buildings	Ellipsis and substitution	Describing buildings	Word stress	
9C Deal with conflict			Sound and spelling: foreign words in English	Dealing with conflict
9D Write a discussion essay				
Review and extension More practice		WORDPOWER *build*		
Unit 10 Occasions				
Getting started Talk about an unusual wedding				
10A Give a presentation or a speech	Regret and criticism structures	Communication verbs	Word groups and main stress	
10B Talk about superstitions and rituals	Passive reporting verbs	Superstitions, customs and beliefs	Consonant clusters	
10C Take turns in more formal conversations			Intonation in question tags	Turn-taking
10D Write a film review				
Review and extension More practice		WORDPOWER *luck* and *chance*		
Communication Plus p. 127	**Grammar Focus** p. 138		**Vocabulary Focus** p. 158	

4

Contents

Listening	Reading	Speaking	Writing
Interview with an amateur photographer	Article: *Lessons Elliott Erwitt has taught me about street photography*	Discussing photography skills; Talking about your favourite photos	
News report: The conclusion of the story of the suspicious encounter	Blog post and email: Two views of a suspicious encounter	Discussing first impressions; Telling a personal story	The first part of a short story
A big presentation		Organising a presentation	✓ Unit Progress Test
Three interviews with volunteers	Advertisement: *You can help!* Application email	Talking about volunteer work in your local area	Application emails; Giving a positive impression
Three monologues: Inventions that would make the world a better place	Article: *Human augmentation – a dream or a nightmare?*	Discussing 'superpowers'; Presenting a new invention	
Radio show: *From my bookshelf*	Article: *Loneliness and temperature*	Talking about what you read online; Explaining how you would overcome a hypothetical problem	
Unsolicited suggestions		Apologising and admitting fault	✓ Unit Progress Test
Four monologues: People express their opinions of their colleagues	Proposal: A team-building programme	Ordering the personality attributes of an effective team member	Proposals; Linking: highlighting and giving examples
Radio interview with a sleep researcher; Radio phone-in programme about waking up at night	Article: *Top tips to help you sleep* Article: *The myth of the eight-hour sleep*	Discussing tips for a good night's sleep; Planning a typical day for someone with a segmented sleep pattern	
BBC interview: Living on a calorie-restricted diet	Article: *Anti-ageing treatments* Interview: *We don't have to get sick as we get older*	Discussing anti-ageing treatments; Presenting your views on health and ageing issues	
An exclusive story		Negotiating	✓ Unit Progress Test
Radio interview: The Stone Age diet	Home page: *Ancestors* restaurant	Discussing what's important when you eat out	Promotional material; Using persuasive language
Podcast: New ideas for 'smart cities'	Article: *If you want to get close to nature, head into the city* Fact file: Biophilic cities	Sharing information about initiatives to improve cities; Presenting ideas for 'smarter' cities	
Conversation: Tourist attractions	Article: *Kazuyo Sejima: Passion and precision*	Describing buildings; Presenting a proposal for the redevelopment of a derelict building	
A leak and a fall-out		Complaining and responding to complaints	✓ Unit Progress Test
Conversation: Life in a rural community in New Zealand compared to life in a city	Essay: Urban migration	Discussing rural and urban living	Discussion essay; Linking: reason and result
Three monologues about giving a presentation	Article: *Don't be boring!*	Discussing what makes a good presentation; Giving a one-minute speech: *Learning from my mistakes*	
Radio interview: Superstitions in sport	Article: *The game before the game*	Discussing superstitions, customs and beliefs; Talk about rituals you or people you know have	
A successful interview		Turn-taking	✓ Unit Progress Test
Four monologues about how people use reviews	Two film reviews: *Knives Out*	Discussing how much reviews influence your choices	Film reviews; Concise description

| Writing focus p. 169 | Verb patterns p. 176 | Phonemic symbols p. 177 | Irregular verbs p. 177 |

CAN DO OBJECTIVES

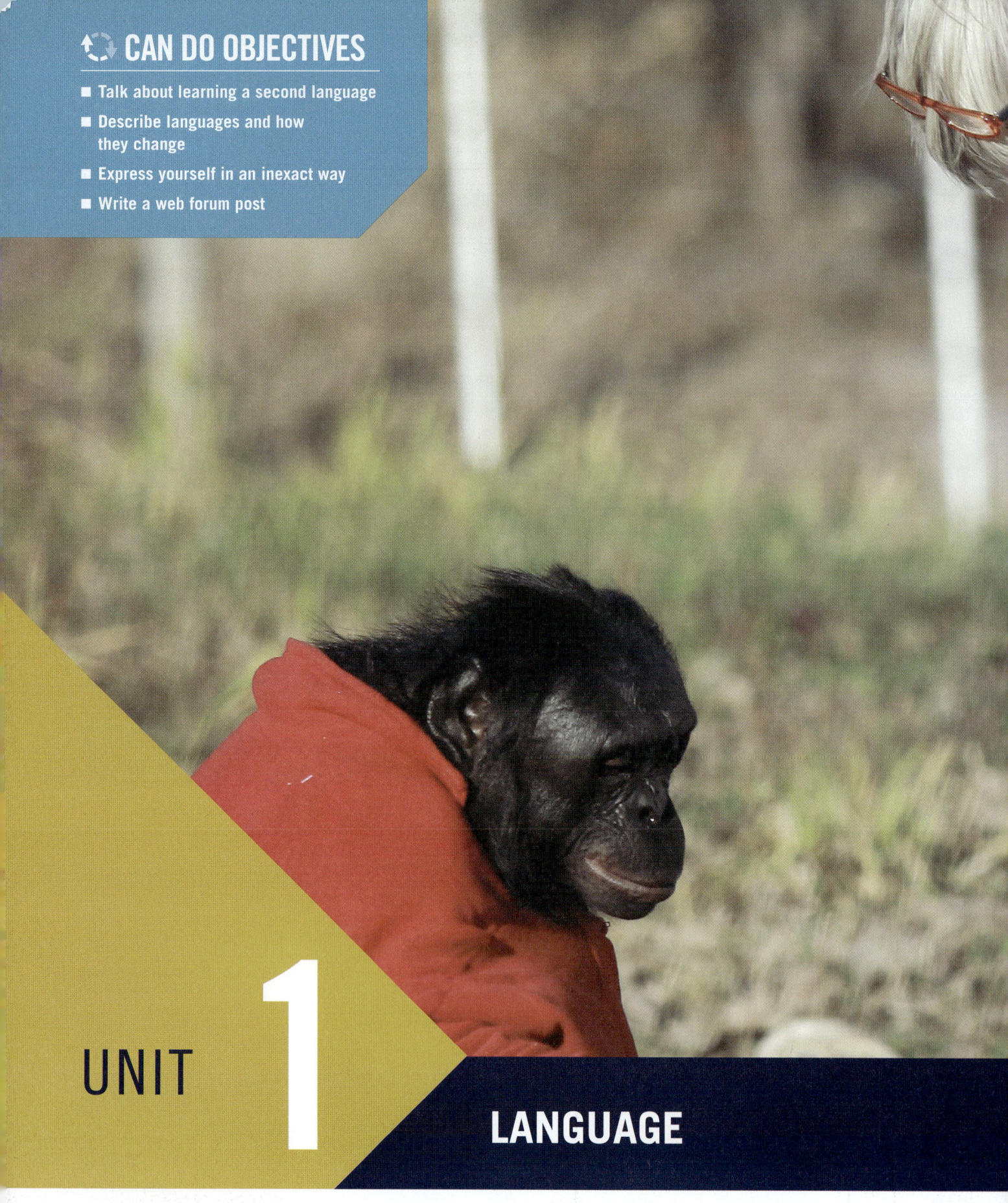

- Talk about learning a second language
- Describe languages and how they change
- Express yourself in an inexact way
- Write a web forum post

UNIT 1
LANGUAGE

GETTING STARTED

a 💬 Look at the picture and discuss the questions.
1. What do you think the ape is being taught to do? How successful do you think this will be?
2. What do you think the benefits of teaching animals language are for … ?
   - humans
   - animals
3. In what ways do you think this ape's language learning experience is similar to or different from a human's?

b 💬 Discuss the questions.
1. In what other situations do humans and animals communicate with each other?
2. Which animals are known for their ability to communicate well with humans?
3. If you could converse with any animal, which one would it be? What would you like to ask it?

7

1A I THOUGHT I COULD PICK UP ITALIAN BY EAR

Learn to talk about learning a second language

- **G** Adverbs and adverbial phrases
- **V** Language learning; Noun forms

1 READING

a Do you agree with these statements about learning a second language? Why / Why not?
1. It's helpful to get feedback from native speakers.
2. Trying to memorise words and phrases is a core part of the learning process.
3. Communicating in another language makes you feel like a more confident person.
4. Learning grammar is a waste of time – I don't even know it in my first language!
5. The biggest reward is being able to relate to people from another culture.
6. Apps on smartphones and tablets have made learning a second language much easier.
7. When you've learned one second language, it's easier to learn another.

b Read Scott's blog post about his language learning experience. Which of the statements in 1a might he agree with?

c Read the text again and discuss the questions.
1. Why do you think Scott wanted to 'put his money where his mouth was'?
2. What is the difference between learning a language by ear and studying it formally?
3. How important is a learner's motivation when learning a new language?
4. How does self-consciousness inhibit learning a new language?

LANGUAGE TEACHERS LEARNING LANGUAGE

Speaking Italian to cats

by Scott Fletcher

How I got my tongue around all those crazy Italian vowels with the help of some friendly cats and a mysterious woman on a train

When I finished my training as an English language teacher, I made a vow not to be one of those instructors who teach their native language but cannot speak another language fluently themselves. I wanted to put my money where my mouth was.

I managed to get a teaching job in the north of Italy in a small city called Aosta, right next to the French and Swiss borders, where there is great skiing. (I really love to ski.) I had studied French at school and university, but my language skills were a little rusty. At the time, I didn't speak a word of Italian, so I packed one of those 'teach yourself Italian' books in my luggage.

I flew direct to Milan, and the culture/language shock hit me as soon as I got off the plane. Still tired, I tried to memorise the phrase *Non capisco l'italiano* (I don't understand Italian), but I couldn't get it into my head. Not a great start.

Aosta is bilingual – Italian and French – and, to begin with, I brushed up on my university French and could get by. I was convinced I'd just be able to pick Italian up by ear. Being surrounded by the language and hearing it all the time meant I'd just kind of absorb it, but no such luck. After three months, I'd finally managed to remember *Non capisco l'italiano*, but not a whole lot more.

So I got out that 'teach yourself Italian' book I had packed and got started on the grammar and vocabulary. And I downloaded some Italian learning apps on my phone. It was hard work, and I struggled to grasp some of the verb tenses and vocabulary. It seemed like I would have to remember a mountain of information if I were ever going to speak properly.

I'd made friends with some students. I sort of tried to talk to them in Italian, but more often than not I got stuck. Their English was far better than my Italian. I remember going to dinner at my friend Matteo's place. His family had a couple of cats, and while Matteo was helping his mother serve up the pasta, I had my own private conversation with the cats. Matteo overheard me, laughed, and said,

'That's right, speak Italian to the cats – only they can understand you.' It was a joke, but I felt crestfallen and could feel my vow to learn another language slipping away.

A few weeks after that, I went on a trip to Venice for a weekend. On the train journey there, I met a teacher of English at a secondary school in Milan. We started chatting, and she asked me how long I'd been in Italy. By this time it was almost five months, and she smiled when I admitted that I couldn't speak Italian yet. I told her I'd been studying on my own, but I had no confidence to speak.

She then said (in Italian), 'Come on. You can speak to me.' She had a very determined look on her face, but also a warmth and friendliness that was somehow encouraging. So I took the plunge. Not very well to begin with, but I gradually began speaking in Italian with more and more confidence.

And that was my breakthrough. In the two hours it took to travel from Milan to Venice, I somehow unlocked everything I had been studying. Why? Basically, I think it had everything to do with the woman I met (I don't know her name, and I've never seen her again), but I felt less self-conscious speaking to someone who wasn't my student or my friend.

2 GRAMMAR
Adverbs and adverbial phrases

a Notice the highlighted adverbials in the text. Add them to the lists below.
1. **Comment** (used to express the speaker's point of view): *clearly, apparently, actually, basically*
2. **Degree** (used to make the meaning stronger or weaker): *very, a little, …*
3. **Manner** (used to say *how*): *slowly, on foot, …*
4. **Time** (used to say *when*): *in the eighties, overnight, …*
5. **Frequency** (used to say *how often*): *never, …*

b What position(s) can each adverbial take in these sentences? Which adverbials change meaning in different positions?
1. a in the end 1, 3   b eventually
   ^{1}I ^{2}managed to hold a conversation in Japanese ^{3}.
2. a extremely   b often
   ^{1}I ^{2}found it ^{3}difficult.
3. a frequently   b all the time
   ^{1}I ^{2}made silly mistakes ^{3}.
4. a slowly   b clearly
   ^{1}I ^{2}would like native speakers to speak to me ^{3}.
5. a naturally   b well
   ^{1}I'm ^{2}a little envious of friends who can already speak the language ^{3}.

c ▶ Now go to Grammar Focus 1A on p. 138.

When I went back to Aosta, my friends couldn't believe it. 'What happened to you?' Matteo asked. I could suddenly speak Italian. I haven't looked back since, and my confidence in speaking has grown enormously. My Italian isn't perfect, but it's fairly fluent and I know the grammar. I did, in the end, manage to put my money where my mouth was.

UNIT 1

d 💬 Think of a skill you have learned at some stage in your life. Plan to talk about it, using some of the adverbs and adverbial phrases from the reading and the box below. Make notes.

in the beginning   obviously   extremely   eventually
properly   clearly   incorrectly   naturally   in the end

Obviously, I was hopeless in the beginning.

In order to do it properly, you have to concentrate on the ball.

Playing a complete game involved a lot of walking, and I was extremely tired afterwards.

e 💬 Describe the experience you had learning the skill without naming it. Can your partner guess what skill you are talking about?

3 VOCABULARY Language learning

a Look at the underlined parts of the texts. Match the words and phrases 1–4 with the definitions a–d.
1. ☐ pick up   3. ☐ grasp
2. ☐ brush up on   4. ☐ rusty

a understand something, especially something difficult
b less able because you are out of practice
c learn something by being exposed to it
d improve your knowledge of something you've partly forgotten

b ▶ Now go to Vocabulary Focus 1A on p. 158.

c Read the questions about your English language learning background. Add two more to ask a partner.

1. When did you first start learning English?
2. How long was it before you could hold a conversation in English?
3. When did you first put your learning into practice?
4. Have you progressed as well as you expected?
5. Have you ever been immersed in an English-speaking culture? If so, what was it like? If not, is there a culture you would like to get to know?
6. How important is it to you to speak accurately? Why?
7. What level of competence would you like to attain eventually?
8. _____
9. _____

d 💬 Work in pairs. Ask and answer the questions in 3c.

UNIT 1

4 LISTENING

a 💬 Discuss the questions.
1 Think about someone you know who grew up bilingual. What was their experience like?
2 What do you think are possible advantages and disadvantages of a bilingual upbringing?
3 What are attitudes towards being bilingual like in your country?

b ▶ 01.06 Listen to Katya being interviewed about her bilingual upbringing on the podcast *Linguistically speaking*. Answer the questions.
1 Which languages does she speak?
2 What was unique about her upbringing?
3 What's her attitude to bilingualism?

c ▶ 01.06 Listen again. Are the sentences true or false? Correct the false sentences.
1 Katya realises that her upbringing was very special and different.
2 Katya's mother used both English and Russian when she spoke to Katya.
3 She wasn't really aware that she was speaking two languages when she was a child.
4 She thinks she might have had some initial problems acquiring Portuguese.
5 She went to special classes to learn to read and write in English and Russian.
6 She found it easy to fit into her school in the UK.
7 She believes being bilingual has given her an ability to concentrate on tasks.
8 She found she struggled learning Mandarin.

d 💬 Imagine you want to give your child a bilingual upbringing. What would you have to do? How easy or difficult would it be? Make notes and compare with your partner.

5 SPEAKING AND VOCABULARY Noun forms

a ▶ 01.07 Complete the sentences with the noun form of the words in brackets. Listen and check.
1 So, I got _____ (expose) to both languages right from the beginning.
2 If I wanted to communicate, I had to use Portuguese. It was a _____ (necessary).
3 There's a _____ (reluctant) on the part of some parents to let their children learn a second language.
4 And my _____ (motivate) was much higher. It's like there's a part of my brain that gets real _____ (please) from engaging with another language.

b ▶ Now go to Vocabulary Focus 1A on p. 158.

c 💬 How can these factors have an impact on learning a second language?
• the right mentality
• financial limitations
• distractions
• opportunities for interaction
• first language interference
• natural competence
• the prestige of knowing a second language

d Choose a person 1–3 from the options below and write five pieces of advice for them.
1 an English speaker who wants to learn your language
2 a friend who wants to pass a state English exam
3 a teenager who finds languages at school a turn-off

e 💬 Work in pairs. Compare your ideas in 5d and prioritise four suggestions that are useful for all language learners.

The most universally useful suggestion here is to invest in a good dictionary.

I couldn't agree more. I also think putting your learning into practice whenever you can is really important.

Katya as a child

Katya today

10

1B LANGUAGE HAS BEEN CONSTANTLY EVOLVING

Learn to describe languages and how they change
- **G** The perfect aspect
- **V** Describing changes

1 SPEAKING

a Look at these words. Which ones do you know? Tell your partner. Look up the words you don't know in a dictionary.

radio babysitter blog selfie in-joke spacecraft sudoku
ecotourism brainwash Bollywood
technophobe environmentalism

b Each word in 1a was first used in a different decade, from the 1900s to the 2010s. When do you think each word first came into the English language, and why? Put them in order.

1900s radio
1910s …

c 01.09 Listen and check your answers. What is the significance of photographs 1 and 2?

d Two more new words in English are *hangry* and *glamping*. Talk about their meanings. Do you know any other words that have come into the English language recently?

2 READING

a Read the introduction to an article about the way English has changed. Which <u>two</u> points does the writer make?
- ☐ English has become less complex over the years.
- ☐ Many changes to language take place gradually, so we may not notice them.
- ☐ Modern technology has helped us see how language is changing.

b Answer these questions.
1 What do you think the words in *italics* in paragraph 1 mean?
2 Can you think of an example of 'the annoying inconsistencies between spelling and pronunciation in English'?

c ≫ **Communication 1B** Work in pairs. Student A: Go to p. 127. Student B: Go to p. 131.

d Look at each pair of sentences below. Do the sentences show a change you read about? Explain the change to your partner.
1 a Shall we meet at 6:00?
  b Do you want to meet at 6:00?
2 a I was fired from my job.
  b I got fired from my job.
3 a She started to cry.
  b She started crying.
4 a I ought to go soon.
  b I need to be going soon.

How quickly is the English language changing?

We all know language changes. People's favourite music was *far-out* in the 1960s, *rad* in the 1980s, *wicked* in the 1990s and *awesome* in 2010. You just need to watch a film from ten years ago to hear phrases that have come and gone.

However, there are far more subtle, ongoing language changes taking place at any given time. These changes may have a hugely significant impact, but can go entirely unnoticed while they are in progress. One lasting change to English that was barely perceptible at the time is known as the Great Vowel Shift. Over a period of 350 years (from 1350 to 1700), the long vowel sounds of English drifted so far that speakers at either end of the period could not have understood each other. However, nobody noticed for about 100 years after it had happened! The Great Vowel Shift was a major contributor to the annoying inconsistencies between spelling and pronunciation in English that have plagued users ever since.

These days, no such important change would go unnoticed. Linguists can now analyse huge collections of text and transcribed speech and identify ongoing patterns of change that in the past would not have been visible for many years to come. Here are some of the less noticeable changes that are occurring in English right now:

UNIT 1

3 VOCABULARY Describing changes

a Read the sentences about language change below. Which words/phrases in **bold** tell the reader … ? You will write some numbers more than once.

a the speed of a change ☐☐☐
b that a change is in progress ☐☐
c how easy a change is to see ☐☐☐
d about something that is decreasing ☐☐
e how big or important a change is ☐☐☐
f that a change is long-term or permanent ☐
g about something that is increasing ☐☐☐☐

> One ¹**lasting** change to English that was ²**barely perceptible** at the time is known as the Great Vowel Shift.
>
> These changes may have a ³**hugely significant** impact, but can go ⁴**entirely unnoticed** while they are in progress.
>
> Here are some of the less ⁵**noticeable** changes that are occurring in English right now:
>
> There was ⁶**a steady shift** towards more frequent use of the verb + -ing, and these forms are still ⁷**on the increase**.
>
> There are far more ⁸**subtle**, ⁹**ongoing** language changes taking place at any given time.
>
> The use of continuous passive verb forms has also seen ¹⁰**a rapid rise**.
>
> Modal verbs are ¹¹**gradually giving way** to other less formal expressions.
>
> Stiff, formal words like *shall* and *ought* are ¹²**on the way out**.
>
> Words that cover the same ground, such as *going to*, *have to*, *need to* and *want to*, are ¹³**taking hold**.
>
> The use of *get* passives has ¹⁴**grown substantially**.

b 💬 Write sentences about real changes in your world. Then compare your ideas with other students.
1 something that is on the way out in your culture
2 a place that has changed substantially in recent years
3 a problem that is on the increase
4 a fashion that has taken hold recently among the younger generation
5 a subtle change to a popular product

4 LISTENING AND GRAMMAR
The perfect aspect

a ▶ 01.10 Listen to four people commenting on the article in 2a and answer the questions.
1 What kind of language change does each speaker focus on?
2 What specific examples does each speaker give?

b 💬 Are the kinds of change the speakers mentioned happening in your first language?

c ▶ 01.11 Name the underlined tenses in sentences 1–5 from the speakers' comments. Match them with uses a–e. Then listen and check.
1 ☐ Language has been changing much faster since people started using the Internet.
2 ☐ I mean, people have stopped using strict rules for punctuation.
3 ☐ In about 50 years, most dialects of English will have died out.
4 ☐ People had been taking photos of themselves before 2013, but they didn't have a single word for it.
5 ☐ The word *wireless* had had a completely different meaning: it used to mean 'radio'.

a an activity that continued prior to a definite point in time in the past
b a state that existed before a specific point in time in the past
c an action that was completed at an indefinite time in the past
d an activity that started in the past and continues until now
e an action that will be completed before a definite point in time in the future

d What do all perfect verb forms have in common? Choose the correct word to complete the rule.

> All perfect verb forms describe actions, states and processes in the time period *before* / *after* a particular point in time.

e ▶ 01.11 **Pronunciation** Listen to the sentences in 4c again and notice the pronunciation of the underlined words. What kind of words are stressed? What kind of words are usually unstressed?

f ≫ Now go to Grammar Focus 1B on p. 139.

g 💬 Talk about words in your own language. Think about:
• a word in common use now that hadn't been invented when you were a child
• a word that people have been using a lot this year
• a word that will have fallen out of use in 20 years' time
• a word that has changed its meaning.

UNIT 1

5 READING AND SPEAKING

a What is unusual about the remarks in pictures 1–3? What would you expect the people to be saying instead?

b 💬 Read the fact file and discuss the questions.
1. What do you think each fact tells us about the speakers' culture or environment? Or the way they think about the world?
2. Which language feature do you think is the most unusual?

c **Language in context** *Expressing meaning*
Read the dictionary definitions and complete the example sentences with the correct form of the highlighted words from the fact file.

1. to decide what the meaning of something is
   It's very hard to _____ the animal's behaviour.
2. to notice or understand the difference between two things
   It's very difficult to _____ **between** the twins.
3. to show the difference between things
   The thing that _____ her **from** the others is her taste in clothes.
4. to explain something more clearly by showing examples, pictures, etc.
   Why don't you include some stories to _____ your points?
5. to show, point or make clear in another way
   She shook her head to _____ that I shouldn't speak.
6. to express a thought, feeling or idea so that it is understood by other people
   Her face _____ her feelings even if her words didn't.
7. to represent an abstract quality or idea exactly
   We need a slogan that _____ the philosophy of our business.

d 💬 What facts about your own first language would you add to the fact file? Think about:
- an area of meaning where there are many more or many fewer words than in English
- an idiom that can't be translated into English
- grammar or vocabulary that might reflect the culture.

Explain your list to a partner.

e 💬 Read the opinion below. Do you agree with this opinion? Why / Why not? Discuss with your partner, giving reasons to support your answer.

Language is the main influence on how people view their world.

FACT FILE:
HOW LANGUAGES ARE SPECIAL

1 Could you move to the east a bit?

2 Stop! The light is dark!

3 A half dozen of the long, yellow, slightly curved, sweet fruit, please.

The **DANI OF NEW GUINEA** only distinguish colours from one another using two words, one for dark colours and the other for light colours.

It is believed that the **INUIT IN NORTHERN CANADA** have about 50 different words for snow and about 40 ways to distinguish different kinds of ice from one another.

ALBANIAN has 27 different words for kinds of moustaches. *Posht*, for example, means a moustache that hangs down at the ends.

HAWAIIAN LANGUAGES have 108 words for sweet potato and 47 for banana.

In the **NATIVE AMERICAN LANGUAGE HOPI**, the verbs do not differentiate between past and present. Instead, the forms of its verbs convey how the speaker came to know the information.

GUUGU YIMITHIRR, a language spoken in northeast Australia, does not have words for 'left' and 'right' as directions at all. Instead, they use north, south, east and west. When they want someone to turn while driving, they'll say, for example, 'Turn a little bit west'.

In the language of **THE MARQUESAN ISLANDS**, directions are indicated with reference to geographical features – which can make them hard to interpret if you don't know exactly where you are. For example, a Marquesan might say that your bicycle is 'downstream of the house' or that you should 'Walk inland, then seaward' to get to your destination.

UNTRANSLATABLE
Most languages have unique words and idioms that are impossible to translate exactly. These words often embody the culture of the people who speak the language. Some examples that illustrate this:

ENGLISH: *cosy* = pleasantly warm and comfortable
GERMAN: *fernweh* = a longing to be somewhere far away
JAPANESE: *mono no aware* = a gentle sadness at the impermanence of things
DUTCH: *uitwaaien* = walking in windy weather for fun
GREEK: *parea* = a group of friends who meet to share ideas and experiences
KIVILA (PAPUA NEW GUINEA): *mokita* = the truth that everyone knows but nobody talks about

13

1C EVERYDAY ENGLISH
Something along those lines

Learn to express yourself in an inexact way
- S Share rough details of an experience
- P Sound and spelling: *ea*, *ee* and *ie*

1 LISTENING

a Discuss the questions.
1 Have you or someone you know worked with a colleague for a long time? Who? How long?
2 What characterises a good working relationship?

b Answer the questions about the picture.
1 Where do you think Sara and Alex work?
2 What do you think their relationship is?
3 What do you think their conversation will be about? Why?

c 01.15 Watch or listen to Part 1 and check your answers in 1b. How and why does Alex think Sara can help him?

d Language in context *Irony and understatement*

1 Match Sara's and Alex's comments a–d with situations 1–4.
   a ☐ Full of the joys of spring, I see!
   b ☐ Don't sound so pleased to see me!
   c ☐ It's not exactly good news.
   d ☐ That'd be something of a surprise.

   1 Sara is expecting the exact opposite to happen.
   2 Alex notices that Sara's greeting is not enthusiastic.
   3 Alex sees that Sara looks unhappy.
   4 Sara has received a worrying message.

2 Why do you think Sara and Alex don't say exactly what they mean? Do people do the same in your culture?

e 01.16 Watch or listen to Part 2. What is the relationship between … ?
- Nadia and Sara
- Sara and Oscar
- Alex and Emma

f 01.16 Answer the questions. Watch or listen to Part 2 again and check your answers.
1 What does Nadia want to talk about?
2 Why does she mention Oscar?
3 What does Nadia want from Sara?
4 What does Alex suggest is Nadia's reason for speaking to Sara?
5 What help does Sara ask Alex for?
6 What's Sara's impression of Emma?

g Discuss the questions about Parts 1 and 2.
1 What do you know about the company Sara and Alex work for? Do you think Sara and Alex do similar jobs?
2 How do you think Sara feels at the end of this episode?
3 What would be a suitable title for this episode of the story?

UNIT 1

2 USEFUL LANGUAGE Expressing yourself in an inexact way

a In informal conversations, we often express things in an inexact way. Read sentences 1–4. Which character said each one? Match the expressions in **bold** with their uses a–d.

1 ☐ 'please' and 'thank you' and **stuff like that**
2 ☐ Max **whatshisname**
3 ☐ six authors, **give or take**
4 ☐ I'm out of here, or **words to that effect**

a used to give an inexact amount
b used to report someone's words in an inexact way
c used when you can't remember someone's name exactly
d used to refer to things of a similar type in an inexact way

b Which three expressions in **bold** below could you use in 1–4 in 2a? Rewrite three ideas in 2a, changing the word order if necessary.

1 There were **somewhere in the region of** 100 people.
2 She said **something along those lines**.
3 **Whatshername** was late, as usual.
4 I need **some bits and pieces** from the shop.
5 I said I'd give **thingy** a lift.

Which two expressions can't you use in 2a? Why not? Match them to their uses:

a ☐ used to refer to things of different kinds
b ☐ used when you can't remember a woman's name exactly.

c Rewrite these sentences using expressions from 2a and b.

1 William Shakespeare, who wrote *Romeo and Juliet*.
2 I went to the market and bought three items.
3 She told me to go away, saying, 'Please would you leave now?'
4 I know a little Polish – 'hello', 'goodbye', the numbers one to ten.
5 I've been to 15 countries.

d ▶ 01.17 Listen and compare your answers in 2c. Are they the same? Practise different ways of saying each sentence in 2b and c.

3 PRONUNCIATION
Sound and spelling: *ea*, *ee* and *ie*

a ▶ 01.18 Listen to the words in the box. What sound do the letters in **bold** make? Is this sound always spelt with two letters?

pl**ea**sed   m**ee**ting   d**e**cent   ser**ie**s

b ▶ 01.19 The spellings *ea*, *ee* and *ie* are not always pronounced with the vowel sound in 3a. Listen and put the words in this box in the correct column 2–6.

cheerful   bear   research   great   friend

1 /iː/	2 /e/	3 /eɪ/	4 /eə/	5 /ɪə/	6 /ɜː/

c ▶ 01.20 What sound do *ea*, *ee* and *ie* have in the words in this box? Add them to the sound groups in 3b. Listen and check. Practise saying the words.

learn   Greek   hear   heard   meaning   meant
increase   steadily   niece   pierce   idea   break
breakfast   early   pear   career   meet

Which is the only short sound in 3b?

4 SPEAKING

a ▶ 01.21 Listen and answer the questions.
1 What experience does the speaker talk about?
2 The speaker says 'the full horror of the situation' dawned on her. What is she referring to?

b ▶ 01.21 Listen again and write down the expressions from 2a and b that you hear.

c Work alone. Plan to talk about an experience you have had, and make notes. Decide what exact details you will give, and what you will mention in an inexact way. Here are some ideas:
- a time when you got to know someone new on a long journey
- a time when you travelled somewhere new on the spur of the moment
- a time when you made an unplanned purchase

d 💬 Work with a partner. Take turns to talk about your experience. Use expressions from 2a and b to mention things in an inexact way.

✓ UNIT PROGRESS TEST

→ CHECK YOUR PROGRESS

YOU CAN NOW DO THE UNIT PROGRESS TEST.

15

1D SKILLS FOR WRITING
You're spot on there!

Learn to write a web forum post

W Expressing opinions

1 SPEAKING AND LISTENING

a Look at these borrowed words from English used in other languages. Why do you think they are used?

1 džús (Slovakian)
2 outdoor (Portuguese, Brazil)
3 lonche (Spanish, Mexico)
4 maiku (Japanese)
5 gol (Spanish)
6 biznismyen (Russian)
7 kampyutara (Hindi)

b Write down some examples of English words that are commonly used in your language. Then discuss the questions.
1 What are the main topic areas of borrowed English words in your language?
2 How do you / people in your country feel about adopted English words?

c You will hear a linguist, Maxwell Kingsley, talking about the dominance of English as a world language. What do you think he will say about the following?
1 the number of people that speak English
2 English as an easy language to learn
3 the Latin language
4 English's effect on the diversity of human languages
5 the only real disadvantage of the dominance of English
6 English as a truly global language

d 01.22 Listen and check. Make notes. Are there any points he makes that you find surprising?

2 READING

a Read the posts on a web forum. Which two people agree with each other?

b Which post … ?
- do you agree with most, and why
- do you think makes the most interesting point

3 WRITING SKILLS Expressing opinions

a Which elements A–E are used by each writer in the web forum?
A agreeing/disagreeing with a previous comment
B stating a new opinion on the topic
C describing cultural trends to support an opinion
D including personal experience to support an opinion
E making a summarising statement

b Write the highlighted phrases in the posts in the correct part of the table.

Disagreement	Agreement
That simply isn't true. That's easy to say, but … How can you possibly think that? That's a load of rubbish. 1 _____ 2 _____ 3 _____	That makes a lot of sense. You've hit the nail on the head. I would go along with that 5 _____
Uncertainty	**Partial agreement / disagreement**
I've got mixed feelings about this. 4 _____	You've got a point, but … It's true that … , but … On the other hand, I do feel … 6 _____

c Look again at the highlighted phrases for disagreement in the forum. Answer the questions.
1 What phrases do the writers use to soften the disagreement phrases?
2 Do you know any other words and phrases for softening your opinions?

d Look at all the expressions in the table. Which ones are informal? Use a dictionary to help you.

e Now go to Writing Focus 1D on p. 169.

Maxwell Kingsley makes the point that although English has become the dominant world language, this isn't a threat to other languages. Do you think he's right?

FLYING B

I'm in two minds about this.
I agree up to a point that there's a benefit to be had from a shared global language – especially the opportunity to travel and speak to other people without constantly having to learn other languages. On the other hand, as people have said elsewhere, I do feel the dominance of English interferes with the uniqueness of many languages, for example, the way words are borrowed from English.

The world is made infinitely more fascinating by having a variety of cultures. Different histories, cuisines, habits, styles of communication ... A huge part of this is our many unique languages and dialects.

Using the English language is by no means the only thing that's been undermining this uniqueness, but it clearly contributes to it.

REPLY →

ÖMER

If you ask me, that's nonsense. I've lived in various countries, and people speak their own languages 99% of the time.
Many do speak English as a second language for international communication, but as far as I can tell, that doesn't have much impact on their cultural identity. It's true that people are constantly bombarded with English slang and popular buzzwords, but they don't matter that much.

Most non-native speakers see English as a simple tool, but they don't use it when they need to convey subtle details and differences.

REPLY →

GABRIELA

Great comment, you're spot on there!
I speak English fluently, but I use Spanish (and Portuguese!) in everyday life, and, as far as I'm concerned, there's no way English is taking over my life. We all know it's a global language, but so what? Some language has to be. I get a lot out of being able to use English, but I'm never going to stop using my own language. Why would I? I don't quite get what the fuss is about here.

REPLY →

HARU

It seems to me all of you are missing the point here. Even if English does replace other languages, it's not the end of the world – just the opposite, in fact. I think that having one international language is a great way to help unify the world and the human race in general. How can we expect cultures to keep peace between each other when they can't understand each other? Unique languages tend to isolate those communities that are most likely to be economically weak.

Our heritage is only history, and history will never and can never be more important than the present or the future.

REPLY →

UNIT 1

f Compare Flying B's and Gabriela's posts. Whose comments are more formal and abstract, and whose are more informal and personal? How can you tell? Think about:
- abstract nouns
- sentence length and structure
- personal examples
- questions and exclamation marks
- colloquial expressions
- first person.

g What style of comment would you post on this forum: formal and abstract or informal and personal? Why?

> 💬 **Writing Tip**
> In order to write good discussion forum comments:
> - Choose a style and keep to it. It can be informal and chatty or it can be more formal and serious, but it's better not to mix different styles together.
> - Before you respond to a comment, read it carefully to make sure your response is relevant.
> - Even if you strongly disagree with someone, try not to be impolite.

4 WRITING

a Read the opinions below and tick (✓) the ones you agree with.

1 ☐ "Countries need to protect their language from the influx of English words."

2 ☐ "The effect of English on other languages has been more positive than negative."

3 ☐ ""International English" used by non-native speakers is destroying the English language."

4 ☐ "If you want to work for an international company, you should learn English."

b Choose one of the opinions and start a discussion forum. Write a comment of about five or six sentences giving your point of view.

c Share your post with another student. Read another student's post and add a comment. It can be a response or a further comment on the topic.

d Respond to or comment on three other posts.

e Read the discussion forum that you started. Which comment do you think is the most interesting?

UNIT 1
Review and extension

1 GRAMMAR

a Correct seven mistakes with adverbials. Sometimes more than one answer is possible.

1 Please slowly try to speak.
2 He will be probably late.
3 We do by hand our washing.
4 We will be living in June in Paris.
5 She made me so loudly laugh.
6 I in the end managed to get in touch.
7 You can compare easily the different brands.

b Choose the correct options.

1 I *have never visited / never visit* an English-speaking country before.
2 *I've been learning / I'm learning* English for ages.
3 I *had been crossing / was crossing* the road when the car hit me.
4 I *have wanted / wanted* to give up at the beginning but kept studying.
5 She *has had / has* her hair cut. Doesn't it look nice?
6 I *had been studying / was studying* for five hours when you got home.

2 VOCABULARY

a Replace the words in *italics* with an expression in the box.

acquire   rusty   brush up on   get to grips with
hold a conversation   immerse yourself in   struggle with

1 Sally really used to *have problems with* phrasal verbs.
2 The best way to learn is to *fully get to know* the culture.
3 Vladimir is amazing: he can *talk* with anyone in English.
4 How do young children *learn* their first language?
5 I'd better *improve* my French before the trip.
6 I can't *understand the complexities of* German grammar.
7 Mum's Spanish must be *worse than it was*.

b Complete the words with the missing letters.

1 Her popularity with teens has seen a r_____d rise.
2 Even a s_____e change in his hairstyle gets comments.
3 There has been a steady s_____t towards part-time work.
4 This will not result in a l_____g change.
5 Black jeans are on the w_____y out.
6 The o_____g changes are affecting productivity.
7 Perhaps the benefits will not be p_____e for a while.

3 WORDPOWER Idioms: Body parts

a ▶ 01.23 Complete the idioms with the words in the box. Listen and check.

shoulders   hands   tooth   nose   tongue   head   neck

1 Mark obviously **has a** _____ **for** business investment; he has never lost us any money yet.
2 I walked across to the photographers, shouting and yelling. I completely **lost my** _____.
3 Colleagues regard Mika as **a safe pair of** _____ who can be relied upon to step in when required.
4 It may happen, but I certainly wouldn't **stick my** _____ **out** and promise anything.
5 After five years' training for this event, he's **head and** _____ **above** the competition.
6 I had to **bite my** _____ when my manager took credit for my work.
7 I will **fight** _____ **and nail** to prevent any scheme which threatens local livelihoods.

b Match the idioms 1–7 in 3a with definitions a–g.

a ☐ take a risk
b ☐ try very hard to overcome opposition and get something you want
c ☐ be good at finding a specific thing
d ☐ stop yourself from saying something
e ☐ lose control of your behaviour
f ☐ someone other people trust to do a good job
g ☐ be a lot better than other competitors

c Complete the questions with the idioms in 3a.

1 In what situations do you think it's important to _____ out?
2 Who do you know who has _____ for something?
3 Who's an actor you think is _____ above most others?
4 How do you react if someone you know loses _____ in front of you?
5 What's something you would fight _____ to prevent?
6 In what situations do you think people should _____ tongues?
7 Who do you know who's a _____ in an emergency?

d 💬 Discuss the questions in 3c.

🔄 REVIEW YOUR PROGRESS

How well did you do in this unit? Write 3, 2 or 1 for each objective.
3 = very well   2 = well   1 = not so well

I CAN …	
talk about learning a second language	☐
describe languages and how they change	☐
express myself in an inexact way	☐
write a web forum post.	☐

CAN DO OBJECTIVES

- Describe extreme sensory experiences
- Talk about plans, intentions and arrangements
- Give advice
- Write a report

UNIT 2

GOING TO EXTREMES

GETTING STARTED

a Look at the picture and answer the questions.
1 Where is the man? Why do you think he's swimming there?
2 What are the possible risks of swimming there? What skills and attributes do you think a person swimming there needs?
3 What do you think this man does immediately after his swim?
4 Would you consider swimming in this location? Why / Why not?

b Discuss the questions.
1 Imagine you're about to interview this man for the local newspaper. Make a list of questions to ask him. Ask your partner and answer their questions.
2 What's the coldest/hottest experience you've ever had? Describe it to your partner.

19

2A I WOULD HAPPILY HAVE STAYED LONGER

Learn to describe extreme sensory experiences
- **G** Comparison
- **V** Multi-word verbs: social interaction

1 SPEAKING

a ▶ 02.01 Listen to six sounds. Note down what you hear and ask and answer the questions.
1 How often do you hear these sounds? Where?
2 How does each sound make you feel?

b ⟫ **Communication 2A** Now go to p. 127.

2 READING

a 💬 Look at the photo, read the caption and discuss the questions.
1 What do you think an anechoic chamber is?
2 Do you think you'd like to go to one? Why / Why not?

b Read about George Foy's visit to an anechoic chamber on p. 21. Was it a positive experience overall?

c Read the text again and answer the questions.
1 Why did George begin his search?
2 What makes the anechoic chamber at Orfield so quiet?
3 Do most people enjoy being in the anechoic chamber? Why / Why not?
4 What physical and mental effects can the anechoic chamber cause in people?
5 Why was George concerned about going into the chamber?
6 What was George's first reaction to being in the anechoic chamber?
7 Did he enjoy all of his time in the chamber? Why / Why not?
8 What does George say people should do to deal with sensitivity to noise?

d Cover the text and try to remember why George mentioned these things.
1 the New York subway
2 a monastery and a mine
3 his blood
4 his scalp
5 beating the record
6 TV

e 💬 Do you think you could have lasted as long as George in the anechoic chamber? Why / Why not?

The anechoic chamber, Orfield Laboratories, Minneapolis
The quieter the room, the more things you hear. You'll hear your heart beating, sometimes you can hear your lungs, and you can hear your stomach gurgling loudly. In the anechoic chamber, you become the sound.

f **Language in context** *Sounds*
1 Match the definitions below with the highlighted words in the text.
   a strange, mysterious and a bit frightening (adj.)
   b so loud you can't hear anything (adj.)
   c to make a sound by repeatedly hitting something hard (v.)
   d to complain in a high, unpleasant voice (v.)
   e the sound an empty stomach makes (v.)
   f a long, loud, deep noise (n.)
   g the sound of a heartbeat (n.)
   h the sound made by using only the breath to speak (n.)
   i units that measure loudness (n.)

2 Underline the adjectives in the article that describe these nouns: *roar, whisper, thump*.

💬 **Learning Tip**
When you make a note of a new word, it's a good idea to note down the collocation(s) as well. You can also look in dictionaries for other collocations to add to your notes.

3 Notice the words *noise* and *sound(s)* in *italics* in the article. What words in the text form collocations with these nouns? What part of speech are they? Use a dictionary to help you.

block out noise (v.), a source of noise (n.), absorb sound (v.)

UNIT 2

I've been to the QUIETEST PLACE ON EARTH
by George Foy

My search started when I was in the New York subway. My children were whining, four trains came screaming into the station at once, and I put my hands over my ears and cowered – the *noise* was deafening. In cities, the ever-present dull roar of planes, cars, machinery and voices is a fact of life. There is no escape from it, and I was beginning to be driven mad by it. I needed to find a place where I could recapture a sense of peace. The quieter this place was, the more relaxing it would be. I decided to go on a mission to discover whether absolute silence exists. I travelled to a monastery and a mine two kilometres underground – both very quiet, but not the quietest places on Earth. The one place I was most excited about visiting was the anechoic chamber at Orfield Laboratories in Minnesota.

This is a small room insulated with layers of concrete and steel to block out exterior sources of *noise* and internally lined with buffers that absorb all *sound*. Even the floor is a suspended mesh to stop any *sound* of footfalls. If a soft whisper is measured at 20 decibels, the anechoic chamber is one sixteenth of that. The anechoic chamber is considerably quieter than any other place on Earth. Ironically, far from being peaceful, most people find its perfect quiet upsetting. Being deprived of the usual reassuring ambient *sounds* can create fear – it explains why sensory deprivation is a form of torture. Astronauts do part of their training in anechoic chambers at NASA, so they can learn to cope with the silence of space. The presence of *sound* means things are working; it's business as usual. When *sound* is absent, that signals malfunction. I had heard being in an anechoic chamber for longer than 15 minutes can cause extreme symptoms, from claustrophobia and nausea to panic attacks and aural hallucinations – you literally start hearing things. A violinist tried it and hammered on the door after a few seconds, demanding to be let out because he was so disturbed by the silence.

I booked a 45-minute session – no one had managed to stay in for that long before. I felt apprehensive for two reasons: would I go mad and tear off my clothes? Or would I simply be disappointed it wasn't as enjoyable as I'd hoped?

When the heavy door shut behind me, I was plunged into darkness (lights can make a *noise*). For the first few seconds, being in such a quiet place felt utterly peaceful, soothing for my jangled nerves. I strained to hear something and heard … nothing.

Then, after a minute or two, I became aware of my own breathing. The *sound* became more and more noticeable, so I held my breath. The dull thump of my heartbeat became apparent – nothing I could do about that. As the minutes ticked by, I started to hear the blood rushing in my veins. Your ears become more sensitive as the place gets quieter, and mine were going overtime. I frowned and heard my scalp moving over my skull, which was eerie, and a strange, metallic scraping *noise* I couldn't explain. Was I hallucinating? The feeling of peace was spoiled by a little disappointment – this place wasn't quiet at all. You'd have to be dead for absolute silence.

Then I stopped being obsessed with my body and began to enjoy it. I didn't feel afraid and came out only because my time was up; I would happily have stayed longer in there. Everyone was impressed that I'd beaten the record, but having spent so long searching for quiet, I was comfortable with the feeling of absolute stillness. Afterwards, I felt wonderfully rested and calm. The experience was nowhere near as disturbing as I had been led to believe.

My desire for silence changed my life. I found that making space for moments of quiet in my day is the key to happiness – they give you a chance to think about what you want in life. How can you really focus on what's important if you're distracted by constant background *noise*? If you can occasionally become master of your own *sound* environment – from turning off the TV to moving to the country, as I did – you become infinitely more accepting of the *noises* of everyday life.

3 GRAMMAR Comparison

a Cover the text. Complete the sentences with the words in the box. Then check your answers in the text.

> considerably   the (x2)   and
> infinitely   nowhere near

1 The quieter the room, _____ more things you hear.
2 _____ quieter this place was, the more relaxing it would be.
3 The anechoic chamber is _____ quieter than any other place on Earth.
4 The sound [of my breathing] became more _____ more noticeable …
5 The experience was _____ as disturbing as I had been led to believe.
6 … you become _____ more accepting of the noises of everyday life.

b Answer the questions about the sentences in 3a.
1 Which sentences contain two comparative forms? Are the two qualities in these sentences independent of or dependent on each other?
2 Which sentence describes something increasing progressively over time?
3 Look at sentences 3 and 5. Which words in the box below are possible in each gap?

> nothing like   slightly   a good deal
> decidedly   not nearly   significantly

c Now go to Grammar Focus 2A on p. 140.

d Think of a place or an event that you had a strong physical or mental reaction to. Tell your partner.
1 Was this place different from your expectations? Why / Why not?
2 How did you feel? Did your feelings change the longer you stayed there?
3 Would you like to go back to this place? Why / Why not?

> The first time I went to a sauna, it was considerably hotter than I'd expected it to be …

UNIT 2

4 LISTENING

a 💬 Discuss the questions.
1 Have you ever gone for a long period of time without speaking? Why? How did you communicate?
2 What are some reasons people choose not to speak for a long period of time?

b ▶ 02.05 Listen to the first part of Lena's story. Why did she decide to stop talking?

c ▶ 02.05 Listen to Part 1 again. Summarise what Lena says about these things.
1 the dinner party
2 her realisation
3 a spiritual vow of silence
4 a public vow of silence

d 💬 What rules do you think Lena should make for herself for her vow of silence? What situations might be difficult?

e ▶ 02.06 Listen to Part 2. Does Lena mention any of your ideas from 4d?

f ▶ 02.06 Listen to Part 2 again. What does Lena say about these people?
- herself
- the person in the café
- her friend
- the woman in the supermarket
- her landlord

How did she feel at the end of her experiment?

g 💬 Discuss the questions.
1 What do you think of the experiment Lena did? Would you try an experiment like this? Why / Why not?
2 Are you surprised by the reactions of the woman in the supermarket and her landlord? Why / Why not?

5 VOCABULARY
Multi-word verbs: social interaction

a ▶ 02.07 Complete the sentences below with the correct particles in the box. Listen and check.

down with to across out (x2)
in off back about

1 Talking is a way of **fitting** _____ – y'know, a way of showing that we belong to a social group.
2 How would I **come** _____ to other people?
3 … people go into some kind of retreat to **cut themselves** _____ from the outside world.
4 … when someone held a door open for me and a little 'thank you' **slipped** _____.
5 The most interesting thing was the way other people **related** _____ me.
6 She **bombarded me** _____ questions.
7 He always **goes on** _____ something when I go and see him …
8 He usually likes to **run** _____ some politician or other.
9 I often felt that my silence **brought** _____ the best in people.
10 I often wanted to, but I had to **hold myself** _____.

My vow of silence

b Copy the table into your notebook. Then write the multi-word verbs you completed in the sentences in 5a in the correct column of the table.

social interaction in general	spoken interaction
fit in	slip out

c ▶ 02.08 **Pronunciation** Listen to the phrase below. What sound connects with the beginning of *across*?
How would I come across to other people?

d ▶ 02.09 Listen to these phrases from 5a again. Where is there consonant–vowel linking? What sounds are used?
1 … cut themselves off from …
2 … and a little 'thank you' slipped out …
3 … goes on about something …
4 … my silence brought out the best …

Practise saying the phrases with consonant–vowel linking.

e 💬 Think of people you can describe using some of the multi-word verbs in 5a. Tell your partner.
Someone you know who:
- comes across well to new people
- relates to other people well
- often goes on about a problem they have
- brings out the best in you
- tends to cut themselves off from the outside world
- sometimes bombards people with questions
- likes to run down famous people.

> 💡 **Learning Tip**
> When you learn new multi-word verbs, thinking of personalised examples can help you remember the new vocabulary. You can record them in your vocabulary notebook.

6 SPEAKING

💬 Read the ideas about communication. Give an example for each statement you think is true.
1 Communication isn't about what you say – it's about how you say it.
2 It's not the silence that's uneasy – it's your own thoughts that fill the silence.
3 Sometimes talking about a problem only makes it worse.
4 Good listeners make good leaders.
5 People who talk a lot often have the least valuable things to say.

2B I'LL BE JUMPING FROM 900 METRES

Learn to talk about plans, intentions and arrangements
- G Intentions and arrangements
- V Verbs of movement

1 READING AND SPEAKING

a ▪ Look at the photo, read the introduction to the article below and look at the four headings A–D. What do you think the article will be about?

b Complete the quiz about zero-gravity flights. Do you think sentences 1–8 are true or false?
1. Zero-gravity flights were invented as part of the Russian Space Programme in the 1950s.
2. These flights take off at an angle of 15 degrees.
3. A zero-gravity flight typically goes as high as the stratosphere – about 20 kilometres above Earth.
4. The flight causes your body weight to change.
5. France, Russia and Switzerland offer zero-gravity flights.
6. Animals have been sent on zero-gravity flights.
7. People on zero-gravity flights often suffer from nausea.
8. You can drink water on a zero-gravity flight.

c ▪ Work in groups of four and compare your answers. What else do you know about zero-gravity flights?

d In your group, each choose a different paragraph A–D in the article about zero-gravity flights. Which questions from the quiz in 1b does your paragraph answer?

The wonder of weightlessness: A short history of zero-gravity flight

Have you ever looked at videos of astronauts with envy? All that weightless floating around looks like fun, doesn't it? Well, now you can do it. Commercial flights which soar high enough for you to experience gravity-free movement are now available. The cabin on these flights is a lot like a well-padded yoga studio, and you take off lying down. Then, just as the plane whooshes to the top of its arc, you begin to float free. It's a bit like scuba diving, but a whole lot more fun. However, it's not a cheap thrill – a ten-minute zero-gravity flight would cost you about £4,000 (but that does include breakfast and lunch!).

A How did it all begin?

It all started in the 1950s when a team of scientists in the USA began work on a secret programme – Operation Paperclip – to give the country a crucial advantage over their competitors in the space race, the Russians, who were also engaged in their own secret space programme at the time. The US scientists worked out that a parabolic flight could simulate the kind of weightlessness their astronauts would feel in space. At that stage, before either country had managed to send someone into space, the scientists were keen to learn what kinds of nausea astronauts might suffer from and how sick it would make them. To begin with, most passengers on these flights were human beings, but since then all sorts of creatures have been sent into the sky. Cats once took a joyride to check their ability to right themselves in a weightless environment. These days there are zero-gravity flight programmes in Canada, Ecuador, Russia and the USA. Europe also has a programme, operating in both France and Switzerland. All of these countries, except for Canada and Ecuador, now offer commercial flights. In fact, the European flight was used in the Tom Cruise film *The Mummy*.

B How does it work?

A zero-gravity flight begins with a bit of a bang. A normal commercial flight takes off at a maximum angle of 15 degrees. A zero-gravity flight zooms off at a 45-degree angle. Almost immediately, you begin to feel less gravity as you hurtle through the air. The flight follows the pattern of an inverted U, in other words, the shape of a parabola. This is why they're also known as 'parabolic flights' (see fig. 1 on p. 24). When the flight reaches the top of the parabola, it reduces the thrust of the engines and tips down, so that the plane goes into free fall. That's when passengers feel an absence of gravity and begin floating and whirling around the cabin. The plane plunges back towards land before pulling its nose up again. The pilot carries out a series of these rising and tipping manoeuvres, and the plane can reach a height of over 8,000 metres. Passengers, however, don't feel the sensation of the plane going up and down. Gravity is still working on the plane, but not the people in it – they're usually just laughing and screaming and having fun! This goes on for seven or eight minutes and then the pilot begins the descent on the downward curve of the flight parabola.

UNIT 2

C Instant weight loss?

So what exactly is weightlessness? Is it like a sudden ten-minute diet? Not at all. In fact, there are two ways of measuring weight. The first way of measuring weight is by the force your body exerts on physical objects such as bathroom scales. The second way of defining weight is all about the way the force of gravity acts on your body – known as G-force. You only become 'weightless' when gravity is taken away, but that doesn't change the actual measure of your weight. On a zero-gravity flight, you experience the second kind of weightlessness. Your body goes into a kind of free fall as you roll around in space. However, there isn't a complete absence of gravity on a zero-gravity flight. One thing that often puzzles people is the fact that satellites maintain an orbit around the Earth even though the astronauts on board are floating around in a gravity-free environment. Why doesn't the satellite just whizz off into outer space? Well, there is still a certain amount of gravitational pull on the satellite from Earth – it doesn't totally escape the pull of our planet. And satellites manage this because their horizontal speed is so fast. So, on a zero-gravity flight there's an absence of G-force for you, but thankfully, not for the aircraft you're in.

D What does it feel like?

It's better not to expect the smooth ride of a large jet engine plane. You can have a sensation of nausea on a zero-gravity flight, but it tends to happen when you don't follow the rules about eating and drinking before the flight. During the first zero-gravity manoeuvre of the plane, you might struggle to lift your head and you could have the sensation that all your internal organs are being pulled to the floor – a bit like being on a roller coaster. Then you'll probably lose control of your limbs and your arms will go floating above your head and you're suddenly whirling around in space. It's likely you'll be laughing out loud and perhaps flipping over and over like a pancake. If there's water on board, a large blob will float by you. There's not much point trying to drink it – the blob will just slide across your face. But overall, a zero-gravity flight gives passengers an extraordinary sense of freedom – it's as though you've been cut free from the world, and it's a sensation of complete elation. Coming back down to Earth is without doubt a bit of a let-down and most people immediately say, 'I want to go again!' And, yes, while some people do feel sick, they almost never regret this experience of a lifetime.

Fig 1: Parabolic flight manoeuvre

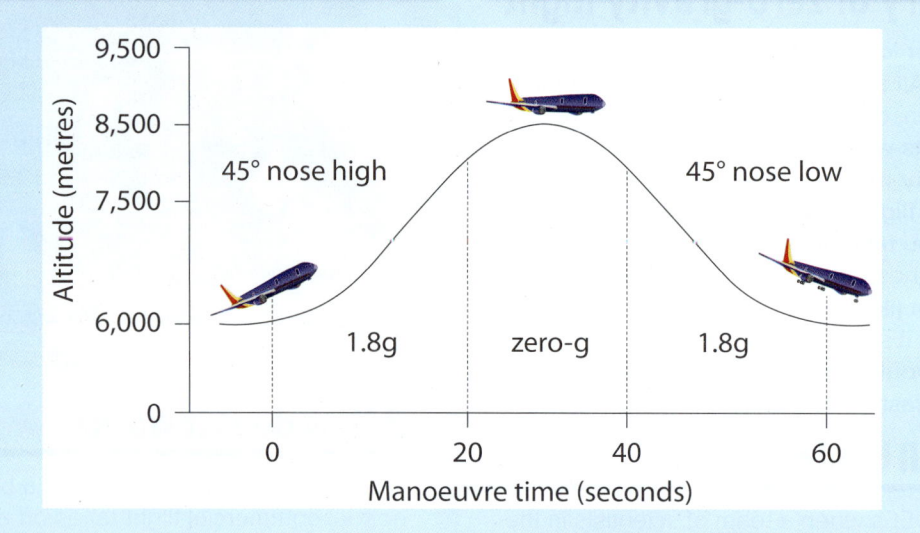

[Graph: Altitude (metres) vs Manoeuvre time (seconds). Parabolic curve showing 45° nose high at ascent (1.8g), zero-g at peak around 8,500m, and 45° nose low at descent (1.8g). Time axis 0 to 60 seconds.]

e Read your paragraph again and make notes.

f 💬 Tell each other about the paragraph you read. Check your answers to 1b.

g **Language in context:** Words and phrases with similar meaning.

1 Which words in the box are used instead of the words and phrases in *italics* in the sentences below? Check your answers in the article.

---
free fall   blob   puzzles (v)   joyride (n)
elation   right (v)   exerts
---

a Cats once took a *trip* to check their ability to *re-position* themselves in a weightless environment.
b The first way of measuring weight is by the force your body *puts* on physical objects.

c Your body goes into a kind of *out-of-control motion* …
d One thing that often *confuses* people is the fact that satellites maintain an orbit around the Earth.
e If there's water on board, a large *mass* will float by you.
f … it's as though you've been cut free from the world, and it's a sensation of complete *happiness*.

2 Why has the writer used the words in the box? Tick (✓) the reasons. The words are … .
a ☐ more exact
b ☐ simpler and easier to understand
c ☐ more descriptive
d ☐ mostly shorter
e ☐ more concise

h 💬 Imagine you received a free ticket on a zero-gravity flight. Would you go? Why / why not?

2 VOCABULARY Verbs of movement

a Look at these sentences and answer questions 1–4.
  a Commercial flights which **soar** high enough for you to experience gravity-free movement are now available.
  b Then, just as the plane **whooshes** to the top of its arc, you begin to float free.
  c Almost immediately, you begin to feel less gravity as you **hurtle** through the air.
  d A zero-gravity flight **zooms** off at a 45-degree angle.
  e The plane **plunges** back towards land …
  f Your body goes into a kind of free fall as you **roll** around in space.
  g Why doesn't the satellite just **whizz** off into outer space?
  h … your arms will go floating above your head and you're suddenly **whirling** around in space.

  The words in **bold** describe movement. Which verbs suggest … ?
  1 speed
  2 the sound that the action makes
  3 a circular movement
  4 a downward movement

b >> Now go to Vocabulary Focus 2B on p.159.

3 LISTENING

a ▶02.11 You are going to hear an interview with Ada, who is going base jumping.
  1 Look at the picture. What do base jumpers do?
  2 What do you think Ada might say about base jumping? Note down a few ideas.
      • before the jump *I've never done it before.*
      • after the jump *I was afraid the parachute wouldn't open.*

  Listen and check your ideas.

b ▶02.11 Answer the questions. Listen again and check.
  1 What do these numbers in the interview refer to?
      a 10   c 900   e 20
      b 300   d 25   f 30,000
  2 What does Ada say about the risks of base jumping?

c 💬 Would you consider going base jumping? Why / Why not?

4 GRAMMAR Intentions and arrangements

a ▶02.12 Both future forms in each pair below are possible. Which sentence did the speakers use, and why? Listen and check.
  1 a So, Ada, you**'re about to go** base jumping.
    b So, Ada, you**'re going to go** base jumping.
  2 a I**'m due to jump** in about ten minutes.
    b I**'m planning to jump** in about ten minutes.
  3 a I**'ll jump** from about 900 metres.
    b I**'ll be jumping** from about 900 metres.
  4 a I**'m definitely going to do** it again.
    b I**'m definitely doing** it again.

b ▶02.13 Complete the sentences below with the words Ada used. Listen and check.

  | intention | planning | aiming | thinking |

  1 I'm also _____ **of trying** a tandem jump sometime.
  2 There is a platform which sticks out over the cliff, and I'm _____ **to jump** off that one.
  3 I'm _____ **to free fall** for exactly 25 seconds.
  4 You come here **with the** _____ **of having** a great experience, and … and that's what you do.

c >> Now go to Grammar Focus 2B on p. 141.

d Prepare to talk about your plans for next year. Are you planning to do / thinking of doing … ?
  • something you've never done before
  • something exciting or risky

  Think how you could use expressions from 4a and b.

e 💬 Tell the other students about your plans. Is anyone planning to do something you'd like to do?

5 SPEAKING AND WRITING

a 💬 Look at the photo of the mountain lake. Where do you think it is? Why might someone want to live there?

b >> **Communication 2B** Now go to p. 132.

2C EVERYDAY ENGLISH
Don't get so wound up about it

Learn to give advice
- S Advise a friend on a tricky situation
- P Emphatic stress

1 LISTENING

a Discuss the questions.
1 In your country, at what age do people usually … ?
  - leave home
  - rent or buy their first property
2 What are the pros and cons of living with … ?
  - relatives
  - people you don't know
  - friends your own age
3 What factors are important in making the decision to leave home?

b Look at pictures a–c. What do you think the connection between them is?

c 02.18 Watch or listen to Part 1 and check your answers in 1b.

d 02.18 Watch or listen to Part 1 again. Answer the questions.
1 What is Emma's problem? Why exactly is Max annoying her?
2 What has she done about it so far?
3 What is Alex's advice to Emma?
4 How do Emma and Alex feel about Max and his book?

e 02.19 **Language in context** *Being tactful or frank*
1 Match the halves of the expressions from Part 1. Listen and check.
   1 ☐ It's like **walking**
   2 ☐ I keep **dropping**
   3 ☐ Why don't you just **tell**
   4 ☐ Don't beat around
   5 ☐ There's a lot to be said for **being**

   a the **bush**.
   b **him straight**, then?
   c **hints**, but he doesn't seem to notice.
   d **upfront about things**.
   e **on eggshells** half the time.

2 Look at the expressions in 1. Which describe being tactful? Which describe being frank?

f Discuss the questions.
1 Do you think Emma is right to drop hints to her brother, or should she stop beating around the bush and tell him straight?
2 Have you ever had the experience of guests who outstayed their welcome? What happened?

2 PRONUNCIATION Emphatic stress

a 02.20 Listen to the sentences below. Underline the main stress in the word groups in **bold**.
1 **Max is due back soon**.
2 **He's getting on my nerves**.
3 Isn't it about time **you asked him to leave**?
4 Did you say **his name is Max**?

Which word in a word group normally has the main stress? Complete the rule.

> The *first / last* word that carries meaning in each word group usually has the main stress.

b 02.21 Sometimes main stress does not follow the rule. Listen and underline the main stress in the word groups in **bold**.
1 **He's not still sleeping on the sofa**, is he?
2 **He is the guy** who wrote *Solar Wind*.
3 **You mean it is him**!
4 **Your brother is the Max Redwood**!

c Look at 2b again and answer these questions.
1 Why don't the phrases in 2b follow the rule?
2 What does Alex mean when he says 'the Max Redwood'?

d Emphasising different words in a word group changes the meaning. Match sentences 1–5 with their meanings a–e. Practise saying the sentences with the correct main stress.

1 ☐ Alex has read Max's <u>book</u>.
2 ☐ Alex has read <u>Max's</u> book.
3 ☐ Alex has <u>read</u> Max's book.
4 ☐ Alex <u>has</u> read Max's book.
5 ☐ <u>Alex</u> has read Max's book.

The speaker is telling us:
a what Alex has done with Max's book
b whose book Alex has read
c who has read Max's book
d that Alex has read Max's book, not his letter, email or blog
e that we are wrong to believe Alex hasn't read Max's book.

e Look at this sentence with the main stress in three different places. Work in pairs. Create a short conversation for each sentence. Then practise your conversation.

<u>I'll</u> give you a ring later.   I'll give <u>you</u> a ring later.   I'll give you a ring <u>later</u>.

26

3 LISTENING

a 💬 Look at picture d. Who do you think says these sentences, Emma or Max?
1. I can't think about any of that right now.
2. There's nothing else to say about *Solar Wind*!
3. Don't get so wound up about it.
4. It's only an interview.
5. I'll just go far far away, take a vow of silence, live on a desert island somewhere …

b 🎬 02.22 Watch or listen to Part 2 and check your answers in 3a.

c 🎬 02.22 Watch or listen to Part 2 again. Answer the questions.
1. Why does Emma think it wouldn't be a problem for Max to move out now?
2. What advantages does Emma mention for Max if he buys his own place?
3. How does Emma suggest Max prepare for the radio interview?
4. How does Max feel about Emma listening to his interview?
5. Why does Max suggest he'll take a vow of silence?

d 💬 Discuss the questions.
1. How would you feel about doing a live radio interview?
2. What are the worst things that could happen?

4 USEFUL LANGUAGE Giving advice

a Answer the questions.
1. Is the farmer's advice in picture e appropriate for the situation? Why / Why not?
2. What would you expect the farmer to say if a train was coming?
3. In what other situations might you use the advice in picture e?

> It might be a good idea to move.

b ▶ 02.23 Match 1–7 with a–g to make sentences from Parts 1 and 2. Listen and check.

1. ☐ **Isn't it about**
2. ☐ **There's a lot to be said**
3. ☐ **Have you thought about the possibility**
4. ☐ **It might be in**
5. ☐ **You might want to**
6. ☐ **Don't** get so
7. ☐ **You might as**

a **well**!
b **time you** asked him to leave?
c have a think about what you could say tonight.
d **of** finding your own place to live?
e **for** being upfront about things.
f wound up about it.
g **your interests to** invest some of it in property.

c Which two expressions in **bold** in 4b sound more polite and formal?

d Complete the advice with the expressions in 4b.
1. You _____ to read up about the company before your interview.
2. Have you _____ working overseas?
3. There's _____ having your own car.
4. You _____ well sell it and get a better one.
5. It might be in _____ keep on good terms with the director.

e 💬 Look at the pairs of sentences from two conversations. Which conversation is more formal? What do you think the context for each is?

Conversation 1
a Isn't it about time you were upfront about it?
b Don't beat around the bush!

Conversation 2
a It might be in your interests to contact a solicitor.
b Have you thought about the possibility of changing the terms?

f 💬 Work in pairs. Use your ideas in 4e to have two conversations.

5 SPEAKING

≫ **Communication 2C** Work in pairs. Student A: Go to p. 127. Student B: Go to p. 131.

UNIT PROGRESS TEST
CHECK YOUR PROGRESS
YOU CAN NOW DO THE UNIT PROGRESS TEST.

2D SKILLS FOR WRITING
Less adventurous students could try paintball

Learn to write a report
W Reports; Linking: contrast and concession

paintball | *pony trekking* | *bungee jumping* | *go-karting* | *tree-top adventuring* | *whitewater rafting*

1 LISTENING AND SPEAKING

a You have to choose a sports activity for a student social programme. Which of the activities in the photos would you choose? Think about:
- appeal of the activity
- skills required
- student safety
- cost
- chances to socialise.

b 02.24 Listen to four students talking about the sports activities on a social programme at a university in Australia. Make notes on their feedback.

Luba, Russia | Mehmet, Turkey | Paolo, Italy | Changying, China

	Positives	Negatives
bungee jumping		
whitewater rafting		
other feedback		

c Think about the students' feedback in 1b. Would you choose the same activities for next year's programme? Which new sports could you choose instead? Explain your choices.

2 READING

a Read the report by a member of the social programme committee and compare the content with your notes in 1b.
1. Which aspects of the students' feedback are included?
2. What negative feedback is not included?

b Are the recommendations similar to your ideas in 1c?

SOCIAL PROGRAMME
REVIEW AND RECOMMENDATIONS OF THE COMMITTEE

1 _____

The purpose of this report is to review options for sports activities that would be suitable as part of an extracurricular social programme for foreign exchange students. Last year we had two activities for exchange students: whitewater rafting and bungee jumping, both of which received mixed reviews. This report is based on feedback on these activities.

2 _____

Even though many students liked the extreme nature of last year's activities, some felt they were too challenging. Many young tourists who come to Australia are keen to do these activities. However, not all our students necessarily have the same ambition. Whitewater rafting was not possible for students who were not confident swimmers. On the other hand, bungee jumping did not require any particular skill or expertise. Nevertheless, the idea of jumping from a bridge was seen by several as being risky.

28

3 WRITING SKILLS
Reports; Linking: contrast and concession

a Add these headings to the correct paragraphs of the report.
- Safety concerns
- Recommendations
- Cost and budget
- Introduction
- Level of challenge

b What phrases are used in the report to give … ?
1. the reason for writing the report
2. recommendations

Are these phrases formal or informal?

c Which word in *italics* in each phrase below is not possible?
1. The *purpose / aim / agenda / objective* of this report is …
2. I would *establish / recommend / suggest / propose* that …
3. My *recommendation(s) / conclusion(s) / suggestion(s) / resolution(s)* is/are …

d Look at the highlighted linkers in the report and decide which word(s) in **bold** in these sentences they could replace.
1. **Unlike** whitewater rafting, bungee jumping is relatively safe.
2. Go-karting is cheaper than skydiving. **Despite this**, skydiving is still more popular with students.
3. You could go pony trekking. **Alternatively**, you could go bungee jumping.
4. **In spite of** the cost, many people go skydiving regularly.
5. **Although** it is very expensive, many people go skydiving regularly.

---

3 _____

Safety issues were raised with both activities. One whitewater raft overturned, and a student suffered a concussion when he hit his head on a rock. Likewise, another student sprained her ankle while getting off the raft.

4 _____

Both activities were quite expensive, so despite the generous budget, we were obliged to ask students to make a contribution, which many were not happy about. The cost of providing transport to the venues for the activities drove the costs up further.

5 _____

For the students who are due to arrive this year, we would recommend that we choose slightly cheaper options and that we offer one extreme sports activity as well as something that is, by comparison, considerably less challenging. In contrast to whitewater rafting, tree-top adventuring is a relatively inexpensive extreme sport with an excellent safety record. Alternatively, less adventurous students could try paintball, which is a low-cost and fun option that does not require any skill. Use of the local paintball venue would cut transport costs, and we would suggest using the savings as a way of subsidising these activities for students.

---

e Match 1–6 with a–f. Underline the linkers of contrast and concession in a–f. Include any prepositions that form part of the linker.
1. ☐ Although extreme sports are generally seen as fun and exciting,
2. ☐ Despite the fact that many students said they were keen to try bungee jumping,
3. ☐ Some students didn't object to paying a small amount for the activity. On the contrary,
4. ☐ When compared to contact sports like rugby and ice hockey,
5. ☐ Regardless of savings we make on transport,
6. ☐ While many students indicated that they have to live on a tight budget,

a. they had assumed they would have to make some kind of contribution.
b. there has been some negative feedback on last year's activities.
c. several said that the activities were affordable.
d. we cannot afford to subsidise very expensive activities.
e. extreme sports begin to look very safe.
f. many failed to reserve a place when this activity was advertised.

f »» Now go to Writing Focus 2D on p. 170.

4 WRITING

a 💬 You are on a committee that has to organise a three-day tourist itinerary for a group of foreign students. Imagine problems previous groups might have had. Think about:
- range of sites visited
- transport
- refreshments
- time to visit sites
- availability of guides
- costs

b Plan a report that discusses these problems and suggests solutions.

> 💡 **Writing Tip**
>
> You probably discussed a lot of ideas in 4a. However, it may not be possible to mention them all in detail in the report. In a report of this nature, you should address three or four key issues, so you may have to prioritise some points over others. It is preferable to mention problems that you can suggest a solution to.

c Write a report of between 250 and 300 words on the tourist itinerary.

d Read another student's report. Do you both mention the same problems and solutions? Which of your problems and solutions are different?

UNIT 2
Review and extension

1 GRAMMAR

a Complete the sentences with one word.
1 The sound quality wasn't as high __as__ I expected.
2 It's a great _____ more expensive to make 3D films.
3 This is by _____ the tastiest meal I've had in months!
4 The higher you go, _____ further you can see.
5 I was getting more and _____ worried by the sounds.
6 Real coffee tastes nothing _____ the stuff from a jar.
7 They didn't make anywhere _____ as much mess as I thought they would.
8 The first place was really noisy, and the second was just _____ bad.

b Choose the correct future form.
1 My brothers *are going to / are thinking of* attempt to climb K2.
2 The race *will begin / is aiming to begin* in five minutes, so get ready.
3 How are you *getting / going to get* there on time?
4 What *will you be / are you* wearing when I see you?
5 The police are *going to / thinking to* speak to those involved.
6 The plane is *due to / about to* arrive in Buenos Aires at 7:00 tomorrow morning.

2 VOCABULARY

a Match 1–5 with a–e.
1 ☐ Unfortunately, she can come
2 ☐ I wish you wouldn't go on
3 ☐ Living in a small village, I felt cut
4 ☐ Don't worry about fitting
5 ☐ A crisis brings

a about the neighbours all the time.
b out the best and worst in people.
c in; your new colleagues are very friendly.
d across as a bit arrogant.
e off and isolated.

b Answer the questions with one word.
1 Would you *stroll* in a park or a train station? park
2 What could *hurtle* past you – a feather or a cat?
3 If something *whirls*, does it travel in a straight line?
4 What could *whoosh* past you – a lorry or a tortoise?
5 Who might *stagger* – someone ill or someone angry?
6 What might *crawl* – a small child or a plane?
7 What could *roll* better – stones or boxes?
8 What surface can you *slide* on – ice or sand?

3 WORDPOWER Idioms: Movement

a ▶ 02.25 Replace the words in *italics* in each sentence with the correct form of a verb in the box. Listen and check.

plunge   whizz   soar   drift   whirl   crawl

1 a After a clever marketing campaign, the company's profits are *going up*.
  b Temperatures *went down suddenly* to a record low of –35° last night.
2 a I sat looking out of the window, letting my thoughts *go where they wanted*.
  b My mind was *full of thoughts going round in my head*, and I simply couldn't decide what to do next.
3 a I'm enjoying my job so much that time seems to be just *going really quickly* past.
  b I hate long-haul flights. Time always seems to *go very slowly* past.

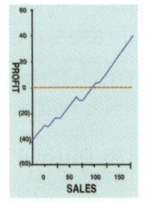

b Match the expressions in **bold** with their definitions.
1 Don't be so scared of going back to university. I'm sure it'll be great. Come on, **take the plunge**.
2 Climbing down the rock surface, I **felt a rush** of adrenalin!
3 If I were offered a job in Japan, I would **jump at the chance**.
4 **I'm on a roll** with my academic work; otherwise I'd be really nervous about my next exam.
5 I know you don't like technology, but I'm sure you'll love this phone if you **give it a whirl**.

☐ get a sudden strong feeling
☐ accept something eagerly
☐ do something you are afraid of
☐ try something for the first time
☐ having a series of successes

c Choose two words or expressions from 3a or 3b and write two sentences, but leave a gap for the word/expression. Read your sentences aloud. Can other students guess what goes in the gaps?

⟳ REVIEW YOUR PROGRESS

How well did you do in this unit? Write 3, 2 or 1 for each objective.
3 = very well   2 = well   1 = not so well

I CAN ...	
describe extreme sensory experiences	☐
talk about plans, intentions and arrangements	☐
give advice	☐
write a report.	☐

CAN DO OBJECTIVES

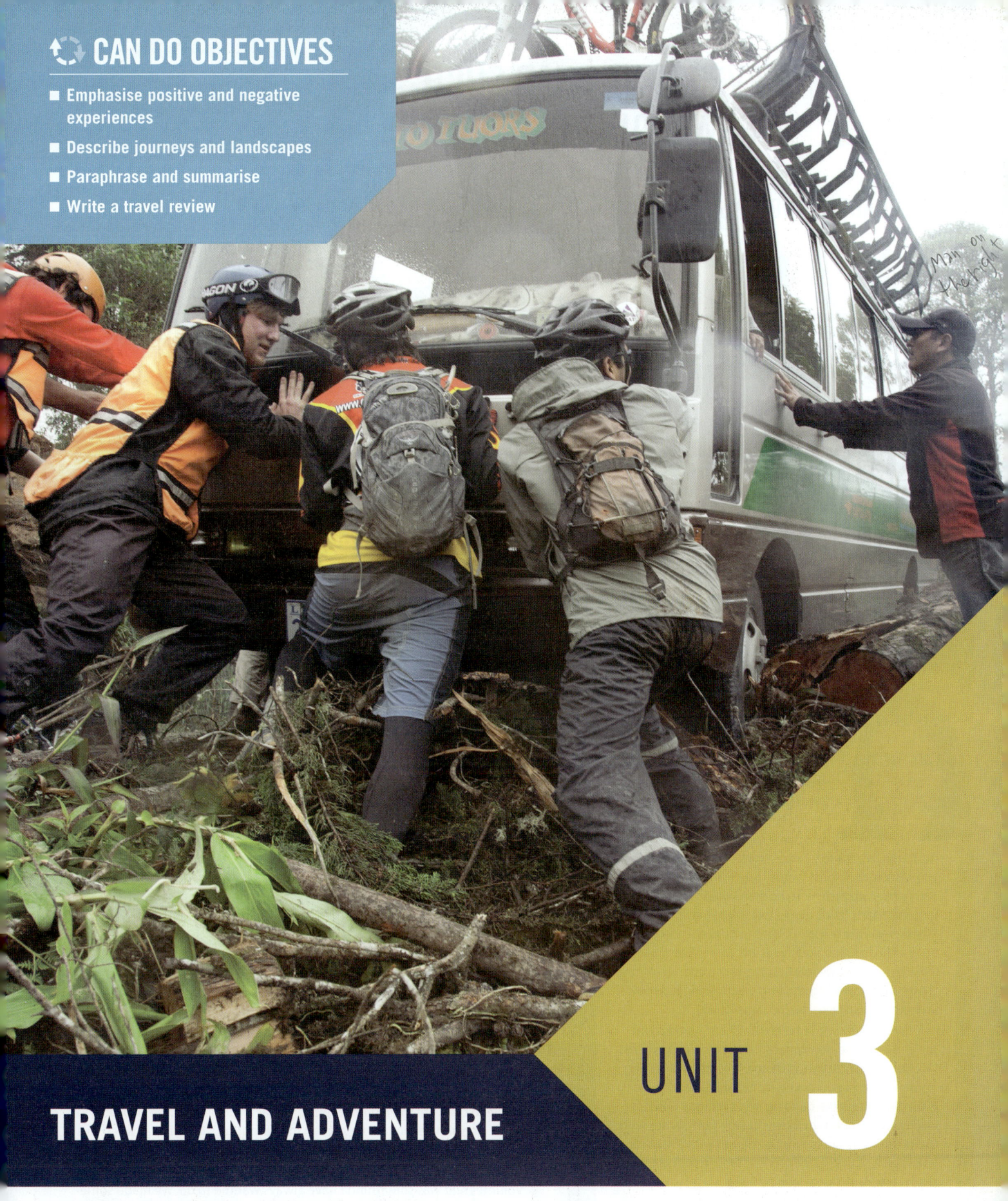

- Emphasise positive and negative experiences
- Describe journeys and landscapes
- Paraphrase and summarise
- Write a travel review

UNIT 3

TRAVEL AND ADVENTURE

GETTING STARTED

a Look at the picture and discuss the questions.
1 What's just happened? Where do you think the bus was going? What factors might have led to the situation?
2 Who do you think the people pushing the bus are? How do you think they feel?
3 What's the man on the right doing? Why?
4 What do you think will happen next?

b Work in pairs. Use your answers to retell the events of the day this photo was taken.

c Would you enjoy the type of trip these people are on? Why / Why not?

3A NEVER HAVE I HAD SUCH A REWARDING EXPERIENCE

Learn to emphasise positive and negative experiences
- **G** Inversion
- **V** Wealth and poverty

1 READING AND SPEAKING

a Which of these volunteer jobs would interest you the most? Why?
1. working at a children's home in Belize
2. coaching sport with schoolchildren in Ghana
3. rescuing and caring for endangered bears in Cambodia
4. conserving coral reefs in the Caribbean

b Have you ever done an activity similar to those in 1a? Where? When? Why? Would you be prepared to use your holiday time to help other people? Why / Why not?

c Read the two reviews of volunteer experiences. Answer the questions.
1. What are the similarities and differences in the two experiences?
2. What specific negatives does each review mention?

THINKING OF VOLUNTEERING ABROAD?

Here are **two inspiring stories** from volunteers who joined ongoing projects organised by POD (Personal Overseas Development), an ethical, non-profit volunteer organisation.

DEBBIE
Teaching children, Ghana

There are a few village life truths that everyone forgets to mention. You will sweat profusely, you will get bitten by a million different insects, you will miss home comforts and no doubt feel frustrated by a fair few things. However, despite all this, you will forget all these worries in a heartbeat. No sooner had I woken up each morning than I would see a smiling face and hear a child's giggle that would melt my heart. Whether you are going to Ghana to build a school or to build a child's future, your heart will break when it's time to leave because the people become your world. Never have I had such a rewarding and truly enlightening experience. Without a doubt, it will be the same for you.

The day starts with breakfast at 7 am. I worked in the kindergarten, so it was off to class for 8:30, where I worked till lunchtime. Afternoons could be anything from extra classes, arts and crafts, sports coaching or even digging on the building site. Evenings were for chilling out around the fire or having yam parties with the neighbours or playing silly games with the other volunteers. Normally we were so tired from the long day that we were all fast asleep by 9 pm.

It's difficult to adjust to the intense heat, and it really does sap a lot of your energy. It's also difficult when you want to do as much as possible to help but find yourself restricted by your own physical shortcomings.

The most rewarding part for me was the relationships that I built; there is no better feeling in the world than having a child run to you in the morning with pure happiness on their face at seeing you.

LINDA AND MALCOLM
Working at a children's home, Belize

My husband and I spent two weeks at a children's home in Belize, and we both thoroughly enjoyed every minute of it. The experience of living with these warm, friendly people was something we will always remember, and we would certainly like to return in a couple of years. We were not really prepared for the intensity of the heat even though we had holidayed in the Caribbean previously.

The children were a joy and such characters, and we created some very special bonds. There was a lot of maintenance work to do, and Malcolm, who was able to carry out more manual work, was at an advantage. We also did a lot of gardening and helping in the kitchen (my favourite). Time off was when you wanted it, and with Belize being such a beautiful place with plenty of history and places to explore, you really need to make the most of it and see all you can.

Volunteering was something I have always wanted to do. We made some great friends and worked out of our comfort zone quite often, which for me made the experience even more special. At no time did we regret the decision to go there.

We loved being with the children, giving them little treats and helping make their environment better. We made them a special meal of burgers and chips, and the enjoyment on their faces made it so worthwhile. Little do children back home realise how the food they take for granted is a genuine treat for children here.

UNIT 3

d Which review would you find more helpful if you were a prospective volunteer? Why?

e Language in context *Unusual experiences*

1 Match 1–8 with a–h to make expressions used in the reviews. Check new expressions in a dictionary.

1	miss home	a	your energy
2	melt your	b	special bonds
3	have a rewarding	c	comforts
4	sap a lot of	d	life skills
5	create some very	e	heart
6	make the	f	and enlightening experience
7	take for	g	granted
8	acquire	h	most of it

2 Complete these expressions with the correct preposition. Check your answers in the reviews.
   1 _____ a heartbeat
   2 _____ of your comfort zone
   3 a feeling _____ self-worth and satisfaction

2 GRAMMAR Inversion

a Notice the phrases in **bold** in the sentences below. Why did the writers use these phrases?

☐ for emphasis   ☐ to soften

1 **No sooner had I woken up** each morning than I would see a smiling face and hear a child's giggle that would melt my heart.
2 **Never have I had such** a rewarding and truly enlightening experience.
3 **At no time did we regret** the decision to go there.
4 **Little do children back home realise** how the food they take for granted is a genuine treat for children here.

One of the great things about volunteering is that you are acquiring life skills and experiences you will get nowhere else. A volunteer does not do the work just to help others, but for themselves, too; to get a feeling of self-worth and satisfaction, to learn and experience the way other people live and how other cultures work, and to be part of their way of life.

b Look at the phrases in **bold** in 2a and complete the rule.

> For emphasis, the writers use a ¹*positive / negative* adverbial and ²*statement / question* word order: adverbial + auxiliary verb + subject + verb

c Think about how the sentences differ. When might you use inversion rather than normal word order? Give an example.

d ≫ Now go to Grammar Focus 3A on p. 142.

3 SPEAKING AND WRITING

a ▶03.02 Listen to the examples. Who or what do you think each person is talking about?
1 **Not only are they the nicest people in the world**, they're the best cooks, too.
2 **Only at the sight of the beach** did it all become worthwhile. — *good use of time*
3 **Not until the end of the holiday** did we realise how attached we had become to them.
4 **Never before** have I seen such enthusiasm and excitement.
5 **Not in a million years** would I have imagined building something from scratch.

b ▶03.02 **Pronunciation** Listen to the examples in 3a again. Does the intonation of the phrases in **bold** … ?
• rise then fall   • fall then rise

c Tell a partner about the highlights of a travel experience. Use the ideas below and inversion after some of the adverbials in the box. Make sure you use the correct intonation.

> rarely …   no sooner …   at no time …
> not in a million years …   only …   not until …

• first impressions of the journey/place
• new experiences you had and your reaction
• a moment when you realised something
• something unique about the experience

> I was staying with a host family. No sooner had I arrived than everybody rushed to greet me.

> I went to India in January. Not in a million years did I think vegetarian food could taste so good.

d Write a paragraph for a blog about your experience. Use two sentences with inversion.

> only by chance …   little …   hardly …
> seldom …   never before …

Little did I know how eventful this holiday was going to be.

Never before had I experienced such heavy rain.

33

UNIT 3

4 LISTENING

a 💬 Imagine you and your friends wanted to start a volunteer project to build a school in a low-income country. What problems could there be?

b ▶ 03.03 Listen to Daniela Papi talking about her experience in Cambodia. Does she mention any of your ideas in 4a?

c ▶ 03.03 Listen again. Summarise what Daniela says about these topics.
1 her initial plans for volunteer work in Cambodia
2 problems with this plan
3 her six years in Cambodia
4 her beliefs after ten years' volunteer work
5 the problems with good intentions and praise

d 💬 Think about the volunteer project you talked about in 4a. What questions would you like to ask Daniela about doing this kind of work?

5 VOCABULARY Wealth and poverty

a Do the words and phrases in **bold** below relate to wealth or poverty? Make two lists. Which word/phrase applies to people with any level of income?
1 Many farmers *are facing real economic* **hardship** after the drought killed all their crops.
2 There's no money to help **impoverished** *communities* build basic facilities like schools and medical centres.
3 In **affluent** *suburbs* like this one, house prices are extremely high.
4 There's a direct relationship between a good education system and the *economic* **prosperity** of a country.
5 Even though I got a pay rise last year, I still *find it difficult to* **make ends meet**.
6 My grandparents used to be *relatively* **well off**, but they lost all their money in bad investments.
7 He lives with his parents and pays no bills, so he has a lot of **disposable income**.
8 In the most **deprived** *areas* of the city, unemployment stands at around 50% and social problems are rife.
9 We can't go on using our credit cards all the time. We have to *learn to* **live within our means**.
10 They lost everything they had in the flood and were *left* **destitute**.

b Answer these questions about the words and phrases in **bold** in 5a.
1 Which noun has the opposite meaning of *hardship*?
2 Compare the adjectives *impoverished*, *deprived* and *destitute*. Which one is more severe than the other two?
3 Compare *affluent* and *well off*. Which one are we more likely to use when we speak?
4 Compare *make ends meet* and *live within our means*. Which expression suggests more of a struggle?
5 Which of these noun phrases has a similar meaning to *disposable income*?
   a living expenses   b spending money

c ▶ 03.04 **Pronunciation** Listen to the sentences in 5a and underline the stressed syllables in the words and phrases in **bold**.

d 💬 Look at the phrases in *italics* in 5a. Think of an example of each from your own knowledge/experience. Compare your ideas with a partner.

> People here faced real economic hardship during the recession.

6 SPEAKING

a Think of someone you know well who would be interested in volunteering. Choose a suitable volunteer project for them or think of another.
1 saving cheetahs from extinction in South Africa
2 conserving the Amazon rainforest in Peru
3 helping build schools in Ghana
4 coaching sport with schoolchildren in Nepal

b What could you say to the volunteer about … ?
- practical preparation   *learn local customs*
- psychological preparation
- positive impact of volunteers
- negative impact of volunteers
- likely personal development and life skills

c 💬 Tell a partner about the person you chose in 6a and what you would say to them about volunteering.

3B I WAS EXPECTING IT TO BE TOUGH

Learn to describe journeys and landscapes
- G Future in the past; Narrative tenses
- V Landscape features

1 READING AND GRAMMAR Future in the past

a 💬 Look at the journey on the map. What do you think it would be like? Talk about:
- what you'd expect to see
- people you might meet
- skills needed
- possible risks.

b Read what Will Millard says about his journey. Answer the questions.
1 Why does Will describe the forest as a *one-off environment*?
2 Why did Will take the trip? How did he travel? Why do you think he chose to travel that way?
3 What would you look forward to on a trip like this? What wouldn't you look forward to?

c Look at the underlined event in the article. Complete each sentence below with a phrase from the box. There is one phrase you do not need to use.

| in the future | in progress | in the past |

When Will arrived in Sierra Leone, this event was _____.
When Will wrote the article, this event was _____.

d Underline six more examples of the future in the past in the article. What four verb forms does Will use?

e Think of other things that Will might have considered before his trip. Write sentences using the future in the past.
I knew that it was going to be difficult.
I was hoping to see some elephants.

f 💬 What do you think will make Will's journey difficult and dangerous?

2 VOCABULARY Landscape features

a What do the highlighted words in the article mean? Which two words are very similar? How are they different? Use a dictionary to help you.

b Complete the collocations below with the words and phrases in the box. Check your answers in the article.

| a tropical | a remote | the heart of the | dense | an untouched |

1 _____ rainforest
    capital
    jungle
2 _____ rainforest
    storm
    island
3 _____ fog
    vegetation
    undergrowth
4 _____ wilderness
    forest
    plate of food
5 _____ area
    forest
    village

c ⟫ Now go to Vocabulary Focus 3B on p. 160.

SURVIVAL ON THE MANO RIVER

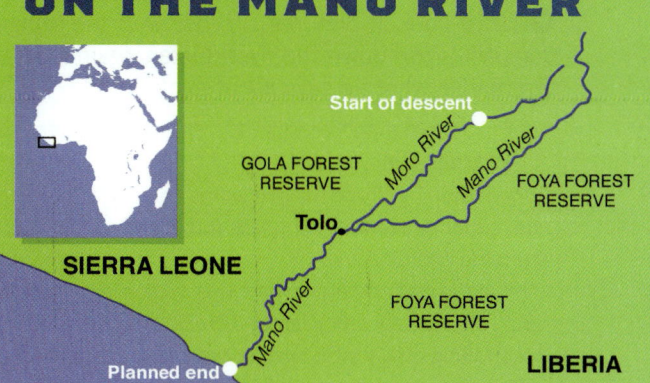

Start of descent
GOLA FOREST RESERVE
Moro River
Mano River
FOYA FOREST RESERVE
Tolo
SIERRA LEONE
Mano River
FOYA FOREST RESERVE
Planned end
LIBERIA

My dream journey became a reality when I received a grant from the Royal Geographical Society to explore the Moro and Mano rivers. The grant was intended to cover expenses, radio training and equipment to record my expedition for BBC Radio 4. I was planning to start at the top of the Gola Forest and make the first descent of the river border of Sierra Leone and Liberia, right through a chunk of Africa's most threatened jungle environment – one of the last untouched wildernesses of the Upper Guinean forest belt. More than a quarter of Africa's total mammal species are found in the belt, with bizarre creatures such as the pygmy hippopotamus found nowhere else on Earth. The need to protect what still remains of this one-off environment could not be more critical.

In Sierra Leone, the Gola Forest is already designated a national park, but I wanted to find out what life in the heart of a tropical rainforest was really like, so I was going to paddle down these rivers, hopefully as far as the sea. I knew that, although I would be in radio contact, I would be on my own in one of the most remote forests in West Africa, and I would be separated from the outside world by dense tropical vegetation. I was expecting it to be tough, but in fact it was to become one of the most difficult and dangerous journeys I have ever made.

UNIT 3

3 LISTENING

a ▶ 03.06 You are going to hear Will Millard describing his trip. Listen to five sounds from the recording. What do you think each sound is?

b ▶ 03.07 Now listen to the whole recording and check your ideas in 3a.

c ▶ 03.07 Look at pictures 1–5 below of the things from Will's trip down the river. Listen again and summarise what he says about each one.

> **Learning Tip**
> When listening, there may be words you don't know. You can either ignore them or guess roughly what they mean from the context.
> *Just at the end of the day there was quite a large **cataract**, and I didn't really fancy taking it on till tomorrow …*
> He's rafting on a jungle river, so we can guess that a *cataract* is some feature of this environment that is difficult to get past.

d Read the sentences below from the listening. Underline examples of the informal conversational style that Will Millard uses.
1 Thanks, mate.
2 Managed to just get my camp sorted.
3 I didn't really fancy taking it on till tomorrow.
4 I guess I'll find out.
5 If I lose the raft, I'm finished.

How could you express the sentences in a more neutral style?

e ▶ 03.08 **Pronunciation** Listen again to part of what Will says. Notice how he pronounces the words in **bold**. Practise saying the phrases a–c.
a … **hit** this big rock …
b … **just** managed to **get** control of it again …
c … it's **got** my shelter on it …

f What would/wouldn't you have enjoyed from this part of Will's journey?

4 READING

a You are going to read about how Will got malaria while he was still in the rainforest. Before you read, discuss these questions.
1 Why would this be particularly dangerous?
2 What do you think his symptoms were?
3 What would he need to do in order to survive?

b Read the text. Check your answers in 4a.

c Read the text again and answer the questions.
1 Why is rafting down rivers a good way to see wildlife?
2 How did he know there were chimpanzees nearby? How close did he get to seeing them?
3 What was he planning to do when he got to the coast?
4 What made him take his symptoms seriously?
5 He says he 'survived thanks to a mix of luck, exceptional local support and money'. What events and facts do you think Will is referring to in this sentence?

I love rafting in rainforests …

This near silent method of travel gives you an unencumbered and discreet approach, perfect for radio, but rivers are also among the best possible places to spot wildlife returning from the forest depths to feed, drink and socialise. This section of the Upper Guinean was one of the finest forests I had ever experienced. It was a storybook jungle, [1]teeming with life.

For a couple of days I had been hearing primates everywhere – in the banksides, up the trees, behind distant ridges, but never quite close enough to see. At dawn I'd hear the piercing, screaming call of a chimp, but it was impossibly far away. The last hour of light would often bring a flash of fur, a scuffle in the bushes, a warning shriek, but nothing more.

After ten days on the river, I believed I was through the worst and started to think about the finish line – where the river enters the Atlantic – and all the fried and liquid-based treats that would be waiting for me at the nearest village.

Then I started to get sick. I tried to [2]shrug it off with ibuprofen and fluid, putting it down to the exertion of paddling daily in the 40°C heat. But as my headache developed into a fever I began to [3]fret, not least because among the last words of warning given to me before heading solo into the bush was the tale of a European woman who had complained of flu-like symptoms, not gone directly to hospital, and died of an undiagnosed haemorrhagic fever 48 hours later. I desperately needed to make contact with someone on the

1 a dragonfly
2 a fish eagle and a catfish
3 a hammock
4 rapids

UNIT 3

d Discuss the questions.
1 How well do you think Will coped with the experience? Would you have coped as well as he did?
2 Do you think what he did was worthwhile? Why / Why not?

e Language in context *Descriptive verbs*

Match the highlighted words and phrases in the text with the meanings below.

a ☐ rub against a hard surface (in order to make a powder)
b ☐ contain large numbers of living creatures
c ☐ pull something heavy
d ☐ physically support
e ☐ bend down with knees bent
f ☐ pull off, like a skin
g ☐ treat something as if it is not important
h ☐ worry (v.)
i ☐ call someone to be present

Sierra Leone bank and find my way to the road, the hospital and proper treatment.

In the morning, I started to paddle out. My headache had worsened to the point that I could barely keep my eyes open in daylight, and the pain in my joints was bordering on the spectacular. My bones felt like they were ⁴grinding to dust with every movement. I had GPS marks for all of the villages along the river but one – Tolo, which had been written on my map in felt tip by one of the Gola Rainforest National Park researchers. It was by far the closest settlement – only a three-hour paddle downstream. The river was much wider and calmer. I was dropping out of the heavy forest and knew I just had to hang on. […]

At noon, a gap in the forest revealed a lone figure – a woman, ⁵crouched down washing her clothes. I was drifting by this point, almost incapable of going through the motions of the strokes. I remember her shouting, then multiple hands on me as I was ⁶peeled from my raft. I was ⁷propped up on a tree-stump stool against a mud-brick house. The chief was ⁸summoned. I might have been the first Westerner to arrive in the village in such a condition, but this place was no stranger to what to do with people carrying my symptoms. My gear was divided up, and I was ⁹hauled through the forest to the nearest village with a motorbike, then on to the roadside and eventually to a hospital.

I survived thanks to a mix of luck, exceptional local support and money. An estimated half a million African people will not be so fortunate this year.

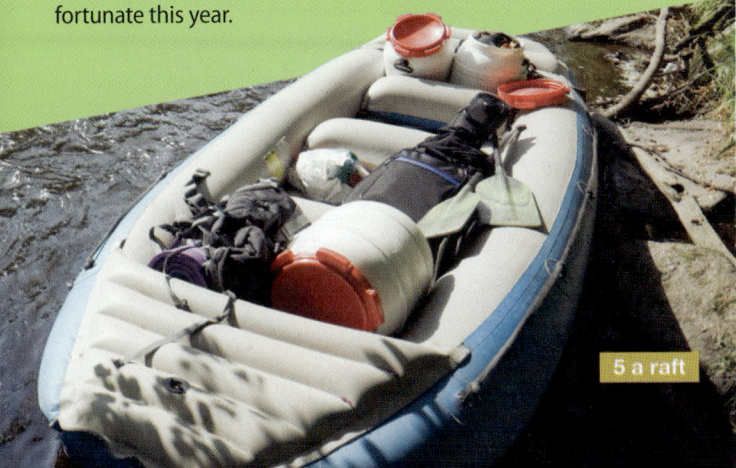

5 a raft

5 GRAMMAR Narrative tenses

a Read sentences 1–7. What is each verb form in **bold**? Why is that particular verb form used?

☐ past simple   ☐ past continuous
☐ past perfect   ☐ past perfect continuous
☐ past simple passive ☐ past perfect passive
☐ *would* + infinitive

1 For a couple of days, I **had been hearing** primates everywhere …
2 At dawn I**'d hear** the piercing, screaming call of a chimp …
3 My headache **had worsened** to the point that I could barely keep my eyes open …
4 … and the pain in my joints **was bordering on** the spectacular.
5 … Tolo, which **had been written** on my map in felt tip …
6 My gear was divided up, and I **was hauled** through the forest to the nearest village with a motorbike …
7 I **survived** thanks to a mix of luck, exceptional local support and money.

b ≫ Now go to Grammar Focus 3B on p. 143.

c How does using a different tense change the meanings of these sentences?

1 For a couple of days, I **had heard / had been hearing** primates everywhere.
2 At dawn, I **heard / 'd hear** the piercing, screaming call of a chimp.
3 The chief **was / was being** summoned.

6 WRITING AND SPEAKING

a Look at the first line of each paragraph in *I love rafting in rainforests* and answer the questions.
1 How do all the paragraphs (except two) start?
2 Which paragraphs start differently? What are the purposes of these paragraphs?

b Think about an adventurous journey you have been on, or one you have seen in a film / on TV or read about. Here are some ideas:
- a visit to a wild or remote place
- falling ill far from home
- travelling by an unusual form of transport
- being alone in an unfamiliar place.

c Write an article about the journey. Use narrative tenses and descriptive vocabulary. Describe:
1 plans that were made
2 expectations before the trip
3 when the main events happened and what happened
4 personal feelings during and after the trip.

I had been looking forward to going to Australia for months …
Last summer, I was staying with friends in Paris …

d Work in pairs. Practise telling the story.

e Work in groups. Tell the story to the others and answer any questions.

37

3C EVERYDAY ENGLISH
To cut a long story short

Learn to paraphrase and summarise

- S Paraphrase and summarise in informal conversations
- P Consonant clusters across two words

1 LISTENING

a Have you ever seen or heard a live broadcast that went wrong? What happened?

b Discuss the questions.
1 What's happening in picture a?
2 What questions do you think Oscar will ask Max during the interview?

c 03.10 Watch or listen to Part 1 and check your answers.

d 03.10 Watch or listen to Part 1 again and choose one true ending for each sentence.
1 The inhabitants of the remote planet in Max's book are aliens who …
   a look very different from humans.
   b look like humans but have a different culture.
   c want to explore other planets.
2 Oscar suggests that Max's ideas might come from …
   a his experiences while travelling.
   b another science fiction novelist.
   c experiences in his childhood.
3 Oscar suggests that Max's next book …
   a will be published in the near future.
   b will be a sequel to *Solar Wind*.
   c will depend on the success of his first book.

e Discuss the questions.
1 How do you think Oscar and Max feel about the success of the interview? Why?
2 Have you ever been interviewed for any reason? How did you feel … ?
   • before the interview
   • afterwards

2 PRONUNCIATION
Consonant clusters across two words

a 03.11 Listen to the words and phrases in the box. Underline the letters which correspond to the consonant clusters given afterwards. Notice that consonant clusters can occur within a word or across two words.

explorers /kspl/   space travel /str/   aliens look /nzl/
long story /ŋst/   bestseller /sts/

b 03.12 Match phrases 1–7 with consonant clusters across two words a–g below. Listen and check your answers. Practise saying the phrases.

1 ☐ deep space   a /kspl/
2 ☐ dense jungle   b /lθkr/
3 ☐ Max Redwood   c /ksr/
4 ☐ science fiction   d /nsf/
5 ☐ six planets   e /nsdʒ/
6 ☐ tourism statistics   f /psp/
7 ☐ wealth creation   g /mst/

c 03.13 Listen to the pronunciation of the phrases in groups 1 and 2. In which group can you hear the letters in **bold** clearly?

1 /t/ or /d/ before a _____	2 /t/ or /d/ before a _____
a Westga**t**e Street	Westga**t**e Avenue
b travelle**d** much	travelle**d** a lot
c remo**t**e planet	remo**t**e area
d differen**t** culture	differen**t** abilities
e Solar Win**d** 2	Solar Win**d** 8
f top-secre**t** classified	top-secre**t** information

d Complete the name of each group in the table in 2c with *vowel* or *consonant*.

e Practise saying the phrases in the table in 2c.

UNIT 3

3 LISTENING

a 💬 Look at picture b and answer the questions.
1 What do you think Emma thinks of Max's radio interview?
2 What do you think she will say to Max about it?

b 🎬 ▶ 03.14 Watch or listen to Part 2. How is Emma dishonest?

c 🎬 ▶ 03.14 Complete the sentences with the words you heard. Watch or listen to Part 2 again and check.
1 I'm sure it wasn't that _____!
2 I'll never be able to show my _____ again!
3 I'll put _____ on.

d **Language in context** *Exaggerating*
1 ▶ 03.15 Complete Max's exaggerations with the words in the box. Listen and check.

outright   complete and utter   totally   blithering

1 It was an _____ disaster!
2 I came across as a _____ idiot!
3 A _____ embarrassment!
4 And my career's _____ ruined!

2 💬 Why do you think Max exaggerated about his interview? In what situations do you think people choose to exaggerate? Why?

e 💬 Discuss the questions.
1 Do you think it's better to be kind or to be honest when people ask your opinion?
2 Have you ever … ?
   • told someone a white lie to avoid hurting their feelings
   • felt someone has told you a white lie to avoid hurting your feelings

4 USEFUL LANGUAGE
Paraphrasing and summarising

a Read the extracts from Parts 1 and 2. Match the expressions in **bold** with their uses below.
1 *What happens next? **Or, to put it another way**, when will Solar Wind 2 be published?*
2 ***All things considered**, I think my first and last radio interview … was a complete and utter embarrassment.*

☐ paraphrase = express the same idea in new words
☐ summarise = express only the main point(s)

b ▶ 03.16 Complete the extracts from Parts 1 and 2 below with the expressions in the box. Listen and check.

in other words   in a nutshell   that is to say
to cut a long story short   what I meant by that was

1 And basically, _____, a group of explorers are visiting a remote planet …
2 … populated by people, _____, aliens!
3 I was planning a trip across Asia but, well, _____, I had to cancel it
4 So _____, it all just came from your imagination, then?
5 _____, you're not allowed to give any dates yet?

c Add the expressions from 4a and b to the correct group below.

Paraphrasing	Summarising

d Complete the sentences with a suitable expression for summarising and paraphrasing and your own idea.
1 We had some ups and downs throughout the trip. All …
2 People there spend a lot of time visiting aunts, uncles, cousins, that is …
3 I had loads of problems on the trip, but to …
4 I'm sorry, I didn't express myself very clearly. What …
5 The novel is quite long and complicated, but in …

5 SPEAKING

Communication 3C Work in pairs. Go to p. 129.

✓ **UNIT PROGRESS TEST**

→ **CHECK YOUR PROGRESS**

YOU CAN NOW DO THE UNIT PROGRESS TEST.

3D SKILLS FOR WRITING
The view is stunning

Learn to write a travel review
W Descriptive language; Writing briefly

1 SPEAKING

a What is the most rewarding place you've been to as a tourist, and what is the most disappointing? Why?

b Read the description of Cusco from a tourist website. How much does it appeal to you as a tourist destination?

2 LISTENING

a ▶ 03.17 Listen to Roberto and Annie talking about Cusco and answer the questions.
1. What do they say about the places in the photos?
2. What similar points do they make?
3. Do you think that Roberto and Annie would both go back to Cusco? Why / Why not?

b ▶ 03.17 Roberto and Annie use descriptive phrases to talk about the city. Which phrases do they use? Match the words in boxes A and B. Then listen again to check.

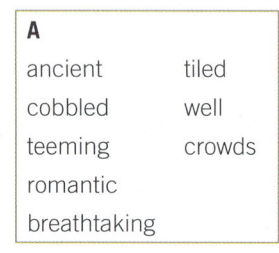

A		B	
ancient	tiled	atmosphere	roofs
cobbled	well	of tourists	streets
teeming	crowds	preserved	view
romantic		walls	
breathtaking		with people	

c Discuss the questions. Consider the issues from the point of view of both residents and tourists.
1. What are the good and bad effects that tourism can have on a city like Cusco?
2. Do you think popular tourist cities should try to limit tourists or charge them to see the city?

CUSCO, PERU
History magic and beauty

to do   to eat   to see   to go

Historic architecture of Cusco

Inca stone walls

It's no wonder that Cusco, high in the Andes mountains in Peru and a jumping-off point for the wonders of Machu Picchu, is on nearly everyone's list of must-see places in South America. It attracts 1.5 million visitors every year and has everything you'd expect of an Andean city …

- a romantic setting in a round valley surrounded by wild mountains
- a historic city centre that you can walk around in a couple of hours, although you'll want to stay much, much longer
- a mind-blowing mixture of Inca and Spanish colonial buildings and dozens of squares and parks
- the magnificent Inca citadel of Sacsayhuamán, with great views across the city
- comfortable accommodation at reasonable prices
- a lively and welcoming street life, with shops, restaurants and atmospheric cafés

3 READING

Read the traveller's review. What further information (beyond the descriptions in the listening) does it include about … ?

- walls and buildings in Cusco
- the Inca citadel

Use your answers in 2a to help you. Underline the information in the review.

4 WRITING SKILLS Descriptive language; Writing briefly

a Find words or phrases in the text which could replace the words in *italics* below.

1. The owners *were very helpful*.
2. Walking along the streets is *very difficult*.
3. Sacsayhuamán is *an attraction you definitely should see*.
4. Climbing the steps *needed a lot of effort*.
5. There are *good opportunities to take photos*.
6. The restaurant had *traditional food from the country*.
7. The food was *not too expensive*.
8. The restaurants in the centre are *more expensive than they should be*.

> **Writing Tip**
>
> When writing a description, try to use words that carry a more precise or an extra meaning. So instead of *through some … lanes which had little shops and cafés*:
> - through some … lanes which were **lined with** little shops and cafés (extra meaning: they were in lines along the sides)
>
> Instead of *zigzag walls with stone doorways in them*:
> - zigzag walls **interspersed with** stone doorways (more precise meaning: they were spaced evenly along the walls, between each section of wall)
>
> You can also convey your attitude by using words with a positive or a negative meaning. So instead of *the city was full of tourists*:
> - The city was **buzzing with** tourists. (= it was full of life; it was good)
> - The city was **overrun with** tourists. (= there were too many of them; it was bad)

b In the review, the writer sometimes omits certain words. What words could you add to these examples to make complete sentences?

1. Only one problem.
2. Took hundreds of photos.
3. Then back down to the hotel for a quick shower.

c Find three more examples of words which are omitted. What is the effect of leaving out words in this way?

1. It seems more formal.
2. It seems less formal and more like conversation.

d Now go to Writing Focus 3D on p. 170.

UNIT 3

★★★★★
Cusco getaway

We stayed at the Hotel Casa Verde – a small hotel in a quiet area just up the hill from the centre. It was fairly basic, but the owners were very hospitable and really put themselves out for us. Our double room was comfortable and spotlessly clean. To our surprise, it cost just £30 per night, including a delicious breakfast with fresh fruit, eggs and excellent coffee.

We spent the morning wandering around the city. Really impressive architecture – massive Inca walls with perfectly interlocking stones which the Spanish used as foundations for their colonial buildings, built in slightly forbidding grey stone. Only one problem – it was quite overrun with tourists (like us!), and the streets near the centre were full of people selling souvenirs, so they were kind of a nightmare to get through. We preferred the quieter lanes leading uphill from the city centre and found a few pleasant little squares where we could sit and soak up the atmosphere away from the crowds.

In the afternoon, we decided to visit Sacsayhuamán, the ruined Inca citadel above the city – a must-see attraction. We set off uphill away from the centre, through some quiet cobbled lanes which were lined with little shops and cafés. Then the hill got steeper and the lane turned into flights of steps leading up through a quiet residential area. Quite rough at such a high altitude (we had to stop every few minutes to get our breath back!), but we got to the top eventually. Great photo ops from the top with views across the whole city and the mountains beyond. The citadel itself is fascinating – massive Inca stones which are fitted so perfectly that you can't get a piece of paper between them (we tried!), and zigzag walls interspersed with perfectly proportioned stone doorways. Took hundreds of photos, and definitely worth the climb up there!

Then back down to the hotel for a quick shower and something to eat. Near the hotel there was a restaurant with authentic cuisine – quite a limited menu but very reasonably priced. I had alpaca stew, which tasted delicious. A much better option than the overpriced restaurants in the city centre!

5 WRITING

a Make a list of tourist attractions in the town and area where you are now. Include:

- attractions you think are worth visiting
- attractions you think are less worthwhile.

b Imagine you spent a day here as a tourist. Choose two or three attractions in the list and write a review. Include comments on your accommodation and somewhere you ate, too.

c Work with a partner. Look at what you both wrote and see how you could improve it by:

- using adjectives and phrases with a stronger positive or negative meaning
- making some sentences shorter by omitting words.

d Read your review to the class. Which reviews do most people agree with?

41

UNIT 3
Review and extension

1 GRAMMAR

a Reorder the words to make sentences.
1. get / plane / was / about / a / John / to / on
2. you / home / did / her / at / rarely / very / see
3. was / that / thought / faint / Amelia / to / she / going
4. account / anyone / told / on / no / be / must
5. next / set / we / early / day / to / were / leave / the
6. on / go / like / would / I / a / no / trip / way / that

b Cross out the verb form that is NOT correct.
1. Kevin *was leaving* / *was about to leave* / ~~would leave~~ on a business trip when he got the call.
2. Originally we *planned to take* / *had been going to take* / *would be taking* the train.
3. As soon as we *arrived* / *had arrived* / *had been arriving*, we checked in.
4. We *had used* / *had been using* / *used* up our supplies and had to find more from somewhere.
5. Our room was terrible, and I *had been complaining* / *might complain* / *complained* to the manager.
6. Travel *was* / *would be* / *had been* cheaper in those days.

2 VOCABULARY

a Complete the sentences with the words in the box.

| affluent | deprived | destitute | disposable |
| hardship | means | prosperity | well off |

1. This neighbourhood is fairly _____, so prices are high.
2. I don't really have much _____ income.
3. You can tell it's a(n) _____ area by the crime rate.
4. The floods left many poorer residents _____.
5. I wouldn't say I'm super-rich, but I am _____.
6. A recession had started, and the years of _____ were over.
7. It is no _____ to live without a car in a big city.
8. We manage to live within our _____ somehow.

b Complete the missing words.
1. Many species live only in the h_____t of the rainforest.
2. Anything might be hiding in the dense v_____n!
3. This is truly an u_____d wilderness.
4. The r_____d coastline is popular with walkers.
5. Once a year the rains bring the a_____d desert to life.
6. Tourists come for the p_____e beaches and gentle sea.
7. They say there are alligators in the s_____p.

3 WORDPOWER Idioms: Landscapes

a Match the expressions in **bold** with definitions a–g.
1. **A** I'm absolutely **swamped** this week.
   B Poor you. Let me know if there's anything I can do.
2. **A** We've had loads of customers this week.
   B It's great, I know. But we're not **out of the woods** yet.
3. **A** What are you going to say to him?
   B I don't know. I'll go over and **get the lie of the land** first.
4. **A** How are you coping with the move and the new job?
   B It's **an uphill struggle**, but I'm just about managing!
5. **A** It seems like when we talk we're always **getting bogged down with** tiny details.
   B So you're not making any progress?
6. **A** I've had cake every afternoon this week!
   B Be careful! It's **a slippery slope** once you start.
7. **A** I paid £100 off our credit card last month.
   B That's just **a drop in the ocean** though, isn't it? You told me you owed a few thousand.

a ☐ a small amount compared to the amount required
b ☐ a series of events that become out of control and create worse problems
c ☐ free from problems/danger
d ☐ wait until you have all the information about a situation
e ☐ get stuck on a particular point and be unable to make progress
f ☐ be overwhelmed by too much work
g ☐ when making progress is very difficult

b ▶ 03.18 Complete the sentences with an idiom from 3a. Listen and check.
1. I made a small donation, but I know it's just _____.
2. She clearly wants to _____ before she makes any big decisions.
3. Regaining popular opinion is going to be _____ for the party.
4. We've just had some great news from the hospital: Sam's _____.
5. I told her borrowing was _____. She's going to have to get a second job.
6. If you can't answer a question, don't _____ it; just move on to the next one.
7. Ever since they put the ad out, they've _____ completely _____ with phone calls.

c 💬 What situation do you think each person in 3b is talking about?

🔄 REVIEW YOUR PROGRESS

How well did you do in this unit? Write 3, 2 or 1 for each objective.
3 = very well   2 = well   1 = not so well

I CAN ...	
emphasise positive and negative experiences	☐
describe journeys and landscapes	☐
paraphrase and summarise	☐
write a travel review.	☐

CAN DO OBJECTIVES

- Talk about using instinct and reason
- Talk about memories and remembering
- Use tact in formal discussions
- Write a profile article

UNIT 4

CONSCIOUSNESS

GETTING STARTED

a Look at the picture and discuss the questions.
  1 What do you think the device does?
  2 Where is the woman? What do you think she's doing?
  3 How do you think the woman feels?

b The woman is using a virtual reality headset to guide her through a story about the food she is going to experience. Discuss the questions.

1 Would you like to try it? If so, what foods would you try it with? If not, why not?
2 What do you think the benefits of this technology could be in the wider world?
3 What technology have you experienced that changes how you perceive things?

43

4A THAT LITTLE VOICE IN YOUR HEAD

Learn to talk about using instinct and reason
G Noun phrases
V Instinct and reason

1 SPEAKING

a What are your five senses? What do you think is meant by a 'sixth sense'? Do you think you have one?

b Do the quiz with a partner and compare your answers.

c Communication 4A Count up how many As and how many Bs you chose. Check your results on p. 131.

2 VOCABULARY Instinct and reason

a Look at these people's statements. Would they be As or Bs, according to the quiz?
1 It's important to be **rational** when making life-changing decisions.
2 **On impulse**, I applied for a new job.
3 I knew **subconsciously** that I was making a mistake.
4 I think it's important to **weigh up** the advantages and disadvantages before you make a choice.

b Replace each expression in **bold** in 2a with a word or phrase from the box.

deep down   consider   objective   on a whim

c Now go to Vocabulary Focus 4A on p. 161.

Do you have A SIXTH SENSE?

How much do you rely on your intuition? Do the quiz and choose A or B. Don't think too long about it – follow your gut!

1 You find yourself a new flat. You like it because …
   A it's got a positive atmosphere and feels like a nice place to be in.
   B the furniture is in good condition and it has everything you need.

2 You meet a new colleague and have a bad feeling about them. You …
   A decide not to trust them – your first impressions are usually accurate.
   B ignore the feeling. You can't tell what people are like from first impressions.

3 The phone rings at home, and you aren't expecting a call. You …
   A have a strong feeling about who's calling.
   B have no idea who's calling until you get to the phone.

4 A close friend, who has been unusually quiet, says they need to talk to you.
   A You probably won't be surprised by what they say – you kind of know already.
   B You have no idea what to expect – it could be anything.

5 When do the best ideas come to you?
   A when you're relaxing or during the night while you're asleep
   B after thinking long and hard about them

6 You wake up from a strange dream. You think …
   A 'This dream is telling me something – I must remember it.'
   B 'What a silly dream!' and go about your day.

7 A new opportunity arises, but it's a major change. Your family and friends advise against it.
   A You go for what you feel is right, in spite of their advice.
   B You drop the idea – they can see the situation more objectively than you.

8 Are you someone who experiences an unusual number of coincidences?
   A Yes, although you don't believe they are simply coincidences.
   B No, and neither does anyone else – coincidences are purely chance events.

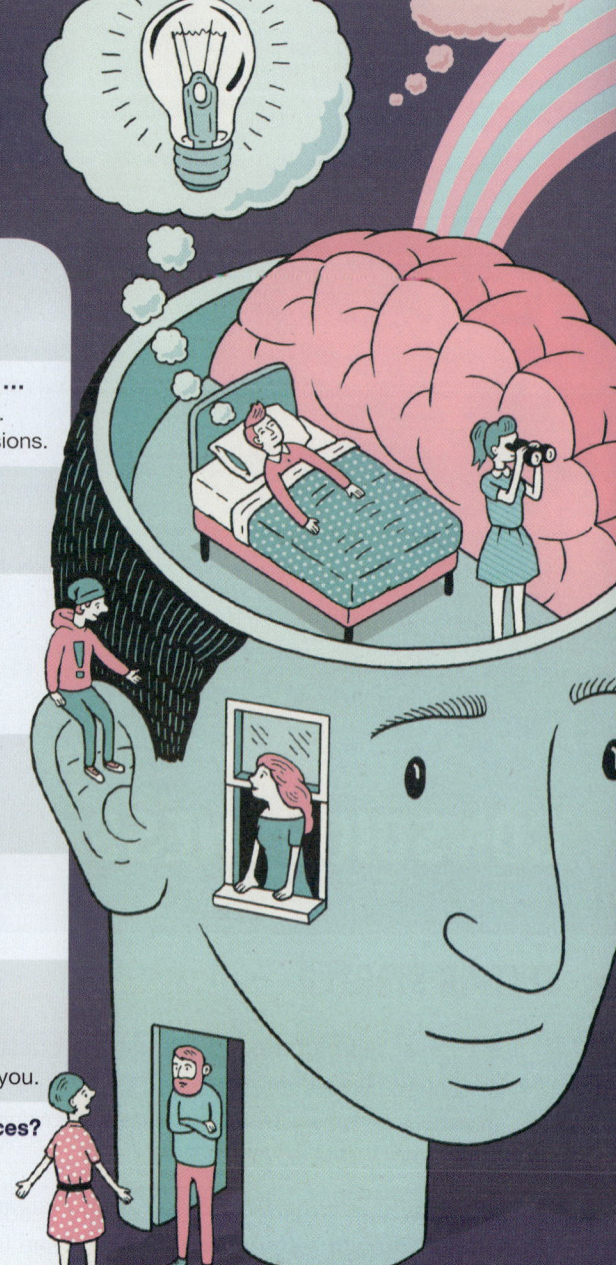

UNIT 4

3 READING

a Read the first part of the article below about gut instincts and discuss these questions.
1 What is the author going to give readers advice about?
2 What are the roles of the left and right sides of the brain, according to researchers?
3 What does the writer suggest is a good way to make decisions?

b Read the rest of the article. Match the headings a–e to the advice 1–5.
a I'm not sure about you.
b This is the one I've been waiting for!
c I've done this a million times before.
d I should try to help.
e I'm in pain.

c Look at the underlined parts of the article. Explain in your own words what the writer means in each case.

d Discuss these questions.
1 Do you agree with the five pieces of advice in the article? Are there any you disagree with? Why?
2 Can you think of situations where it might be better not to follow your gut instincts?

4 GRAMMAR Noun phrases

a Match the noun phrases 1–6 from the article with their type a–f.
1 ☐ a funny feeling in your stomach
2 ☐ that narrow parking space
3 ☐ humanity's oldest survival mechanisms
4 ☐ an irresistible urge to ask
5 ☐ gut feelings
6 ☐ commonly reported indicators

a noun + noun
b noun + 's + superlative + compound noun
c article + adjective + noun + preposition + possessive + noun
d determiner + adjective + compound noun
e adverb + adjective + noun
f article + adjective + noun + infinitive

b Rephrase these noun phrases using the patterns in brackets.
1 a meeting which happens by chance (article + noun + noun)
= a chance meeting
2 the dreams of my friend who is close (possessive + adjective + noun + 's + noun)
3 a day that you will remember (article + noun + to + infinitive)
4 a dream that is so vivid it disturbs you (article + adverb + adjective + noun)
5 thoughts that are dark and secret (adjective + adjective + noun)
6 the capacity of humans to imagine things (article + adjective + noun + for + noun)

c Now go to Grammar Focus 4A on p. 144.

Learn to
TRUST YOUR GUT!

You have an irresistible urge to ask a complete stranger to go for a coffee. You decide on a whim to buy a property you've never visited. You feel an inexplicable certainty that you should not get on that plane.

Following your gut feelings could either be the best thing you ever did or end in disaster. On the other hand, ignoring these instincts could have exactly the same outcomes. How can we know when to trust our intuition and when to let our heads rule?

Psychiatrists assert that the home of intuition is in the right hemisphere of the brain. While the conscious left brain edits the world into a logical and coherent whole, the right brain picks up the big picture and reacts spontaneously. Too often the left brain dismisses the urges of the right as irrational, while we remain blissfully ignorant of the process.

In order to use intuition more effectively, we can tune in to the physical symptoms that let us know it is operating. Clammy palms, a tingle up the spine or a funny feeling in your stomach are all commonly reported indicators that the intuitive right brain is in action. When you notice this feeling, take the time to evaluate it and give yourself a choice.

And to help you on your way, here are five instances where the gut is almost always right.

1 _____
It seems so much like common sense that it could be the left brain talking. When you hear that little voice in your head nagging you to go for a check-up, do yourself a favour and go. If you don't, you could be letting yourself in for trouble down the road.

2 _____
First impressions are not just about hair and shoes. Tune in to that all-important feeling you get when you meet a new person, and you are using one of humanity's oldest survival mechanisms. Our ancestors knew instinctively who to trust and who not to – and so do you. Crossing the street to avoid a stranger is not going to hurt anyone's feelings, and it may just keep you safe.

3 _____
Use your instinct to tell you when those around you are in need of your support. Our urge to help others is often outbid by other priorities, like getting somewhere on time or not wanting to appear nosy. But these instincts are just as much survival mechanisms as our fears, and who knows when you may need a hand yourself one day?

4 _____
Trust your gut to get you through the most stressful of occasions. When you're under pressure, it's easy to forget how to do even things you're an expert at. So use intuition to guide you into that narrow parking space or to cook that special meal. Under stress it's way more reliable than your conscious brain.

5 _____
Never discount your gut instincts in the lead-up to a decision that could affect the course of your future life. These are the times to really use your whole brain. If your right brain says, 'Yes! Yes! Yes!', there's a good chance that's the decision you'll be happiest with in the long run.

45

UNIT 4

5 LISTENING

a You will hear a discussion about the way doctors diagnose patients. How much do you think doctors rely on their gut instincts?

b ▶04.04 Listen to the discussion. What do the speakers agree on? Choose 1, 2 or 3.
1 Doctors rely too much on their gut instincts, and this can be a problem.
2 Unfortunately, doctors don't pay attention to their gut instincts.
3 Doctors often rely on their gut instincts, and this is useful.

c ▶04.04 Listen again and choose the correct option in *italics*.
1 When we have inner doubts, they are *often / not usually* just signs of worry.
2 Most doctors will admit to *having / following* gut instincts.
3 Ann Van den Bruel has done research into *how often doctors use gut instinct / how accurate gut instinct is*.
4 Doctors' gut feelings about children's infections often turn out to be *correct / incorrect*.
5 Margaret McCartney thinks that gut instincts are *important / unscientific*.
6 Doctors tend to follow their gut instincts when they are *more / less* sure about their diagnosis.
7 Doctors from different countries seem to have very *similar / different* experiences.
8 Doctors in general practice have to rely on their instincts *less / more* than hospital doctors.

d In what ways has the discussion changed your mind about the question in 5a?

e Language in context *Doubt and uncertainty*

1 ▶04.05 Complete the sentences with the words in the box. Then listen and check your answers.

pattern   doubt   jars   worriers
feeling   bones   fit   anxieties

1 That **uneasy** _____ that you get when you think there is something that you should be doing.
2 More often than not these are **groundless** _____ that simply reflect that many of us are **born** _____.
3 All may appear well on the surface, but you're left with **a nagging** _____ that all is not quite as it seems.
4 It's almost like recognising that this person just **doesn't quite fit the** _____, but you're not quite sure in what way.
5 Other doctors will say that they **feel it in their** _____ that something's just not right.
6 It's just this idea that you get: something that _____, something that just **doesn't quite** _____ properly **together**.

2 Which words and phrases in **bold** are connected with these things?
a a feeling that things aren't OK
b worrying more than you need to
c not being able to make sense of things
d knowing something intuitively

6 SPEAKING

a Read each dilemma. What would you do? Is what you would do and what you should do the same in each case?
1 You are a judge. You are due to sentence a criminal that you have seen in your court before. On that occasion, he was found not guilty of a serious crime due to a lack of evidence – but your gut told you differently. Do you give him the maximum sentence this time?
2 You are a junior web designer, and your boss has asked you to present a web design for a potentially important client. You've been given detailed information about the colour and design preferences of your client's target market, but you feel that this would result in a sterile and boring design that wouldn't get you the contract. Do you insist on presenting your preferred design instead?
3 You are interviewing candidates for a six-month contract. One candidate is very well qualified and performs well in the interview, but there's something about him that makes you uneasy (you can't quite put your finger on it). The choice is between him and someone who doesn't look so good on paper and was very nervous in the interview, but who you have a good feeling about. Who would you go for?

b How could gut instinct play a part in these roles?
- politician
- CEO of a large company
- airline pilot
- parent

c Choose one of the jobs in 6b or a different job and write a dilemma like those in 6a. Swap dilemmas with other students and discuss the dilemma you receive.

4B HE GOT HIMSELF LOCKED IN A SHED

Learn to talk about memories and remembering

G Structures with *have* and *get*
V Memory

1 LISTENING AND GRAMMAR
Structures with *have* and *get*

a 💬 Discuss the questions.
1 What kind of stories do you and your family and childhood friends tell about your childhood?
2 What was a particularly funny/proud/scary moment?

b ▶ 04.06 Listen to Tommy, Marissa and Clara talk about their childhood memories. Answer the questions.
1 What's the significance of photos a–c? Summarise what happened in each memory.
2 Why do you think these memories are still so clear for the speakers?

c 💬 Do you relate to any of the people telling the stories? Why / Why not?

> I can't really relate to Clara. I was a very confident child!

d Compare the meaning of each pair of sentences. Is there a difference?
1 a **My parents were having the kitchen renovated.**
   b My parents were renovating the kitchen.
2 a **I had all my toys stolen.**
   b All my toys were stolen.
3 a **He got himself locked in the garden shed.**
   b He got locked in the garden shed.
4 a **His disappearance got everyone looking for him.**
   b He got everyone to look for him.
5 a **She had me sitting on my own.**
   b I was sitting on my own.
6 a **He got me to play when nobody else could.**
   b He played with me.

Match the sentences in **bold** with the uses a–d below.
a the subject's possessions were harmed by somebody else ☐
b the subject paid somebody else to do a job ☐
c the subject caused somebody to do something ☐ ☐
d the subject caused what happened to them ☐

e Copy the table into your notebook. Then add the sentences in **bold** in 1d. Answer the questions.

Subject	Verb form 1	Object	Verb form 2
They	had	their roof	fixed.
We	got	our car	broken into.

1 Could *get* be used instead of *have* in each sentence with *have*? If so, does it change the meaning?
2 Could *have* be used instead of *get* in each sentence with *get*? If so, does it change the meaning?

f ⟫ Now go to Grammar Focus 4B on p. 145.

2 SPEAKING

a ▶ 04.09 Pronunciation Underline the stressed syllables in these sentences. Then listen and check. What kinds of words are usually unstressed?
1 I had my bike stolen.
2 They had me doing all the cleaning for weeks.
3 I had my arm broken in a football match.
4 She had me doing all her homework.
5 It got me thinking about what I'd done wrong.
6 I got myself locked out of the house.
7 I got my mum to say I was sick.
8 My brother got me punished unfairly.

b 💬 Think of two or three childhood incidents like the examples in 2a. Use these questions to help you remember. Tell your partner about them.
• Who was there?
• Where were you?
• Did anyone get into trouble? Who?
• Did something cause the problem?
• How was the situation resolved?
• What was the outcome?

UNIT 4

3 LISTENING AND READING

a ▶ 04.10 Listen to Marissa's story again, and then listen to her brother Charlie's version. Note down the differences.

b 💬 Discuss the questions.
1 Does your family have any stories that there are different versions of?
2 What's your earliest memory? How reliable do you think it is?
3 What reasons can you think of for inaccuracies in … ?
  • childhood memories
  • the memories of witnesses in criminal cases
4 How good are you at remembering events? Do you think you would make a good witness in a criminal case?

c Student A: Read the text *False childhood memories*. Answer the questions.
1 Why are many of our early childhood memories wrong?
2 What causes us to invent memories?
3 How can we tell if someone's memory is probably true or not?

Student B: Read the text *How eyewitness evidence can be unreliable*. Answer the questions.
1 What causes witnesses of a crime to get things wrong?
2 What factors make police line-ups an unreliable way of identifying a criminal?
3 How are police trying to improve eyewitness testimony?

d 💬 Tell your partner about the text you read. Was there anything you found particularly interesting or surprising?

e In pairs, guess the meaning of the highlighted words and expressions in both texts. Then check your ideas in a dictionary.

FALSE CHILDHOOD MEMORIES

Does this sound familiar? You're talking to your mother about the wonderful time that your grandmother visited. You were about three years old. Your mother then interrupts to tell you that your grandmother never came to that house because by the time you were born she was not well enough to travel. But you remember it all so clearly, and there's a photograph to prove it! You find the photo of your grandmother at your family home and then you note the date: a year before you were born. How is that possible? A lot of our so-called childhood memories are things that we have made up. They might relate to a family story we've heard or a photo we've seen, and we embellish that information and turn it into our own memory. However, they bear little resemblance to the real event. And the more we talk about it, the more plausible the story seems. So when someone contradicts us, it comes as a shock.

Scientists have proved that this is a natural phenomenon. Very few people can remember events that happened before the age of two. This is because our brains are developing so quickly as we learn to understand the world around us and communicate that there aren't enough brain cells left to make the kinds of neural connections we need to establish long-term memories.

So if it's physiologically impossible, why do we spend so much time making memories up? It all has to do with narrative. Humankind thrives on stories. We like to know and talk about the story of our lives, and if there are any missing gaps in the early years, we're very good at filling them in. We'll even borrow events from family members and make them our own. In short, our memories are very malleable.

Brain scan studies have been done that show that the neural activity of false memories looks very similar to that of real ones. So how can we tell if a childhood memory is real or fake? It's all in the detail. If someone has a complex memory of an event that includes different actions and lots of sensory information, then it's more likely that it'll be fake.

So the next time you're disagreeing with a sibling over what really happened when you were a child, chances are that you're probably both wrong and the truth lies somewhere in the middle, or maybe will never be known.

HOW EYEWITNESS EVIDENCE CAN BE UNRELIABLE

It's a classic scene in any courtroom drama. It looks like the defendant is going to go free, but at the last minute, the prosecution produces a witness who swears that they saw the defendant commit the crime. There's nothing more convincing than eyewitness testimony. This is what sways the jury.

Convincing it may be, but is it accurate? Research has shown that eyewitness testimony is actually quite fallible. Our memories aren't like smartphone cameras that record visual information with precision. Nor are our memories neutral. They are susceptible to influence from our belief systems, our sense of who we are, and how we feel about the world.

Psychologists also point out that most people who see a crime experience some kind of shock or trauma. This, in turn, prevents us from forming accurate memories of the events, and it also means we forget things far more quickly than we assume. However, we are also very good at fusing bits of visual information and then reconstructing events, so what we 'remember' is often not what happened but what we would like to think happened. Frequently, when a crime takes place, the police arrive at the scene of the crime and immediately talk to any witnesses. Police always ask for a physical description of the perpetrator of the crime, and they will often invite the witness to the police station to look at photographs.

The police investigation proceeds, and the witness may then be invited back to identify the perpetrator in a line-up. By this stage, time has elapsed, and the witness might assume someone in the line-up must be the person they saw. The pressure of the situation makes them feel they need to choose someone, even if they don't really recognise anyone in the line-up. Or, while they are trying to decide, the police officer might direct their gaze at one of the suspects. Body language can easily influence the witness's choice.

Police are being more cautious and are starting to record the identification procedure so that it can be shown in court. The jury can see whether the identification process was carried out in a neutral manner. Even so, police may plant information about a criminal inadvertently, and our memory often plays tricks on us. By the time we're called to the witness stand in court, what we think we perceived may not be completely accurate; it may not be the full story.

4 VOCABULARY Memory

a Match the collocations 1–6 with their definitions a–f.

1. a vague memory
2. a painful memory
3. a vivid memory
4. a photographic memory
5. a lasting memory
6. a distant memory

a. permanent
b. it still makes you unhappy
c. it happened a long time ago
d. unclear
e. you can remember anything perfectly
f. with clear sensations

b In which collocation in 4a is the meaning of *memory* different? What's the difference?

c Now go to Vocabulary Focus 4B on p. 161.

d Ask and answer the questions.

1. How clearly do you remember the time before you went to school?
2. If you think of your home town, what's the first thing that comes to mind?
3. Which holidays do you have lasting memories of? What kind of things do you remember most vividly? (food/people/sights)
4. If you cast your mind back five years, what's the first thing you remember?
5. When was the last time an appointment slipped your mind?
6. Are there any sounds or smells that trigger a memory for you? What exactly?
7. What's a memory of a close friend that you'll always treasure?

5 SPEAKING

a **Communication 4B 1** Test your memory. Student A: Go to p. 132. Student B: Go to p. 130.

b Work in small groups. What can you do to improve your memory? Make a list of ideas.

- get more sleep

c **Communication 4B 2** Go to p. 133 and read the fact file.

d Discuss the questions.

1. What information in the fact file was useful / not useful for you?
2. What things do you find easier / more difficult to remember than others? Why?
3. In education, what kinds of things do you think need to be memorised?
4. Is it a good idea to use technology to help us remember things?

4C EVERYDAY ENGLISH
I see where you're coming from

Learn to use tact in formal discussions
- S Give opinions tactfully
- P Homophones in words and connected speech

1 LISTENING

a Discuss the questions.
1 What makes a media interview successful?
2 Who is responsible for making an interview work – the interviewer or the interviewee?

b 04.13 Watch or listen to Part 1. Who does Nadia think is responsible for making an interview work?

c 04.13 Look at the list of topics that were mentioned in Part 1. Who mentioned them and what did they say about them? Watch or listen to Part 1 again and check your answers.
1 Max's writing
2 professionalism
3 a sequel to *Solar Wind*
4 the number of listeners

d Discuss the questions.
1 How would you describe Oscar's and Sara's responses to Nadia's feedback?
2 Are you surprised by their responses?

e 04.13 **Language in context** *Idioms 1*
Answer the questions below. Watch or listen to Part 1 again and check your answers.
Nadia says that Max wasn't *particularly forthcoming*.
a What idiom with the word *blood* does Oscar use with the same meaning?
b What idiom with the word *nut* does Sara use?

2 USEFUL LANGUAGE
Being tactful in formal discussions

a Match the expressions in **bold** from Part 1 with their uses a–c.
1 ☐ Well, **if you don't mind me saying so**, it was like trying to get blood out of a stone.
2 ☐ **I see where you're coming from, but** guys, I think we're forgetting something here.
3 ☐ Look, **don't take this personally**, Oscar. I'm trying to be constructive.
4 ☐ **I do take your point, but** I'm not sure there's anything more I could've done.
5 ☐ **I beg to differ**. I agree Redwood wasn't particularly forthcoming, but my feeling is that there's always a way.
6 ☐ **No offence intended**, Oscar, **but** I couldn't understand why you were asking about a sequel.
7 ☐ **With all due respect**, Sara, I don't think you're in a position to tell us what does and doesn't make a good interviewer.

a soften direct criticisms
b present contradictory opinions
c soften strong/unpopular opinions or bad news

b 04.14 Listen to 1–3 and match the expressions in **bold** with their uses in 2a.
1 ☐ You can be a bit heavy-handed from time to time. But **I mean that in the nicest possible way**.
2 ☐ **I'm afraid I have to say**, if we go down this road, it'll be a disaster.
3 ☐ **That's not the way I see it**, I'm afraid. There were several ways to avoid this outcome.

c Work with a partner. Make the discussions below more tactful, using expressions from 2a and 2b. Act out your discussion for other people in the class.
1 A My article was rather clever.
 B It was potentially offensive.
 A People shouldn't be so sensitive.
 B You need to be more tactful.
2 A I think I handled that meeting quite well.
 B You allowed Leon to talk for too long.
 A You could have interrupted him and helped me out.
 B It was your job to chair the meeting.

50

3 PRONUNCIATION Homophones in words and connected speech

a ▶ 04.15 *See* and *sea* are homophones – two different words with the same pronunciation. Listen to these phrases and find the words which are incorrect. Write the correct homophone. Sometimes there is more than one in each phrase.

1 with all ~~dew~~ respect *due*
2 I mean it in the nicest possible weigh
3 it's knot about being fare
4 the virus gets into the sells
5 a pear of pants
6 I can still see the hole seen
7 eyewitness testimony carries grate wait
8 it may bare little resemblance to the truth

b Phrases can also be homophones. Complete these homophones.

1 great eye = grey _____*tie*_____
2 known aim = no _____
3 way cup = wake _____
4 fork aches = _____
5 lock tin side = _____

c ▶ 04.16 Listen and correct the homophones in these sentences. Notice that the end of one word may change because of the sound at the beginning of the next.

1 How do ewe thing kit went? *How do you think it went?*
2 if few don't mime me saying sew
3 I think we all knee two learn from this
4 know a fence in ten did
5 we knee to bay rim mined

d Complete the advice.
If you hear a word which doesn't seem to make sense in context, …

4 LISTENING

a 💬 Look at the picture below. What do you think Sara is asking Alex to do?

b 🎥▶ 04.17 Watch or listen to Part 2 and check your answer in 4a.

c 🎥▶ 04.17 Watch or listen to Part 2 again and answer the questions.
  1 What has been the same about Nadia's behaviour and what has been different?
  2 How do you think Sara feels when she is asking Alex for Max's phone number? Why?
  3 What advice does Alex give Sara? Why?

d 💬 If Sara follows Alex's advice, what do you think the consequences will be?

e **Language in context** *Idioms 2*
  1 ▶ 04.18 Complete the idioms with one word in each space. Listen and check your answers. What do the idioms all express?
    1 _____ me about it!
    2 You're _____ me!
    3 You've _____ the nail on the head!
  2 ▶ 04.18 Underline the main stress in the idioms in 1. Listen again and check. Practise saying the idioms.

5 SPEAKING

Communication 4C Work in pairs.
Student A: Go to p. 127.
Student B: Go to p. 133.

UNIT PROGRESS TEST
CHECK YOUR PROGRESS
YOU CAN NOW DO THE UNIT PROGRESS TEST.

4D SKILLS FOR WRITING
So what was her breakthrough moment?

Learn to write a profile article

W Organising information; Showing time relationships

1 SPEAKING AND LISTENING

a Think about these questions and note down your ideas. Then ask and answer the questions.
1. Have you ever been interviewed for any kind of article or TV programme? If so, what was it for?
2. If someone were to interview you about your interests, work or talents, what do you think the interview would be about?
3. Think of one interest or ability you have. Where do you think it comes from? Can you remember when and how it first started? Were there any particular people or events that influenced you?

b You are going to hear an interview with a singer, Noni-K. Here are some key things she mentions about her life. Why do you think they are important in her career?
1. She was shy as a young teenager.
2. Her family moved from South Africa to London when she was a child.
3. She moved back to South Africa when she was 17.
4. She started sharing music with friends.
5. A friend let her use his studio.
6. She recorded her first album.

c 04.19 Listen and summarise what Noni-K says about each of the things in 1b.

2 READING

Read the article and answer the questions. Use your answers in 1c to help you.
1. What further information does the article give about Noni-K's life and career?
2. Was there any information in the interview that the writer didn't include in the article?

3 WRITING SKILLS Organising information; Showing time relationships

a In addition to describing Noni-K's life, the article includes:
- direct quotes (things Noni-K said)
- the 'setting' of the interview (outside a recording studio)
- her appearance at the interview (clothes, manner).

1. Find two examples of direct quotes in the article.
2. What is the effect on the reader of including direct quotes and details of the setting and her appearance?

Best known for her recent album *Breakout*, Noni-K is one of the most exciting new talents on the South African music scene. She talks to Saul Winthorpe about how she got to where she is now.

Within a single year, Noni-K has moved from only being known locally to being one of the hottest new names in South African hip-hop. In a field that has traditionally been dominated by male artists, she is one of a new generation of female singers who are establishing themselves in South Africa and internationally. Noni Kamari, better known by her stage name Noni-K, is a multifaceted vocalist with a body of work which ranges from hip-hop to soul, and which embraces her own personal growth, both as a person and as a performer.

When I meet her outside the studio in Johannesburg where she is recording her second album, she is wearing the same casual clothes – baggy, light-grey jumper and black trousers – that are her trademark style on her YouTube videos. She seems surprisingly relaxed about her sudden success. She's also refreshingly personal and uninterested in commercial success. 'I make the music I believe in,' she tells me. 'For me, it's a way to see who I am. And if it speaks to other people, that's cool too, but that's not really what I'm doing it for.'

We talk about her early teenage years and whether she'd always enjoyed performing. She tells me that she was actually quite shy as a young teen, partly because her family moved to the UK when she was eight,

UNIT 4

b What verb tenses does the article use … ?
1 to talk about her current success
2 to describe what happened during the interview
3 to talk about events in her life in the past

c Compare these sentences with the same ideas in paragraph 2 of the article.

> I meet her outside the studio in Johannesburg. She is recording her second album. She is wearing the same casual clothes. She's wearing a baggy light grey jumper and black trousers. These clothes are her trademark style on her YouTube videos.

1 What differences are there in the way the ideas are expressed?
2 Why do you think the writer chooses the style used in the article? Tick (✓) one or more reasons.
   a ☐ to make it sound more formal
   b ☐ to show how different ideas are connected together
   c ☐ to make the paragraph read more smoothly

d Cover the text. Combine the information in each item below into single sentences.
1 She tells me that she was actually quite shy as a young teenager. This is partly because her family moved to the UK when she was eight. First, they moved to Bristol. Subsequently, they moved to London.
2 Through friends, she got to know a circle of people in Johannesburg. They were sharing ideas in music. Before long, she was creating songs in a new, more experimental style.

Compare your sentences with the ones in the text. Are they similar? Which are more effective?

e Which of the highlighted expressions in the text means … ?
1 immediately (x1)
2 after a short time (x2)
3 some time later (x3)

f Underline the time expressions in these examples. Add them to lists 1–3 in 3e.
1 No sooner had I started singing than I realised it was what I'd always wanted to do.
2 Not until many years later did she become famous.
3 The instant I heard her music, I knew she was an exceptional talent.
4 In time, she started singing in a greater variety of styles.
5 She went on a tour of the main cities of South Africa, which was closely followed by a tour of Asia.

g What is unusual about the structure of sentences 1 and 2?

h ⟫ Now go to Writing Focus 4D on p. 171.

4 WRITING

a Prepare to be interviewed by another student about an interest or a talent.
1 Look at the notes you made in 1a and think of some questions you would like your partner to ask you.
2 Think of a suitable venue for your interview (your workplace, a café …).

b Take turns interviewing each other and take notes. Use the questions your partner suggested and add others of your own. You could ask about:
- how it started
- early influences
- involvement of family and friends
- achievements
- plans.

> 💬 **Writing Tip**
> When taking notes:
> - Write down key points as you listen to help organise your ideas later – just enough to remind you of what your partner said.
> - What is the most interesting part of your interviewee's story? Make sure you highlight this in your notes – it could be a good way to begin the article.

c From your notes, write an article about your partner. Use the Noni-K article as a model and include a few direct quotes from your interview.

---

first to Bristol and subsequently to London. Because of this, she always felt like a bit of an outsider. It wasn't until she moved back to South Africa at the age of 17 that she started to feel more confident about performing. 'There's so much happening here,' she tells me. 'The moment I arrived I knew I'd found the place I wanted to be. It felt like coming home.' Through friends, she got to know a circle of people in Johannesburg who were sharing ideas in music and before long she was creating songs in a new, more experimental style. Shortly afterwards, she got together with two other musicians and they started performing regularly. Gradually, they got better known, but it was only when she released her first album, *Breakout*, that she suddenly became a sensation in South Africa and beyond. And her popularity shows no sign of waning any time soon. Noni may only be making music for herself, as she says, but she's also spreading joy to her thousands of followers.

BREAKOUT

Noni-K

UNIT 4
Review and extension

1 GRAMMAR

a Correct the mistakes in the sentences.

1. A published recently article has caused a political uproar.
2. For dessert there were delicious strawberry filled with cream tarts.
3. We need a new bed. Our one old is broken.
4. Every table's corner was covered in papers and documents.
5. If you ever get a chance see them in concert, I recommend it.
6. A friend of the wife of John is also interested.
7. The recently elected leader of the council's name is Mr Singh.
8. I have to tell him a difficult something this evening.

b Choose the correct options.

1. The house *got / had* burgled and almost everything was taken.
2. Only Jason could *get / have* himself lost in a supermarket.
3. We'll have *done the repairs / the repairs done* by a specialist.
4. *Get / Have* Pam to tell you why she left university.
5. It's as painful as *to have / having* a tooth taken out.
6. Wait five minutes until I've got the baby *dressed / to dress*.
7. The police officer *got / had* them give their details.

2 VOCABULARY

a Match the sentence halves.

1. ☐ It was a difficult climb, and I'll think
2. ☐ Usually I'm quite rational, but sometimes I act on
3. ☐ I don't know why, but I've got
4. ☐ I'll give you some time to think
5. ☐ In a situation like this, you need to weigh up
6. ☐ There was no logic; it was just my gut
7. ☐ Sometimes you think everything is all right, but

a. impulse and do something I later regret.
b. subconsciously you know it isn't.
c. it over and make up your mind.
d. instinct telling me what to do.
e. twice about doing something like that again.
f. the pros and cons and come to a decision.
g. a hunch that Samuel stole the necklace.

b Correct the mistakes in the sentences.

1. My childhood is just a far memory to me now.
2. I have a photographer's memory; I can remember things really easily.
3. A vocabulary notebook is a good way to freshen up your memory of new words.
4. I can only foggily remember my first lesson in this English class.
5. When I think of fast food, the word *unhealthy* comes in mind.
6. I have some hurtful memories from my school days.
7. People's birthdays often leave my mind.
8. Some photographs I have stimulate the memory of some wonderful experiences.

3 WORDPOWER *mind*

a ▶04.20 Complete the phrases in **bold** with the verbs in the box. Listen and check.

speak   read   cross   bear   put

1. Don't hold back, please. _____ **your mind**.
2. Thanks for telling me. I'll _____ **it in mind** when I'm making my decision.
3. I wish you'd tell me what the problem is. I can't _____ **your mind**.
4. You can do anything if you _____ **your mind to it**.
5. It didn't _____ **my mind** to tell you.

b Match the phrases in **bold** in 3a with definitions a–e.

a ☐ think of, remember
b ☐ give your true opinion
c ☐ try hard, using your brain
d ☐ know what somebody is thinking
e ☐ consider useful information

c ▶04.21 Match 1–5 with a–e. Listen and check.

1. ☐ I'll double check I locked the door.
2. ☐ I can't cope with doing it right now.
3. ☐ I know you've got doubts.
4. ☐ Look at the state of my hair!
5. ☐ She's stressed out.

a. I'm not **in the right frame of mind**.
b. Please try to **keep an open mind**.
c. It gives me **peace of mind**.
d. She **has a lot on her mind**.
e. I swear it **has a mind of its own**.

d 💬 Choose a sentence from 3a or 3c and continue the conversation with other students. When your conversation ends, choose a new sentence.

🔄 REVIEW YOUR PROGRESS

How well did you do in this unit? Write 3, 2 or 1 for each objective.
3 = very well   2 = well   1 = not so well

I CAN . . .	
talk about using instinct and reason	☐
talk about memories and remembering	☐
use tact in formal discussions	☐
write a profile article.	☐

CAN DO OBJECTIVES

- Talk about crime and punishment
- Talk about job requirements and fair pay
- Recall and speculate
- Write an opinion essay

UNIT 5

FAIRNESS

GETTING STARTED

a Look closely at the picture and discuss the questions.
1. Where is the man? Why do you think he is there?
2. What might the role of the dog be in this place?

b The man is participating in a pet therapy programme for offenders. Discuss the questions.
1. In what ways could working with animals benefit prisoners?
2. What other kinds of activity might be beneficial for people while they are in prison?
3. Why do you think some criminals leave prison and reoffend while others don't?

5A A PLACE WHERE YOU HAVE TO LOOK OVER YOUR SHOULDER

Learn to talk about crime and punishment
G Relative clauses
V Crime and justice

1 READING

a What do you think life in a typical prison is like? Think of examples from your country or from films and TV programmes.
   1 What does a prison look like?
   2 What are the conditions like? (cells, food, facilities, activities for prisoners)

b Look at the photos of Halden Prison in Norway and discuss the questions.
   1 What do you think the conditions are like? (cells, food, facilities, activities for prisoners)
   2 What kinds of crimes do you think the prisoners here might have committed?

   Read the article and check your answers.

c Read the article again and answer the questions.
   1 On arrival, what two things does the writer notice?
   2 How does Norway aim to deal with criminals?
   3 Does the writer think the prison is like a hotel? Why / Why not?
   4 What are the aims of the design of the prison?
   5 How are inmates motivated to do activities? Why?
   6 What aspect of prison life does Kent find difficult?
   7 What surprised the visiting prison warden?
   8 What is the writer's impression of the atmosphere at Halden?

d Work in pairs. Try to find the meaning of the highlighted words and phrases in the article. Use a dictionary to check your answers.

e Do you agree with Kent's statement in *italics* in the article? Should prison be more about punishment or rehabilitation? Why?

Can we have a swimming pool?
LIFE AT HALDEN PRISON
by Amelia Gentleman

Halden Prison smells of freshly brewed coffee. It hits you in the ¹communal apartment-style areas where prisoners live together in groups of eight. The other remarkable thing is how quiet the prison is. There isn't any of the angry banging of doors you hear in British prisons, not least because the prisoners are not locked up much during the day.

Halden is one of Norway's highest-security jails. Up to 252 criminals, many of whom have committed some of the most serious offences, can be held there. Since it opened in 2010, at a cost of 1.3bn Norwegian kroner (over £100 million), Halden has acquired a reputation as the world's most ²humane prison. It is the flagship of the Norwegian justice system, where the focus is on rehabilitation rather than punishment.

Halden has attracted attention globally for its design and comfort. Set in a forest, the prison blocks are a model of ³minimalist chic. At times, the environment feels more like a Scandinavian boutique hotel than a maximum security prison. Every Halden cell has a flat-screen television, its own toilet (which, unlike standard UK prison cells, also has a door) and a shower, which comes with large, soft, white towels. Prisoners have their own fridges, cupboards and desks in bright new pine and huge, ⁴unbarred windows overlooking mossy forest scenery.

Obviously the hotel comparison is a stupid one, since the problem with being in prison, unlike staying in a hotel, is that you cannot leave – hidden behind the silver birch trees is a thick, tall, concrete wall, impossible to ⁵scale.

Given the constraints of needing to keep ⁶high-risk people ⁷incarcerated, creating an environment that was as unprisonlike as possible was a priority for Are Høidal, the warden of Halden, and the prison's architects. Høidal says, 'We felt it shouldn't look like a prison. We wanted to create normality. If you can't see the wall, this could be anything, anywhere.'

2 GRAMMAR Relative clauses

a Match the captions with photos a–d in the article.

   1 ☐ Norwegian prison officers are tasked with rehabilitating the men in their care, the result of which is a 20% reoffending rate, compared with almost 50% in England and Wales.

   2 ☐ The prison has a mixing studio in which prisoners can focus their creative energy on music.

   3 ☐ Welcome to Halden Prison, Norway, inside the walls of which prisoners receive comforts often likened to those of boutique hotels.

   4 ☐ The prisoners, some of whom have committed the most serious crimes imaginable, are provided with plenty of opportunities for physical exercise.

b Underline the relative clause in each caption in 2a. Is it defining or non-defining? How can you tell?

c Compare the clauses below with the examples in 2a. What features of the clauses in 2a are more formal?
   1 which results in a 20% reoffending rate
   2 where prisoners can focus their creative energy on music
   3 where prisoners receive comforts often likened to those of boutique hotels
   4 who in some cases have committed the most serious crimes imaginable

d ⇒ Now go to Grammar Focus 5A on p. 146.

UNIT 5

> **Halden prison has been compared to the finest hotel.**

Prisoners are unlocked at 7:30 am and locked up for the night at 8:30 pm. During the day, they are encouraged to attend work and educational activities, with a daily payment of 53 kroner (£4.50) for those who leave their cell. 'If you have very few activities, your prisoners become more aggressive,' says Høidal. 'If they are sitting all day, I don't think that is so good for a person. If they are busy, then they are happier. We try not to let them get [8]institutionalised.'

Kent, a 43-year-old office manager serving a three-year sentence for a violent attack, is sitting in the prison's mixing studio. He admits he's enjoying being able to focus on his music, but says, '*Halden prison has been compared to the finest hotel. It is not true.* The real issue is freedom, which is taken away from you. That is the worst thing that can happen to you. When the door slams at night, you're stuck there in a small room. That's always a tough time.'

As we walk around the compound, an inmate comes up to ask Høidal, 'Can we have a swimming pool?' He laughs and remembers the shock of a prison warden who visited recently and was horrified to see that the inmates didn't stand to attention when Høidal came past, but instead [9]clustered around him, seizing the chance to list their complaints.

The inmates tell Høidal they're annoyed by recent changes to the routine, but they are respectful when they [10]address him. He listens politely, agrees that in prison [11]minor irritations can become major frustrations, but remarks that people outside the building would laugh at the trivial nature of their complaints.

Maybe I'm not there long enough to sense hidden anger or deep despair, but Halden doesn't feel like a place where you have to look over your shoulder.

e What do you think prison life should be like? Complete the sentences with your own ideas.
  1 Prisoners should *have their own / share a* cell, in which there should be: _____ _____ _____ _____.
  2 Prisoners should *have to do / have the option of doing* some kind of work, for which they should be paid _____ per week.
  3 The guards, _____ of whom should be trained in _____, should be paid _____ per week.
  4 Prison meals, _____ of which should be _____, should be served _____ times a day.
  5 The prison grounds …
  6 Visitors …

f 💬 Compare your ideas in 2e with other students. Whose prison is more like Halden?

57

UNIT 5

3 VOCABULARY AND SPEAKING
Crime and justice

a ▶05.03 Make the names of crimes by matching words and phrases from A with those in B. Then check the meanings in a dictionary. Listen and check.

A		B	
1	violent	a	corruption
2	tax	b	stolen goods
3	possession of	c	assault
4	credit card	d	fraud
5	bribery and	e	evasion

b ▶05.04 **Pronunciation** Listen to the words below and notice the four different pronunciations of the letter *s*.

/s/ a**ss**ault   /ʒ/ eva**s**ion   /z/ po**ss**ession   /ʃ/

c ▶05.05 Which sound in **bold** in the words below is different in each group? Listen and check.

1 a**ss**ault   assa**ss**in   mi**ss**ion   dismi**ss**
2 eva**s**ion   deci**s**ion   explo**s**ion   impre**ss**ion
3 po**ss**ession cou**s**in   compari**s**on   rea**s**on
4 posse**ss**ion permi**ss**ion vi**s**ion   Ru**ss**ian

d 💬 Take turns giving definitions and examples of the crimes in 3a. Can your partner guess the crime?

e ≫ Now go to Vocabulary Focus 5A on p. 162.

4 LISTENING

a Match the descriptions 1–5 with the pictures a–e.
1 ☐ This cereal offender was tripped up by his breakfast habit.
2 ☐ An honest fraudster turned himself back in after escaping prison.
3 ☐ This fake fan was caught by an immigration officer.
4 ☐ A boxful of bees taught a would-bee burglar a painful lesson.
5 ☐ These thieves thought they were clever, but the emergency services operator they accidentally dialled was smarter.

b ▶05.08 Listen to the news stories and check. Then, in pairs, explain what's happening in each picture.

c ▶05.08 Listen again. In each story, how were the criminals caught, or how do police hope to catch the criminals?

d **Language in context** *Crime*
Work in pairs. Try to find the meaning of the words in **bold**. Use a dictionary to check your answers.
1 … he **forged** the passport – it's a fake.
2 … he has been **detained** in a local juvenile detention centre …
3 They had this great plan to **pawn** them for cash …
4 … guess who was waiting? The police, of course, with the **handcuffs** ready!
5 Someone manages to **smuggle** in a mobile phone for him …
6 … the fraudster turns into an honest man – he **hands himself in**.

e 💬 There are two puns in the sentences in 4a. A pun is a joke that relies on words with two different meanings. One example is 'cereal offender', because it sounds like 'serial offender', which refers to someone who repeatedly commits the same crime. Find and explain the other pun.

f 💬 Discuss the questions.
1 Which crime do you think is the most serious?
2 Which criminal(s) do you think is/are the least competent?
3 Do you find any of the stories funny? If so, which ones?

5 SPEAKING

a 💬 Work in pairs. Discuss the criminals 1–4. Decide on a fair form of punishment/rehabilitation for these crimes. Is there any further information you would need to make a judgement?
1 A 90-year-old man who is found guilty of income tax evasion over a period of 50 years.
2 A woman found guilty of causing death by dangerous driving. She swerved to avoid a pet cat and caused the death of a motorcyclist.
3 An airport employee who stole valuable items from suitcases that were left on carousels. She sold them for cash or gave them away as presents.
4 A 17-year-old who has been caught shoplifting trainers. It's the first time he's been caught, but at his home the police find a large collection of sportswear.

b 💬 Work in groups of four. Are your suggestions for consequences similar? If not, can you agree on the consequences for each criminal?

5B IT'S ESSENTIAL TO HAVE THE RIGHT QUALIFICATIONS

Learn to talk about job requirements and fair pay
- **G** Obligation, necessity and permission
- **V** Employment

1 LISTENING AND VOCABULARY
Employment

a 💬 What would you regard as a 'good job'? How easy is it for people to find a good job these days?

b ▶ 05.09 Listen to four people talking about employment. What field does each person work in or want to work in?

Mike, UK
Olivia, Mexico
Andrew, UK
Karen, Germany

c ▶ 05.09 Listen again and match the statements to the speakers. Some statements apply to more than one speaker.

Who … ?
1 is concerned that their good luck won't last
2 has had trouble getting a good job since qualifying
3 faces a lot of competition in their field
4 is reluctant to accept unpaid work
5 is unhappy with their working hours

d 💬 Discuss the questions.
1 What advice would you give each of the people?
2 Do you know anyone who is in a similar position to any of these people? What has their experience been?

e Andrew says: 'There have been a lot of redundancies in the **financial sector**.' Answer the questions.
1 What is meant by a *sector*?
2 What jobs can you think of in each sector in the box?

| financial | agricultural | construction | public | retail |
| manufacturing | transport | energy | industrial |

3 What other sectors can you think of?

f Which of the words in the box in 1e have verb forms? Which are adjectives?

g ▶ 05.10 **Pronunciation** Listen to sentences 1 and 2. Match the stress patterns to the words in **bold**.
☐ oO   ☐ Oo

1 We are proud to **present** our new IT equipment to you today.
2 The new manager received a welcome **present** from the IT department.

Why is the word *present* stressed differently in sentences 1 and 2? Do you know any other noun and verb pairs that follow the same stress pattern?

h ▶ 05.11 Listen to these words used as nouns and verbs in two sentences, a and b. Which sentence contains the noun? Which sentence contains the verb?

1 increase   ☐ noun   ☐ verb
2 import   ☐ noun   ☐ verb
3 record   ☐ noun   ☐ verb
4 export   ☐ noun   ☐ verb
5 contract   ☐ noun   ☐ verb

i 💬 Discuss the questions.
1 What do you think are the advantages and disadvantages of working in each of the sectors listed in 1e?
2 Think of a job you would like to have. In which sector does this job belong?

2 SPEAKING

a 💬 Discuss the benefits in the employment terms and conditions.
1 To which job could the benefits apply?
2 Which would be the most motivating for you?

> **TERMS AND CONDITIONS**
> - six-month sabbaticals
> - four 'personal days' – four days a year when the employee can miss work without giving a reason
> - unlimited holidays (provided they don't have an impact on the business)
> - three-monthly performance review
> - performance-related pay
> - equal paternity and maternity leave
> - equal pay for 16-year-olds and older new employees
> - free sport facilities in the workplace
> - flexitime
> - unlimited free healthy snacks and drinks

b 💬 Imagine you ran a small business. What kind of business would it be? What benefits would you offer your employees? Why?

UNIT 5

3 READING AND SPEAKING

a 💬 Read the headings and look at the photos. What do you think each job involves? Read and find out.

b 💬 Apart from the salary, are there any similarities between the two jobs? Consider these aspects:
- lack of privacy
- risks and dangers
- working hours
- qualifications and training
- getting along with other people
- impact on family life.

c 💬 Could you imagine doing either of the jobs? Why / Why not?

4 GRAMMAR
Obligation, necessity and permission

a Look at these examples from the job descriptions for the bomb disposal diver.
1. If possible, you should have a few years' diving experience.
2. You must be given a diving assessment and a diving first-aid course.
3. You have to live with five to ten people in close proximity for a month or longer.

In these particular sentences, is there any difference in meaning between … ?

a *must* and *should*   b *must* and *have to*

b Complete the sentences below with the obligation phrases in the box. Then check your answers in the texts.

| be called on | it's essential | are obliged | expect you |
| it's advisable | be required | a mandatory requirement |

Bomb disposal diver
1. Companies will _____ to be a certified diver.
2. Certification is _____.
3. You'll _____ to have an explosive ordnance disposal qualification.

Pet food taster
4. _____ to keep pet owners in mind.
5. You will _____ to actually sample the food.
6. _____ to have a degree.
7. You _____ to taste it even though you suspect it's going to be disgusting.

c 💬 Answer the questions.
1. How can the sentences in 4b be rephrased using *must*, *have to* or *should*? What other changes to the sentences are required?
2. Why do you think the author chose to use expressions other than modal verbs?

d ≫ Now go to Grammar Focus 5B on p. 147.

BOMB DISPOSAL DIVER

TYPICAL SALARY: In the private sector, you can earn up to £100,000 a year working just two months out of every three.

THE JOB: Being a bomb disposal diver involves descending to the seabed and searching for unexploded bombs, shells, grenades and landmines, and then either safely recovering and collecting the weapons, or securely disposing of them.

QUALIFICATIONS: To dive offshore, companies will expect you to be a certified diver, and, if possible, you should have a few years' diving experience. On top of that, you must be given a diving assessment and a diving first-aid course, and also undergo offshore survival training. These qualifications are a mandatory requirement, and you should expect to pay at least £15,000 for all these courses.

And that's just the diving. To be able to dispose of the bombs safely, you'll be required to have an explosive ordnance disposal (EOD) qualification and several years of experience.

TO SUCCEED AS A BOMB DISPOSAL DIVER, YOU NEED … to stay calm in stressful situations. 'You're pretty much on your own at depth, with zero visibility, working to a very narrow timescale,' says Daniel Roantree, an EOD diver. And you have to live with five to ten people in close proximity for a month or longer, so if you don't like living in small confined spaces with lots of other people, forget it. Personal space is something of a luxury.

WORST THING ABOUT THE JOB: Expect to be away from home at least six months of the year.

'You're pretty much on your own.'

'It helps if you have a sophisticated palate.'

PET FOOD TASTER

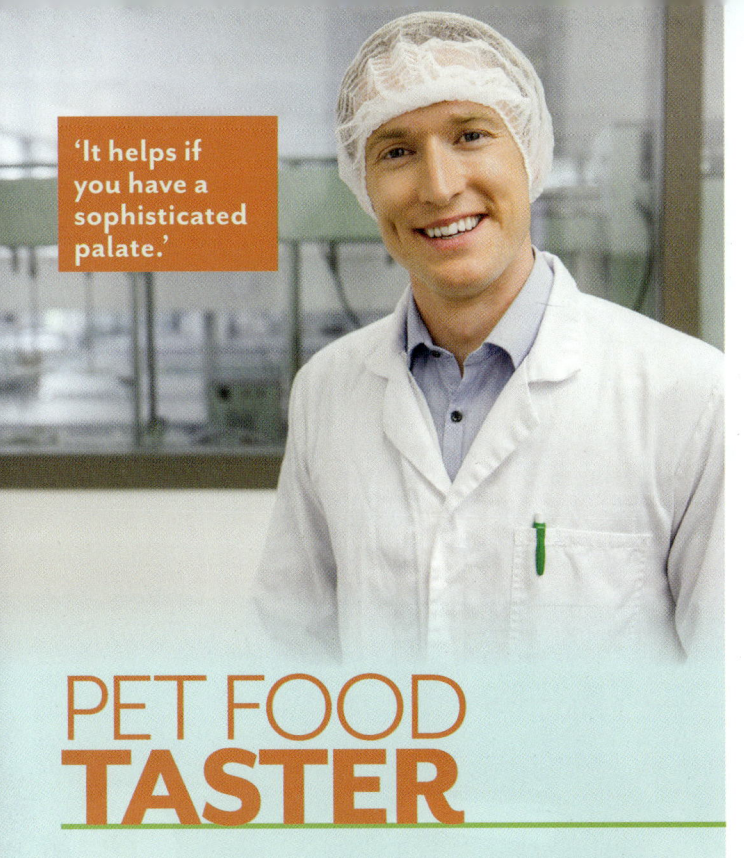

TYPICAL SALARY: At the beginning of their careers, pet food tasters earn just over £25,000 a year. However, if you're particularly talented at working out what it is that pet animals want to gobble up, you can earn up to £74,000 a year.

THE JOB: In reality, the job doesn't involve eating endless bowlfuls of pet food. It's more about testing it for its nutritional value and coming up with ways of making the food enticing for pets. This means paying attention to the smell of pet food – this is what makes it so appealing to animals. But also, it's advisable to keep pet owners in mind. The smell shouldn't be too overpowering because owners don't want their houses smelling of fish or liver. At some stage in the process, you will be called on to actually sample the food, but the good news is you don't need to swallow. After the tasting, you can spit it out.

QUALIFICATIONS: Having sharp taste buds isn't enough to become a pet food taster. It's essential to have a degree and you'll probably need a PhD. Why? Well, a large part of the job involves scientific research and report writing, so you need to be well qualified to do that.

TO SUCCEED AS A PET FOOD TASTER, YOU NEED ... to be quite creative and come up with good ideas for new kinds of pet food. You don't have to be able to think like an animal, but you do need to understand them and what's likely to get them rushing to their food bowl. It also helps if you have a sophisticated palate and know to check not only for taste but also texture and consistency.

WORST THING ABOUT THE JOB: You'll sometimes be given something new to try that doesn't smell very good. Unfortunately, you are obliged to taste it even though you suspect it's going to be disgusting. It usually is. Also, it's a job with a lot of deadlines. It seems like pets are an impatient lot – always looking for the next new taste sensation.

UNIT 5

5 READING AND SPEAKING

a **Communication 5B** Student A: Read the text on p. 129. Student B: Read the text on p. 130.

b Work with your partner. Exchange information about the jobs. Explain:
- how much the job pays
- what it involves
- what qualifications and skills you need
- any negative aspects of the work.

c In groups, talk about the four jobs you read about.
1 What is it about each job that makes it so well paid? Is it connected with … ?
   - personal sacrifice
   - specialist skills and knowledge
   - unusual talents
   - responsibility
   - danger
2 Which is the most/least appealing job for you? Why?
3 Who in your group would be most suitable for each of the four jobs (assuming you had the necessary qualifications and training)? Why?

d Think about your own job or occupation, or one you would like to have. Use these phrases to describe the requirements of the job to your group.

> It's essential to …   (They) expect you to …
> You are obliged/required to …
> You may be called on to …
> It's up to you to …   It's advisable to …
> … is a mandatory requirement

Which of the jobs that you read about seems the most demanding? Why?

6 SPEAKING

a Work with a partner. Choose a job from the list below and decide what value you think the job has and what a fair salary would be.
1 a nurse
2 a primary school teacher
3 an investment banker
4 a Premier League footballer
5 a police officer

Think about:
- how much the person works
- qualifications and training
- the importance of the job
- the amount of responsibility the person has.

b **Communication 5B** Go to p. 131.

61

5C EVERYDAY ENGLISH
I'd hazard a guess

Learn to recall and speculate
- S Deal with a situation without the facts
- P Main stress

1 LISTENING

a Discuss the questions.
1 Do you find it easy to talk to people you've just met? Why / Why not?
2 Look at strategies a–e for talking to new people. Which of these do you use? Do you do anything else in particular?

> a Open the conversation by commenting on something else that's happening around you.
> b Pay them compliments where possible.
> c Ask for personal information about where they live and what they do for a living.
> d Try to be funny, but don't make jokes about other people. Always laugh at their jokes.
> e Look for opportunities to empathise with them.

b 05.13 Watch or listen to Part 1. What strategies from 1a does Sara use? Note down some specific examples.

c What do you think the impact of Sara's conversation strategies will be on Max?

d 05.14 **Language in context** *Temporary states*
1 Match a–c with 1–3 to make phrases from Part 1. Listen and check.

a ☐ on a temporary   1 ups and downs
b ☐ hopefully, I'll snap 2 basis
c ☐ we all have our   3 out of it soon enough

2 Which phrases in 1 mean … ?
   a everybody experiences good times and bad times
   b stop behaving in a negative way
   c not permanently

e 05.15 Watch or listen to Part 2 and answer the questions.
1 What does Max think it's easier to write?
2 What had Sara assumed Max was doing?
3 What reason does Max give for his interview with Oscar being a disaster?

2 PRONUNCIATION Main stress

a 05.16 Listen to Max's lines below. Each pair of word groups ends with the same word, but it only receives the main stress in the first. Why?
1 a When your detective solves the <u>murder</u>,
  b you just invent <u>another</u> murder.
2 a He hadn't even read my <u>book</u>.
  b Hadn't even <u>opened</u> my book.

Choose the correct word to complete the rule.

> The last word or phrase in a word group which gives *new* / *repeated* information is stressed.

b 05.17 <u>Underline</u> where you think the main stress in these pairs of word groups is. Listen and check.
1 a It's dangerous enough being a diver,
  b let alone a bomb disposal diver!
2 a I don't think wealth distribution in this country is fair –
  b quite the opposite of fair, in fact.
3 a I haven't got the right qualifications –
  b in fact, I've hardly got any qualifications!
4 a Halden is more than just a prison –
  b it's the world's most humane prison.

Practise saying the sentences.

3 LISTENING

a ▶ 05.18 Watch or listen to Part 3. How does Sara's meeting with Max nearly end in disaster?

b ▶ 05.18 Watch or listen to Part 3 again and answer the questions.
1. What did Max think Sara's job was?
2. Why does Max say he wouldn't have agreed to meet a journalist?
3. What two reasons does Sara give for wanting to interview Max?

c Why do you think Max considers doing another interview?

4 USEFUL LANGUAGE Recalling and speculating

a ▶ 05.19 Complete the expressions from Parts 1, 2 and 3. Listen and check.
1. You're staying with Emma at the moment, **if my memory _____ me correctly**?
2. **I was _____ the impression that** you were writing another book?
3. **No _____ you heard that** from that guy from the radio interview.
4. **What _____ out in my mind most is** that that interview was a total disaster!
5. **I'd _____ a guess that** he hadn't even read my book.
6. _____, you're a technician, like Emma's boyfriend, right?
7. **I think I _____** Emma saying that her boyfriend's a technician at City FM.
8. _____ you'd known, would you still have agreed to meet with me?

b Which expressions in 4a are used for recalling events? Which are used for speculating? Are there any which could be used for both?

c ▶ 05.20 Read this conversation. Find five mistakes and correct them. Listen and check.
A So when are you starting your new job? I was over the impression that you were starting next week.
B Oh, no. That would be too soon. I need a holiday first!
A But, if my mind serves me correctly – you went to Spain last month for a long weekend, didn't you?
B Who told you that?! I hazard a guess it was that sister of mine!
A Yeah, I think I remember she saying something along those lines.
B Well, you can't have too much of a good thing, can you? Presuming, you need a holiday too. Why don't you come with me?
A Well, I can't remember the last time I had a break. Why not?

d Practise the conversation in 4c with a partner.

e Recall your first day at school, or your first day in a job. Complete the sentences with your own ideas. Then tell a partner.
1. What stands out in my mind is …
2. I think I remember …
3. If my memory serves me correctly, …

f Discuss the questions. Use expressions from 4a to speculate.
1. Why do you think writers sometimes suffer from writer's block?
2. Why do you think some famous writers avoid giving interviews?

5 SPEAKING

▶▶ **Communication 5C** Work in pairs.
Student A: Go to p.128. Student B: Go to p.131.

☑ **UNIT PROGRESS TEST**

→ **CHECK YOUR PROGRESS**

YOU CAN NOW DO THE UNIT PROGRESS TEST.

5D SKILLS FOR WRITING
It's a way of making the application process more efficient

Learn to write an opinion essay

W Essays; Linking: addition and reinforcement

1 LISTENING AND SPEAKING

a Discuss the questions.
1. Do you use social media? If not, why not? If so, how often do you post comments about your work or studies? What kind of things do you say?
2. Do you think it's a good idea to post comments about work or study on social media? Why / Why not?

b You are an employer. You see these comments written by employees to their colleagues. How would you feel? What action (if any) would you take?

> Couldn't face it today – called in sick. Having a lovely day at the beach! ☺
>
> Our merger with Bookman & Associates looks imminent #superfirm #merger
>
> This year's pay offer – a miserable 1% increase. Do management live in our world or not?
>
> Things a bit slow at work today – spent all day online 'doing research'.

c Discuss the questions.
1. Have you ever heard of anyone losing a job because of something they did on social media? What did they post? Do you think that dismissal is fair punishment for work-related posts? Why / Why not?
2. What other types of post on social media wouldn't employers approve of?

d ▶ 05.21 Listen to Mario and Laila talking about job applications and social media. What differences are there … ?
1. in the experiences they have had
2. in their attitudes and opinions

Mario

Laila

e Read the opinions from Mario, Laila and their interviewers below. Tick (✓) the opinions you agree with and compare with a partner.

- ☐ It's essential that we project a positive image at all times – both in person and online.
- ☐ Demanding to see my social media – that's just a bit too *Big Brother*-ish for my liking.
- ☐ I don't really see a problem with employers having a look at my social media posts.
- ☐ I think that people tend to forget that just about anything you post online can be accessed in one way or another.
- ☐ If you don't want people to read it, then don't post it.

2 READING

a Read an essay about companies that research their job applicants on social media. Answer the questions.
1. Why do companies feel it's appropriate to use social media to find out about job applicants?
2. What are the reasons some job applicants are worried about this practice?
3. What position does the writer of the essay take on this topic?

b Do you agree with the writer's opinion? Why / Why not?

Social media and RECRUITMENT

1 These days, an embarrassing photo on a person's social media profile might make all the difference when trying to land a top job. Increasingly, companies are examining applicants' social media profiles for information to use in the selection process.

2 Young adults, many of whom have grown up with social media, are usually comfortable about sharing their lives online. Recently, however, some job applicants have voiced privacy concerns in relation to social media. They insist that their private life is private and is no business of any employer. In addition, they complain that companies go 'trawling' for negative information about applicants rather than getting a balanced general impression. They also express concern that they may be judged on the behaviour of their friends and family. What's more, some fear that employers may discriminate against them on the basis of factors such as their medical history or age.

2d ago

3 WRITING SKILLS Essays; Linking: addition and reinforcement

a What is the function of each paragraph in the essay? Match these descriptions with the paragraphs 1–4.

- [ ] to present ideas and opinions for one side of the argument
- [ ] to state the writer's final, balanced opinion of both arguments
- [ ] to present ideas and opinions for a second, contrasting side of the argument
- [ ] to outline the topic of the essay and get the reader's interest

b How does the writer create interest in the introduction?

a [ ] by stating their opinion on the topic
b [ ] by referring to interesting facts and figures
c [ ] by making a surprising statement
d [ ] by clearly outlining the issue to be discussed

Which of the above are appropriate ways to begin an introduction to an essay? Why?

3 Employers argue that they are breaking no laws by researching their employees on social media – the information they are seeking is freely available. Moreover, as well as being a valuable tool for employers, social media provides information for the job applicant about the company they hope to work for. Above all, employers claim, their research makes the application process more efficient and allows them to filter out unsuitable applicants.

4 While I agree that online research is a two-way process, I believe it is unfair for employers to judge an applicant's suitability solely on the basis of their social media posts. In particular, I understand applicants' concerns about 'trawling'. Besides actively seeking negative information, the system clearly creates opportunities for employers to discriminate. I think the time has come for guidelines or laws to restrict the research employers can do. Furthermore, checks need to be made that their decisions are fair and transparent.

c How does the writer conclude the essay?

a [ ] by stating their balanced opinion
b [ ] by briefly summarising key points
c [ ] by outlining a possible course of action
d [ ] by introducing interesting new information

Which of the above are appropriate ways to conclude an essay? Why?

d How many supporting arguments does the writer give for each side in paragraphs 2 and 3?

e Notice the highlighted linker in paragraph 2. Underline more linking words and phrases in the essay that add information or reinforce an argument by adding a supporting idea.

f Write the words you underlined in 3e in the correct column of the table. Which linker highlights the most important argument?

Adds an idea in a new sentence	Adds two ideas in the same sentence
In addition	as well as

g Underline the linkers in these sentences and add them to the table in 3f.

1 Beyond researching the applicant on social media, employers usually contact previous employers for references.
2 It is standard to conduct a search of criminal records in addition to the methods mentioned above.
3 It is often argued that a time-efficient process is best for all involved. Besides, time saved is money saved.

h » Now go to Writing Focus 5D on p. 172.

4 WRITING

a 💬 In some countries, employers are able to fire an employee without giving any reason for dismissal. Do you think this is fair? Talk about it in small groups.

b Make notes of the ideas from the discussion in 4a. Organise your notes into opinions in favour of this idea and against it.

> **Writing Tip**
>
> When writing an essay on a controversial topic, it can help to talk to other people and note down opinions, even when these are not your own. Alternatively, brainstorm ideas from two different points of view. Your essay will be more interesting if you consider both sides of the issue and outline a range of opinions.

c Write an essay on the fairness of employers dismissing employees without having to give a reason. Consider the points of view of both employers and employees and include your own opinion.

d Swap essays with a partner. Do you mention the same points? Is your opinion the same?

UNIT 5
Review and extension

1 GRAMMAR

a Complete each sentence with one word.
1. The crime _____ she committed was very serious.
2. There are several reasons _____ they hid the money.
3. There are various theories, some of _____ are very hard to believe.
4. Interview anybody _____ fingerprints were found there.
5. We'll find them _____ they are.
6. They accused each other, _____ which case one must be lying.

b Cross out one word or phrase in each sentence that is NOT correct.
1. It is *advisable / obliged / essential* to register for courses well in advance.
2. You *are expected / are required / had better* to attend 80% of the classes.
3. You are not *allowed / permitted / obliged* to throw litter outside.
4. *It's up to you whether you / You have no choice but / You are under no obligation to* sign up for the course but I would recommend it.
5. Module 2 is optional, so you *mustn't / don't have to / are not obliged to* do it.
6. Once I *had to / must have / was required to* take a four-hour practical exam.
7. Students *should / ought to / obliged to* make a study timetable.
8. I *was supposed to / had better / had to* be at the office at 9:00, but I overslept.

2 VOCABULARY

a Complete the sentences with the correct words. The first letter is given.
1. Criminals should be brought f_ace-to-face_ with their victims.
2. C_____ service is a more effective punishment than prison.
3. People who drink and drive should be permanently b_____ from driving.
4. Credit card f_____ usually happens because people are careless.
5. Tax e_____ is not a crime, just creative accounting.
6. It is wrong for prisoners to be held in solitary c_____.
7. Group c_____ will not help the most serious offenders.
8. No one should s_____ more than 20 years in prison.

b Match the jobs 1–4 with the correct sectors a–d.
1. ☐ social worker   a construction
2. ☐ builder   b agricultural
3. ☐ investment banker c public
4. ☐ farmer   d financial

c 💬 Discuss the advantages and disadvantages of each of the types of work in 2b.

3 WORDPOWER Idioms: Crime

a ▶05.22 Complete the idioms in **bold** with the words in the box. Listen and check.

doubt   shoulder   the law   red-handed
murder   good   in crime   lightly

1. Halden doesn't feel like a place where you have to **look over your _____**.
2. People who are **up to no _____** are often very good at lying.
3. I guess the inspectors need to be inspected. If there aren't the proper controls, they **get away with _____**.
4. The jury decided to **give** the accused **the benefit of the _____** and came back with an innocent verdict.
5. Last week, he **caught** a thief _____ loading sections of copper wire into a car.
6. A new film about famous **partners** _____, Bonnie and Clyde, hits cinemas this weekend.
7. He **got off** _____; he only had to repay the money. He didn't go to prison.
8. The High Court **lays down** _____, and all the local judges have to follow its decisions.

b ▶05.23 Complete the exchanges with the idioms from 3a. Listen and check.
1. **A** I can always tell when my children are _____. They have a guilty look on their face.
   B I never can. Unless I _____ them _____, I can never work out if they've been naughty or not.
2. **A** He may have made up his story about feeling sick, but I'm going to _____ him _____.
   B OK, but if you trust him too much, he'll try and _____.
3. **A** He's found himself a _____ in a boy called Jim from school, and now he never comes home at a reasonable time any more.
   B You should _____. He's only a teenager.
4. **A** You really _____ at work after messing up that big order. I can't believe they didn't take it more seriously.
   B I know, I can't stop _____ now. I'm sure that can't have been the end of it.

c 💬 Tell a partner about a time when:
- you caught somebody red-handed
- you had to lay down the law to someone
- you gave someone the benefit of the doubt.

🔄 REVIEW YOUR PROGRESS

How well did you do in this unit? Write 3, 2 or 1 for each objective.
3 = very well   2 = well   1 = not so well

I CAN …	
talk about crime and punishment	☐
talk about job requirements and fair pay	☐
recall and speculate	☐
write an opinion essay	☐

66

CAN DO OBJECTIVES

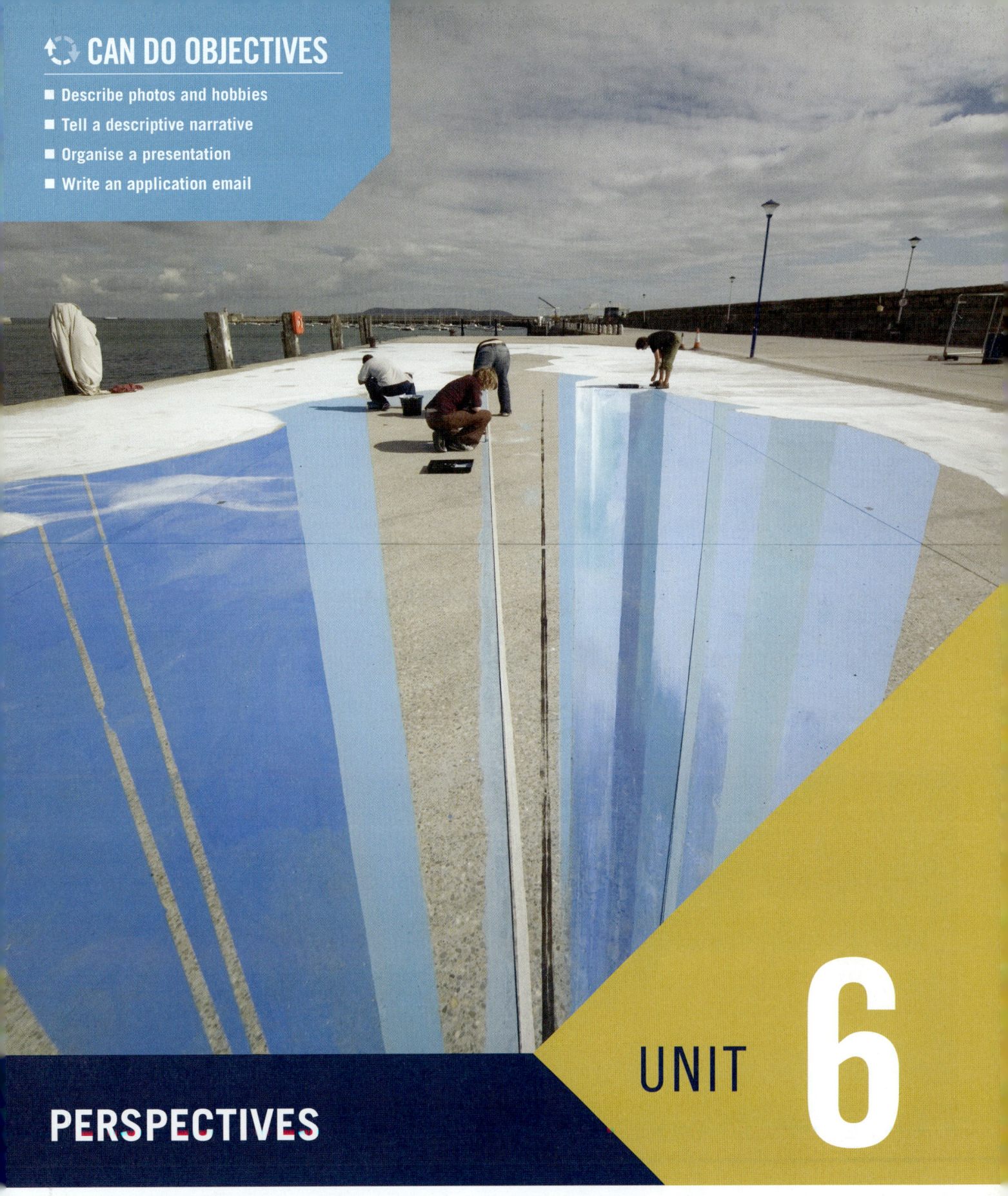

- Describe photos and hobbies
- Tell a descriptive narrative
- Organise a presentation
- Write an application email

PERSPECTIVES

UNIT 6

GETTING STARTED

a Look at the picture and answer the questions.
1. What are the people doing? Why do you think they're doing it?
2. How long do you think it has taken them? How long do you think it will stay there?
3. What impact do you think it will have on passers-by?

b Discuss the questions.
1. Are there any examples of street art in your town or city?
2. How do you think your community would react to having a piece of street art like the one in the photo on their street?

67

6A WE ALL SEEM TO LOVE TAKING PICTURES

Learn to describe photos and hobbies
- G Simple and continuous verbs
- V Adjectives: describing images

1 SPEAKING AND READING

a Discuss the questions.
1 What do you usually use to take photos – your phone or a camera?
2 Do you take a lot of photos? Why / Why not?
3 What do you usually do with the photos?
4 Do you think you're good at taking photos? Why / Why not?

b Have you ever heard of the photographer Elliott Erwitt? Read the fact file on p. 69. What kind of photographs does he take?

c What do you think are important skills for photographers? Think about these things:
- what you choose to photograph
- the way the photos look
- the equipment you use
- your attitude and personality.

d Read the article. Are any of your ideas from 1c mentioned?

e Read the article again. Answer the questions.
1 Why shouldn't street photographers plan much?
2 What should be the aim of a street photograph, according to Elliott Erwitt and the writer?
3 What do you think Elliott Erwitt means by 'visual garbage'?
4 What attributes does the writer think are most important in a street photographer?
5 What does the writer mean when he talks about keeping an alien mindset?

f Discuss the questions.
1 How are Erwitt's methods and style evident in the photo of the Villa Borghese Gardens? What do you think of the photograph?
2 Answer the question at the end of the article: As an alien – what would you find intriguing, amusing or nonsensical?
3 Look at the titles of the 'lessons' (1–4) in the article. Are they relevant to other skills and/or jobs that you know about?

2 VOCABULARY Adjectives: describing images

a Work with a partner. What do the highlighted adjectives in the article mean? Check your ideas in a dictionary.

b Now go to Vocabulary Focus 6A on p. 163.

Villa Borghese Gardens, Rome 1969 by Elliott Erwitt

UNIT 6

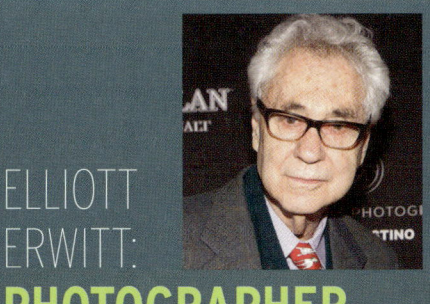

ELLIOTT ERWITT: PHOTOGRAPHER FACT FILE

- born in Paris, brought up in Italy, moved to the USA aged 10
- began photography career in the 1950s
- known for advertising and street photography, particularly ironic black-and-white shots of everyday life
- invited to join the internationally famous photography agency Magnum in 1953

Lessons Elliott Erwitt has taught me about STREET PHOTOGRAPHY

by Eric Kim

If you are not familiar with the work of Elliott Erwitt, you may perhaps have seen some of his iconic work from around the globe (the picture on the right was taken by him). He had one of the longest careers of any photographer, spanning over 50 years. What I most appreciate about Elliott Erwitt is his wry sense of humour when looking at the world – as well as his straightforward philosophies about photography. In this article, I share some of his thoughts and advice.

1 DON'T PLAN TOO MUCH – WANDER AROUND

I think that as a street photographer, sometimes I fall into a trap of planning too much. I generally try to focus my attention on projects (having a preconceived project in mind when shooting in the streets), but I often find it also takes away from the shooting experience. One of the best things about street photography is to be a *flaneur* – someone who wanders around without a specific destination in mind.

ERWITT *I don't start out with any specific interests; I just react to what I see.*

Takeaway point: Let your curiosity lead you. Just go out and shoot whatever you find interesting. Go down roads that may seem a bit foreign, and you might be lucky enough to stumble upon great street photography shots.

2 FOCUS ON CONTENT OVER FORM

Great photos are a combination of content (what is happening in the frame) as well as form (composition). But which is more important? Content or form?

ERWITT *My wish for the future of photography is that it might continue to have some relevance to the human condition and might represent work that evokes knowledge and emotions. That photography has content rather than just form. And I hope that there will be enough produce to balance out the visual garbage that one sees in our current life.*

Takeaway point: We often find fascinating characters in the street and take photos of them, but the compositions may not be so good. On the other hand, we might take well-composed photos of a street scene, but there is nothing going on in the photo – it is boring and without soul.

I agree with Erwitt that we should, as street photographers, put more emphasis on content over form. I feel that photos that evoke emotions and the human condition are far more powerful and meaningful than just photos with good composition.

3 DON'T TAKE THINGS TOO SERIOUSLY

When one thinks about the photography agency Magnum, some adjectives that come to mind are gritty and raw.

However, Erwitt's style was vastly different. He didn't go out and take photos in conflicts or war. His photos tended to be more playful, humorous and amusing.

ERWITT *Well, I'm not a serious photographer like most of my colleagues. That is to say, I'm serious about not being serious.*

Takeaway point: Don't take yourself and your street photography too seriously, and remember – at the end of the day you want to enjoy yourself.

4 HONE YOUR SKILLS OF OBSERVATION

Erwitt was inspired to go out and take pictures when he saw a photograph by master photographer Henri Cartier-Bresson. He realised it was an act of observation that made the photo great, and that he could do something similar.

ERWITT *The picture seemed evocative and emotional. Also, a simple observation was all that it took to produce it. I thought, if one could make a living out of doing such pictures that would be desirable.*

Takeaway point: One of the things that is the most beautiful about street photography is that it doesn't rely on having an expensive camera or exotic lenses. Rather, it comes down to having an observant and curious eye for people and the world around you.

Therefore, cultivate your vision and way of seeing the world. I recommend that you always carry a camera with you because you never know when the best street photo opportunities will present themselves to you.

A fun exercise: Pretend that you are an alien from another planet, and you have come to the planet Earth for the first time. Imagine how strange human beings would seem – and the urban environment they have built for themselves. As an alien, what would you find intriguing, amusing or nonsensical?

Always keep that mindset to be amazed by what you see around you.

UNIT 6

3 LISTENING

a 💬 Who do you know who is passionate about their hobby? What does the person's hobby involve?

b ▶ 06.03 Listen to Monika, an amateur photographer. Do you think Monika is passionate about photography? Why?

Monika, amateur photographer

A recent photo taken by Monika

c ▶ 06.03 Listen again and answer the questions.
1 What motivated Monika to learn more about photography? Why did she decide to take a course?
2 How has she improved since she started the course?
3 Why does Monika like the photo she took, on the right?
4 How does she describe her other favourite photograph?

d 💬 Do you think Monika would agree with Elliott Erwitt's lessons? Why / Why not?

4 GRAMMAR
Simple and continuous verbs

a ▶ 06.04 Which verb form in *italics* did you hear in the interview with Monika? Listen and check.

So, ¹*do you feel / are you feeling* more confident with your camera now?
It ²*depends / is depending* on the types of photo that I want to take.
Have you ³*discovered / been discovering* any bad habits since you ⁴*started / were starting* your course?
I ⁵*always choose / 'm always choosing* the wrong shutter speed.
I ⁶*think / am thinking* I have two pictures that are my favourite pictures.
One of them is part of a course project that I ⁷*work / 'm working* on at the moment.
So I chose this building that is meant to be demolished. Actually, it ⁸*is demolished / is being demolished* now.

b Look at the verb forms in the sentences in 4a. Match each example 1–8 with one or more descriptions below.

The verb is … .
- simple for a verb not usually used in the continuous ☐
- simple for a completed action ☐
- simple for general truth or attitude ☐ ☐
- continuous for a temporary action ☐ ☐
- continuous for a bad or annoying habit ☐
- simple or continuous depending on the meaning of the verb ☐

c Look at the verb forms 1 and 5 in 4a again. In each case, is the alternative verb form possible? If so, would the meaning be different?

d ⇒ Now go to Grammar Focus 6A on p. 148.

e In each sentence below, find a verb that would be better in the continuous and change it.
1 My little brother always asks me to play computer games with him, but I find them really boring.
2 By this time next month, I'll have played volleyball for three years.
3 These days everyone appears to use a tablet in class rather than writing in a notebook.
4 I often make mistakes when I'm not careful.
5 I've looked for a good grammar app, but I can't find one that's free.

f 💬 Change the sentences in 4e to make them true for you. Compare your ideas with a partner.

5 SPEAKING

a 💬 Discuss the questions.
1 What is your favourite photo of yourself? Describe it to your partner. Say why you like it.
2 What's the best / funniest / most beautiful photo you've ever taken? What's the story behind the picture?

b 💬 What kind of visual art interests you most? Think about:
- painting
- interior design
- drawing
- sculpture
- cartoons
- fashion.

c 💬 Tell your partner about:
1 how you became interested
2 what specifically you like
3 where and how often you look at it
4 any ways you can learn more about this.

d 💬 Do you and your partner share any interests in this area?

6B A PERSON WAVING FOR HELP

Learn to tell a descriptive narrative
- **G** Participle clauses
- **V** Emotions

1 VOCABULARY Emotions

a Which of the adjectives in the box are positive? Which are negative? Check new words in a dictionary.

helpless	disillusioned
overjoyed	overexcited
satisfied	gleeful

b ▶06.07 Look at the adjectives in **bold**. Match the feelings 1–8 with their continuations a–h. Listen and check.

1. ☐ I was absolutely **devastated**.
2. ☐ I felt very **frustrated**.
3. ☐ I was terribly **restless**.
4. ☐ I felt extremely **jealous**.
5. ☐ I felt a bit **insecure**.
6. ☐ I was totally **speechless**.
7. ☐ I feel so **ashamed**.
8. ☐ I felt absolutely **petrified**.

a It was the most beautiful thing I'd ever seen.
b I needed to get in touch, but I couldn't track her down.
c My behaviour at the party was unforgivable.
d It was the biggest game of the year, and we had played appallingly.
e I was the only person at the party who was over 40.
f My brother had money, friends and now a charming wife.
g I couldn't concentrate on my book or TV or work.
h There was a snake crawling across my foot.

c Write sentences like 1b a–h for the emotions in 1a. Read them to other students. Can they guess the feeling?

d ▶06.08 **Pronunciation** Listen to these pairs of sentences from 1b and mark the main stress. How is the stress different in the a and the b sentences? Which show stronger feelings?

1 a I'm absolutely devastated.
  b I'm absolutely devastated.
2 a I felt extremely jealous.
  b I felt extremely jealous.
3 a I feel so ashamed.
  b I feel so ashamed.

e Take turns reading aloud your sentences from 1c, showing strong feelings. Ask your partner questions to continue the conversation.

2 READING

a Read one of the two eyewitness accounts of the same incident. Student A: Read the blog *Brad's view*. Student B: Read the email *Martha's view*. Tick (✓) the things below that are included in your story.

☐ a man wearing a cap   ☐ a group of kids
☐ a police officer   ☐ a speeding car
☐ a blonde woman   ☐ a gun

BRAD'S VIEW

I haven't really enjoyed being here in the capital since I arrived a couple of weeks ago to do some training. I miss my friends, and the training is boring. Left to my own devices, I've ended up spending a lot of time sitting in cafés, so I've been feeling disillusioned by my time away. Also, in big cities there's some really weird stuff that goes on.

This morning I was sitting quietly in a café with my coffee, waiting for my training session to begin. I noticed this guy. He looked like he might have been in his 50s, but it was hard to tell because he was wearing dark glasses and a baseball cap. He was taking photos of the buildings, stopping to look around between shots. To me it looked like he was casing the joint or something.

Looking directly at him, I saw him go up to this woman. I couldn't see her well, and all I know is that she had blonde hair and she was tall. He was talking to her and kind of leaning into her – his body language was very strange.

Then all of a sudden, this group of kids burst out of the metro and swarmed around the man and the woman. But I could see that the man and woman were sort of holding on to each other, scheming something together.

Signalling to someone driving past, the woman puts her hand up. A car screeches to a halt, and they both seemed to make a dash for the car. It's like they're making a getaway together. And the car takes off at top speed.

The whole thing took less than a minute, and it's the kind of situation you would just overlook if you weren't paying attention. But who were these people? And what exactly were they up to? Why all the photography? Disturbed by what I saw, I couldn't concentrate on my training all day. It all just makes me feel very insecure about life in big cities.

I guess I should have reported it, but I don't like to get involved. I only have another five days here, and there's no point getting pulled into something like this. It makes me feel very on edge and restless. Yes, I can't wait to get away from all this intrigue.

71

MARTHA'S VIEW

Advice

Hi Chelsea,

Hope everything's going well at uni.

Am just sending you this message to get your advice. I was on my way to work a couple of hours ago, and I saw something that I've been thinking about ever since. I'm not sure what to do about it.

Anyway, waiting at the bus stop, I just happened to notice this woman. She was blonde and tall and very elegant, and I couldn't help noticing her beautiful cashmere coat. She was walking towards me, and I remember thinking I'd get a good look at the coat as she went by.

Then right out of the blue this man just sort of leapt in front of her and stopped her in her tracks. I couldn't see his face – he was wearing a baseball cap and sunglasses, but he was quite solidly built. And the woman had this look of panic on her face – she looked petrified!

I almost got up to help, but then this group of kids came running out of the metro station, on some kind of school trip and all a little overexcited at the prospect. Laughing and pushing, they surrounded the man and the woman. It looked like the man was holding on to the woman, and her arm went up in the air like a person waving for help when they're in trouble in the sea.

At that point, I jumped up and started moving towards them. When I was only a few metres away, a car pulled up out of nowhere and the man and woman got into the car. But there was something awkward about the way they did that. Was the woman being forced in? It all happened so quickly and with the kids getting in the way, it was difficult to tell. The car just sped off. I tried to get the registration number, but I wasn't quick enough. I felt utterly helpless and very frustrated.

I'm just not sure what to do about this. I keep playing the scene over in my mind. What did I see – a mugging or an abduction? I keep thinking about that woman. Pushed into the car like that, she could be in danger, and I'm the only one who knows. Do you think I should contact the police about this?

Let me know what you think.

Love, Mum

b Read your text again and make notes on what happened so you can tell another student.

c Work in A and B pairs. Tell each other about your story. What do you think happened?

3 GRAMMAR Participle clauses

a Compare the underlined participle clauses from the story with the clauses in *italics*. Do they have exactly the same meaning? How are the participle clauses different in form from the clauses in *italics*?

1 <u>Left to my own devices</u>, I've ended up spending a lot of time sitting in cafés.
   Because I've been left to my own devices …
2 This morning I was sitting quietly in a café with my coffee, <u>waiting for my training session to begin</u>.
   … while I was waiting for my training session to begin.
3 Anyway, <u>waiting at the bus stop</u>, I just happened to notice this woman.
   Anyway, as I was waiting at the bus stop …
4 <u>Pushed into the car like that</u>, she could be in danger.
   Because she was pushed into the car like that …

b In 3a, which are present participle clauses and which are past participle clauses?

c What comes before the participle in the clause below? Which clause in *italics* (1 or 2) has the same meaning? What kind of clause is this?

   … her arm went up in the air like <u>a person waving for help</u>
   1 *… like a person who was waving for help*
   2 *… because she waved to a person for help*

d <u>Underline</u> more examples of participle clauses in both texts.

e Complete the extracts from fiction below with the participle clauses in the box. What do you think the stories are about?

   having finished her breakfast   crying her eyes out
   pulled from behind   into a darkened room
   approaching the house   wanting to reassure him

1 At the sound of a car _____, they grabbed the bags and fled.
2 On my last visit to the camp, I found a small girl _____.
3 _____, I whispered, 'You'll be fine.' But I knew it wasn't true.
4 _____, Amaranth walked down to the front and entered the Grand Hotel. 'Where better to sit and be seen?' she thought.
5 _____, he tried to turn around to see who had caught him.

f Which participle clauses in 3e … ?
   a ☐ ☐ show the sequence of events
   b ☐ ☐ give a reason for an event
   c ☐ ☐ describe an action in progress

g Think of other participle clauses that could complete the extracts in 3e.

   At the sound of a car entering the car park, …

h ▶▶▶ Now go to Grammar Focus 6B on p. 149.

i Add three or more participle clauses to the story below to make it more interesting.

   I walked down the street. I went into a café. I ordered a cup of coffee and a sandwich. I saw an old friend. I went over to say hello to him. I said goodbye. I went out of the café.

   Compare your ideas with other students.

4 LISTENING

a ▶ 06.11 Listen to the news story about the situation you read about in 2a. Does the story match your interpretation of what happened?

b ▶ 06.11 Listen again and answer the questions.
1 Who is Sione Leota?
2 How serious was Mr Leota's medical condition?
3 What do we find out about the woman who helped him?
4 Why doesn't anyone know who the woman is?
5 What appeal does the newsreader make? Why?

5 SPEAKING AND WRITING

a Think of a situation that happened to you or someone you know where first impressions were mistaken. Make notes.

b 💬 Tell another student your story.

c Write the first part of the story that outlines only the first impressions. You can write your story or your partner's, if you prefer it. Remember to use:
   • adjectives to describe feelings and reactions
   • participle clauses.

d Swap your story with a different student. Read aloud each other's stories and try to guess what the outcome was and which first impressions were mistaken.

6C EVERYDAY ENGLISH
First and foremost

Learn to organise a presentation
- S Present an application for a grant
- P Intonation in comment phrases

1 LISTENING

a Discuss the questions.
1 Who are the most famous people in the world today? What are they famous for?
2 In what ways can you measure a person's fame?
3 How is fame today different from … ?
- 10 years ago
- 50 years ago
- 100 years ago

b 06.12 Sara is giving a presentation about the science fiction author Max Redwood. How do you think these numbers will be relevant?

half a million   8   300,000

Watch or listen to Part 1 and check.

c 06.12 Answer the questions. Watch or listen to Part 1 again to check.
1 Why does Paul need to decide on whether they should interview Max again?
   a Nadia is convinced they shouldn't be interviewing Max again.
   b There's a chance things might go wrong again.
   c Paul is coming to their next team meeting.
2 What point is Sara illustrating with the facts and figures?
   a Max is famous for good reasons.
   b Max will attract new listeners to City FM.
   c Max's popularity is on the increase.
3 What angle does Sara propose to take in her interview?
   a She's going to ask about the detail of his next book.
   b She's going to discover the source of his inspiration.
   c She's going to look at what real-life events feature in his writing.
4 How does Sara propose to make the second interview a success?
   a She will use her charm to relax him.
   b She will adapt her approach on the day.
   c She will prepare carefully with Max before the interview.

d Language in context *Idioms 1*
1 What do you think these idioms mean?
   a I really think this **is worth a shot**.
   b I'll just have to **cross that bridge when I come to it**.
2 Can you think of situations in your own life when you might use these idioms?

2 USEFUL LANGUAGE
Organising a presentation

a 06.13 Complete Sara's opening to her presentation. Listen to the extract to check. Can you paraphrase the phrases you completed?

Yes, that's right – an _____ author but not a _____ one, as poor Oscar discovered.

Do you think that her opening was successful? Why / Why not?

b 06.14 Complete these expressions from Part 1. Listen and check.
1 **My focus today is** _____ this second interview.
2 **Let me talk you** _____ why our listeners want to hear more …
3 _____ **and foremost**, he wrote his book from a bench …
4 **One** _____ **is clear** – Max Redwood is on the road to becoming an international best-selling author.
5 **Turning now** _____ the focus of the interview …
6 _____ **specifically**, I propose to find out …
7 **So to recap** _____ what I've been saying …
8 **If you'd like me to** _____ on anything I've just said …

c Answer the questions.
1 Which of the words in **bold** in 2b can be replaced with … ?
   - take
   - moving on
2 Which of the expressions in 2b can be used … ?
   - to introduce a presentation
   - to highlight ideas
   - to sequence ideas
   - at the end of a presentation
3 Can you think of other expressions you can use in presentations?

UNIT 6

3 LISTENING

a 🎬 ▶ 06.15 Watch or listen to Part 2. What good idea does Alex have?

b 🎬 ▶ 06.15 What are the sentences below in response to? Watch or listen to Part 2 again and check.
1 **Sara:** Pretty good, on the whole.
   Alex asks Sara how her meeting with Max went.
2 **Sara:** Not to worry.
3 **Alex:** Great!
4 **Sara:** Actually, no.
5 **Sara:** You might be on to something there.

c 💬 Do you know any books or films with a sequel or prequel? How successful are they?

d **Language in context** *Idioms 2*
Match the expressions a–c from Parts 1 and 2 with meanings 1–3.
a ☐ labour the point
b ☐ more to the point
c ☐ a bit of a sore point

1 a subject that someone prefers not to talk about because it makes them angry or embarrassed
2 repeat an idea more than is desirable/necessary
3 more importantly

4 PRONUNCIATION
Intonation in comment phrases

a Look at the phrase in **bold** from Part 1. Without it, would the sentence make sense?
   Now **as luck would have it**, I bumped into Max the other day.

b ▶ 06.16 Listen to the sentence in 4a. Does the intonation of the comment phrase fall then rise (↘↗) or rise (↗)?

c ▶ 06.17 Listen to the intonation in the comment phrases in the pairs of sentences below. Tick (✓) the sentences, a or b, which have rising intonation.
1 a ☐ Pretty good, **on the whole**.
   b ☐ **On the whole**, pretty good.
2 a ☐ It's a bit of a sore point, **actually**.
   b ☐ **Actually**, it's a bit of a sore point.
3 a ☐ **More to the point**, he's agreed to do a proper interview.
   b ☐ He's agreed to do a proper interview, **more to the point**.

d Complete the rules with *fall–rise* or *rising*.

   When comment phrases are at the beginning of a sentence, they have a _____ intonation. When they are at the end of the sentence, they have a _____ intonation.

e 💬 Practise saying the sentences in 4c.

5 SPEAKING

a 💬 Your school has applied for a grant, and to secure it you need to give a presentation to the funding body's director detailing:
• what kind of grant is required (arts, sports, technology, environmental)
• how much money is needed
• two or more specific things your school will spend the grant on
• the impact the grant will have on the school and its students.

In pairs, plan your presentation. Here are some ideas:
• an arts grant to fund a film project or trip to an exhibition
• a sports grant to install a gym or to equip a football team
• a technology grant to buy an interactive whiteboard, or tablets and ebooks
• an environmental grant to create a conservation area or improve recycling capabilities.

b 💬 Take turns to practise giving the presentation. Think about a successful opening and use expressions from 2b.

c 💬 In new pairs, give your presentations. Decide whether you will award a grant to your partner or not.

✓ **UNIT PROGRESS TEST**

→ **CHECK YOUR PROGRESS**

YOU CAN NOW DO THE UNIT PROGRESS TEST.

75

6D SKILLS FOR WRITING
I enjoy helping people

Learn to write an application email

W Application emails; Giving a positive impression

1 SPEAKING AND READING

a How much do you know about volunteer work in your local area? Which of these activities do you know about? Give yourself a score between 0 and 5 for each one (0 = I know nothing about it; 5 = I know a lot about it).

- ☐ helping old people
- ☐ helping homeless people
- ☐ providing food for people
- ☐ working with children
- ☐ improving the environment
- ☐ helping disabled people

b Look at the pictures and the names of various community volunteer projects. What do you think each one might involve? Think about:
- what the volunteers do
- the aim(s) of the project, and how it might help people.

c Read the online advert about the projects and check your answers.

YOU CAN HELP!

Ever wanted to help out in the community but weren't sure how? Check out these exciting projects in your local community. If you think you can help and you have the right skills, contact Sandy Marks at sandy@localprojects.net.

TREES FOR CITIES

Everyone would like their city to have more trees, but who is going to plant them? In this project, we work with children of all ages and show them how to plant their own trees. As well as improving their local environment, the work helps them learn more about nature. So far, we've planted more than 500 trees around the city – and we aim to plant many more!

SENIOR CITIZENS' MUSIC CAFÉ

We organise afternoons of music and dancing for elderly people who are suffering from diseases such as Alzheimer's. Music and dance can help them get more enjoyment out of life, and experience greater social contact. Music has also been shown to improve memory and slow down memory loss. If you like music and dancing, come along and help us put on these sessions!

FOOD FOR LIFE

Thousands of people in the city can't afford enough food. Meanwhile, supermarkets are throwing perfectly good food away. We collect food from shops and restaurants, and distribute it to the people who need it most – entirely for free. If you've got a car or a bike, come along and get involved.

LANGUAGE EXCHANGE

We arrange for people to meet up for free language lessons – they can choose to practise English or another language, either with a regular partner or in an informal group. It gives people new skills whilst also helping to bring the community closer together. We're always looking for good English speakers to help.

EDIBLE PLAYGROUNDS

One in three children leaves school overweight from eating unhealthy food. We are working with inner-city schools to show children how they can use their school playground to grow fruit and vegetables. Growing their own food helps children to connect with their environment and gives them valuable life skills and self-confidence.

76

2 LISTENING

a **06.18** Listen to three interviews with volunteers and answer the questions.
   1 Which project is each speaker talking about?
   2 What further information do you find out about the three projects?

b 💬 Imagine you could be involved in two of the projects in 1b. Which would you choose and why? Think about:
   - your interests
   - your skills
   - your experience in the field.

   Compare your answers with a partner.

3 READING

a Read the application email and discuss the questions.
   1 In what ways do you think Helen is suitable as a volunteer?
   2 Which projects is she most suitable for, and why?
   3 Is she unsuitable in any way?

Dear Sandy,

1 I'm writing to reply to your advert for volunteers for local community projects. I'd be really interested in working with you, either part-time or full-time.

2 As I live locally, I often read and hear about the work you do in the community. I really like the way you work at a local level and contribute so directly to the needs of ordinary people. I also think it's great that you focus on small-scale, low-cost projects, so that as much money as possible reaches the people who need it.

3 I finished school in July with four 'A' levels and I have applied to study social sciences at university next year. During my last school year, I took part in a research project on the topic of local housing. As part of my research, I interviewed local people of different ages and this taught me a lot about issues that affect our community.

4 I also have some experience of working with children. During my last summer holidays, I volunteered abroad, helping to run a summer camp for children from poor families. I helped to organise sports events and competitions, and I went with the children on excursions.

5 I think I'd fit in well as a volunteer on your projects. I'm sociable and outgoing, and I'm good at getting on with people of all ages. I'm also good at solving problems, and I enjoy helping people.

I'm attaching a recent photo and my CV. I'm also sending you a copy of my school project on local housing, which I hope you find interesting.

Looking forward to hearing from you.

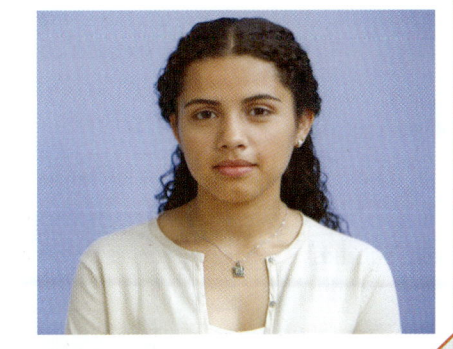

Yours sincerely,
Helen Biggs

---

4 WRITING SKILLS
Application emails; Giving a positive impression

a Read the application email again and match the paragraphs (1–5) with their purposes.
   - ☐ to give examples of relevant practical experience
   - ☐ to state her qualifications and relevant study experience
   - ☐ to demonstrate enthusiasm for their organisation
   - ☐ to summarise additional strengths
   - ☐ to state the reason for writing

b Look at the underlined phrases in these sentences. Find equivalent phrases in the email and note them down.
   1 This is a reply to your advert.
   2 I want to work for you.
   3 I'm going to study social sciences at university next year, if they accept me.
   4 I know a bit about working with children.
   5 Here's a recent photo.
   6 Here's a copy of my school project.
   7 Hoping you reply soon.

   How are the underlined phrases different from those in the email? Which are more effective? Why?

c Do you think the style Helen is using is … ?
   1 very formal 2 fairly informal 3 very informal
   What features of the email helped you decide?

d One of Helen's aims is to give a positive impression of herself. Underline the phrases she uses about herself which give a good impression.

e Now go to Writing Focus 6D on p. 172.

5 WRITING

a Look at the projects described in 1c. Choose one or two that you think you could help with and write an application email. Make sure you:
   - organise what you write into logical paragraphs
   - use appropriate phrases for writing an application email
   - give a positive impression so they will want to employ you as a volunteer.

b Swap your email with another student. Read their email. Would you be interested in offering them a job as a volunteer? Why / Why not?

77

UNIT 6
Review and extension

1 GRAMMAR

a Match the sentences that go together.
1. ☐ Do you come from Tokyo?
2. ☐ Are you coming from Tokyo?
   a Yes, it'll be a long flight.
   b Yes, I've always lived there.

3. ☐ Emily always consults me on everything.
4. ☐ Emily is always consulting me on everything.
   a She is very considerate.
   b She can't think for herself.

5. ☐ My sister hasn't written for ages.
6. ☐ My sister hasn't been writing much.
   a She has been very busy recently.
   b I haven't had a single message from her.

7. ☐ Joan just told me what happened.
8. ☐ Joan was just telling me what happened.
   a Unfortunately, you interrupted her.
   b But it was nothing I didn't already know.

b Rewrite the underlined phrases as participle clauses.
1. My friend knows the people <u>that were involved</u> that day.
2. <u>I didn't want to seem rude, so</u> I pretended to agree with her.
3. A friend who I hadn't seen for ages was on the train <u>that was approaching platform 5</u>.
4. <u>Since he didn't understand Spanish</u>, he struggled to communicate.
5. <u>While we were waiting</u> for the tour to start, we looked at the pictures <u>that were displayed</u> in the foyer.
6. I <u>used just my hands and</u> felt my way across the dark room.

2 VOCABULARY

a Correct the spelling mistakes.
1. The Sydney Opera House is an ikonic building.
2. The play is quite humourous.
3. Her photographs are very playfull.
4. The images he creates are flawles.
5. A black-and-white picture can be really envocative.
6. I found his work very meanful.
7. The jungle scenes are wonderfully ecsotic.

b Complete the sentences with the correct word. The first letter is given.
1. John was j_____ of Brad's new car.
2. I was p_____ when I saw how high up we were.
3. I felt too a_____ to stand up and admit I was wrong.
4. Without my phone, I feel completely h_____.
5. Millions of teenage fans were d_____ to hear about the boy band breaking up.
6. I often feel r_____ when it's too cold to go out.
7. The kids were really o_____ at the party.

3 WORDPOWER Idioms: Feelings

a Match comments a–f with pictures 1–6. Where are the people and why are they saying this?

a ☐ 'They loved it, but I just had to **grin and bear it**.'
b ☐ 'I'm **over the moon** to have won.'
c ☐ 'My noisy neighbours really **get on my nerves**.'
d ☐ 'It had changed so much. I **couldn't believe my eyes**.'
e ☐ 'Tony thinks he's great but he really **gets my back up**.'
f ☐ 'I can't cope! I'm **at the end of my tether**.'

b Match the idioms a–f in 3a with definitions 1–5.
1. ☐ have no strength or patience left
2. ☐ tolerate, put up with
3. ☐ be very pleased and happy
4. ☐ ☐ be made angry by something/someone
5. ☐ be very surprised

c 💬 Complete the questions with the correct words or phrases. Ask and answer the questions.
1. What do people do that _____ your _____ up?
2. When was the last time you were at the _____ of your _____?
3. If you don't like your meal in a restaurant, do you _____ and _____ it, or say something?
4. Have you been _____ about some good news recently? When?
5. Have you ever seen a price tag so high that you couldn't _____ your _____?
6. Which noises really _____ on your _____?

↻ REVIEW YOUR PROGRESS

How well did you do in this unit? Write 3, 2 or 1 for each objective.
3 = very well   2 = well   1 = not so well

I CAN . . .	
describe photos and hobbies	☐
tell a descriptive narrative	☐
organise a presentation	☐
write an application email.	☐

CAN DO OBJECTIVES

- Speculate about inventions and technology
- Emphasise opinions about the digital age
- Apologise and admit fault
- Write a proposal

UNIT 7
CONNECTIONS

GETTING STARTED

a Look at the picture and answer the questions.
1. Where is the girl? What is she doing there? Why?
2. How do you think she feels about her situation? Do you think she feels more or less connected with her peers and teachers? Why?

b Discuss the questions.
1. What is your personal experience of working or learning from home?
2. How do you stay connected with colleagues or classmates if you can't see them face-to-face?
3. A hybrid working, or learning, model is one where people split their time between home and the workplace or classroom. What are the advantages and disadvantages of this model? Make a list.

7A IT MUST HAVE SEEMED LIKE SCIENCE FICTION

Learn to speculate about inventions and technology

- **G** Speculation and deduction
- **V** Compound adjectives

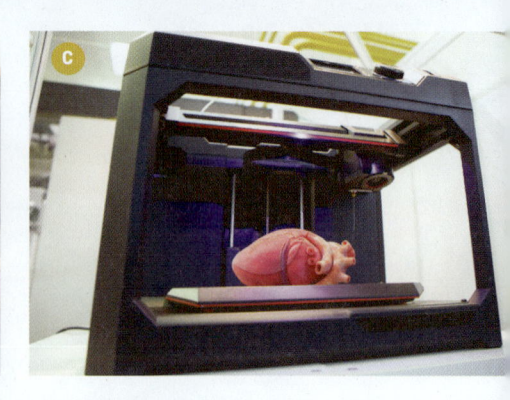

1 READING AND SPEAKING

a 💬 Imagine you could have <u>two</u> of the 'superpowers' below. Which would you choose and how would they be useful? Are there any you would not want? Why?
- ability to read people's thoughts
- X-ray vision
- arms with super strength
- legs that can run as fast as a bike
- skin that can't be wounded
- body parts that can be replaced or upgraded

b 💬 Which of the things in 1a do you think might become reality over the next few decades? What kind of technology do you think would need to be developed?

c 💬 Read the headline of the article. What do you think 'human augmentation' means? Why do you think it might be 'a dream or a nightmare'?

d Read the article. Which numbered paragraph 1–4 does each of the photos a–d go with?

e Read the article again and answer the questions.
1. Which of the things in 1a does the article predict might become reality?
2. Why does the article mention glasses, hearing aids and plastic surgery?
3. Why might people want to replace their own limbs with bionic ones?
4. What are the two main directions of BMI research? Which do you think is more useful, and why?
5. How could haptic gloves be useful in training astronauts and medical staff?

f 💬 Imagine all these developments became reality in your lifetime. Which do you think …?
- would be the most useful to you personally
- would be the most fun
- would raise ethical problems

HUMAN AUGMENTATION – A DREAM OR A NIGHTMARE?

Of all the new developments in technology, it is often the ideas about how to improve the human body that many people find either the most exciting or the most disturbing. When scientists start talking about using telepathy to control computers, or replacing our legs and arms with bionic limbs, or using gene-editing technology to modify the human genome, people understandably start to feel scared. Are we really ready to treat our bodies as pieces of hardware?

Many people would say 'no' without any hesitation. But it's worth remembering that human augmentation is nothing new: in fact, we may have been trying to augment, or improve, ourselves from the moment we invented tools, if not earlier. Glasses were an invention that allowed short-sighted people to augment their bad eyesight, and hearing aids were designed to augment people's bad hearing. Plastic surgery, though once remarkable, is now commonplace. So perhaps we should also be more open-minded about potentially life-enhancing inventions.

Here we look at some of the ground-breaking ideas in human augmentation that are already being developed and which may seem quite normal a few decades from now.

1 **'People will replace their limbs with bionic limbs.'**
   Now: Functioning artificial limbs are already being produced for people with disabilities, and the German company Bionic Systems has developed exoskeletons which skiers or people doing backbreaking work in industry or agriculture can attach to their bodies to increase their strength and help them perform better.
   The future: Samantha Payne, founder of the British robotics firm Open Bionics, believes that it will soon be possible to create artificial hands and arms which will function with more precision, efficiency and strength than our own. When that happens, people might well decide to swap their own hands, arms or legs for bionic limbs which give them extra abilities.

2 **'We'll be able to bring the brain online.'**
   Now: A number of start-up companies are designing so-called 'brain–machine interfaces', or BMIs, which allow direct communication between our brain and a computer by using a headband which measures brain

80

2 VOCABULARY Compound adjectives

a Look at these compound adjectives from the article.
lifelike = appearing real, similar to real life
self-confident = confident about yourself

Match the highlighted compound adjectives in the article with these meanings.
1 making you feel happier or able to live better
2 able to accept new ideas
3 tiring and needing a lot of physical effort
4 not able to see things that are far away
5 completely new and different from other things or ideas

b What other compound adjectives do you know with … ?
1 self-…   2 …like   3 …(-)minded   4 life(-)…

c Now go to Vocabulary Focus 7A on p. 164.

d Work in groups. Take turns thinking of a compound adjective. Don't tell the other students. Instruct the student whose turn it is to do things in a way that demonstrates the adjective.

Try to guess which adjectives other students chose.

3 SPEAKING AND GRAMMAR
Speculation and deduction

a Look at the phrases in **bold** in the extracts from the article and answer the questions.
1 We **may have been trying** to augment, or improve, ourselves from the moment we invented tools.
2 People **might well decide** to swap their own hands, arms or legs for bionic limbs.
3 Because of their cost, haptic gloves **are unlikely to be** widely **used** in the foreseeable future.
4 They **could** eventually **be used** for more everyday applications.
5 Who knows if before long we **might be shaking** hands with business colleagues on the other side of the world!
6 The idea of replacing someone's heart **must have seemed** like science fiction.
7 Most of these devices are still very expensive, but costs **may start** coming down as the technology advances.
8 These new bionic organs **are almost bound to perform** better than their biological counterparts.
  a How much certainty does each sentence express? Write the numbers by the descriptions below.
    • this is certain or nearly certain _____
    • this isn't certain, but it's probable _____
    • this is possible but not at all certain _____
  b Which phrases refer to the past, and which to the future?
  c Which phrases use the following verb forms? Write the numbers below.
    • modal verb + infinitive _____
    • modal verb + *have* + past participle _____
    • modal verb + *be* + -*ing*
    • adjective + *to* + infinitive _____

b ▶ 07.04 Rewrite sentences 1–8 in 3a using the phrases below. Listen and check.
1 It's possible …   5 … may be able …
2 It's likely …   6 … almost certainly …
3 … it's not very likely … 7 … probably …
4 There's a good chance … 8 … sure …

c Now go to Grammar Focus 7A on p. 150.

d Use the verbs in brackets to speculate or make a deduction. Use at least one phrase from 3a or 3b.
1 The inventor of the Internet (foresee) the impact of his invention.
2 Memory implants for humans (be) just a few years away.
3 The development of humanoid robots (have) a major impact on the way we live.
4 Using BMI to monitor thoughts (pose) a threat to people's privacy.

e Discuss these questions about your speculations or deductions in 3d.
1 Did you use the same phrases to express your ideas?
2 Do you agree with each other's statements? Why / Why not?

---

activity. It's already possible to use BMIs to carry out simple tasks, such as changing TV channels.

The future: According to Brian Johnson, founder of Californian start-up Kernel, we will soon be able to use BMIs not only to control machines but also to monitor our thoughts, in the same way that we can now monitor our location or our jogging performance with our smartphones or smartwatches. In other words, our brains would go 'online'! So we (and possibly other people) could monitor whether we're depressed or if we're feeling self-confident, whether we're paying attention during a meeting, or whether we're too tired to drive home from work.

3 **'We'll be able to touch and feel online.'**
Now: Several robotics companies have developed virtual reality gloves, or 'haptic' gloves, which, when used with a virtual reality headset, give you the experience of touching simulated objects, including sensing textures, shapes and weight. The experience is so lifelike that users often can't believe they haven't really held the object in their hand. So far, haptic gloves are at an experimental stage and their immediate applications are for professional simulations where it's important to know how things feel, for example in training astronauts or medical professionals.

The future: Because of their cost, haptic gloves are unlikely to be widely used in the foreseeable future, but they could eventually be used for more everyday applications such as computer gaming, online shopping and perhaps even person-to-person communication. Who knows if before long we might be shaking hands with business colleagues on the other side of the world!

4 **'We'll be able to get replacement organs.'**
Now: Only 60 years ago, the idea of replacing someone's heart must have seemed like science fiction, but this is now standard procedure. It's also becoming normal for surgeons to fit people with robotic devices that mimic and replace specific organs, such as the eyes and the heart. Most of these devices are still very expensive, but costs may start coming down as the technology advances.

The future: Writer Zoltan Istvan believes that more body parts and organs will become replaceable over the next few decades and eventually these new bionic organs are almost bound to perform better than their biological counterparts. This could mean that we will be able to do things we never dreamed of before, for example climbing Mount Everest at 80 or having perfect sight and hearing for the whole of our lives. And like computer programs, these organs could be constantly upgraded as technology develops, so we might, for example, simply go online to download an eye or a heart upgrade.

UNIT 7

4 LISTENING

a 💬 The photos illustrate three issues people have with the modern world. What do you think they are?

b ▶ 07.08 Listen and check your ideas in 4a. What invention is each speaker proposing? Write one sentence to summarise each idea.

c ▶ 07.08 Listen to each idea again. What impact does each speaker intend their idea to have?

d 💬 What kind of person do you think each 'inventor' is? What experiences might lie behind their idea?

> He might be a bit idealistic.

> Yes, and he must have been tricked into believing false information at some point.

e ▶ 07.09 You will hear an expert comment on each idea. Are they likely to think it's a good idea? Listen and check.

f ▶ 07.09 What is the point that each expert makes? Choose a or b. Then listen again and check.
1 a ☐ The app would be misleading because there is no such thing as the truth.
  b ☐ The app would not necessarily be able to check what the truth really was.
2 a ☐ It would be impossible to make the filter reliable enough to be safe.
  b ☐ It would be dangerous to filter out things that are important for safety.
3 a ☐ In choosing someone for a job, you need to see them to know what they're really like.
  b ☐ You will still make judgements about the person even if you can't see their face.

g ▶ 07.10 **Language in context** *Information*
1 Complete the sentences from the recording with the words in the box. Listen and check.

fact   falsehoods   misinformation
disseminated   conceal   filters   claims

a Politicians, media pundits, writers and students get away with _____ that are not based on _____.
b We would hopefully get away from the infuriating _____ that are being widely _____.
c Bad ideas would be seen as a joke, rather than being the source of _____ and perpetuating ignorance.
d It just _____ everything that comes in and out.
e … when someone is interviewed for a job, that they should have to _____ their appearance.

2 Which words in the box refer to … ?
1 information that is true (x1)
2 information that may be true (x1)
3 information that isn't true (x2)
4 sharing or hiding information (x3)

h 💬 Which invention appeals to you the most? Why?

5 SPEAKING

a 💬 Work in small groups. Think of an invention or a new idea. It could be:
- something that would make life easier or better
- something that irritates you that you would like to change
- a social problem that your idea would solve
- something that would be fun or interesting.

Develop your idea together and write notes.

Take turns rehearsing what you will say. Limit what you say to 60 seconds.

Choose one person from each group to present your idea to the class within 60 seconds.

> Our idea for making life easier is …

> The invention we thought of is …

b 💬 Which idea do you think is the best? Why?

7B WHAT I ENJOY IS A HEART-TO-HEART CHAT

Learn to emphasise opinions about the digital age

G Cleft sentences
V Nouns with suffixes: society and relationships

1 SPEAKING AND LISTENING

a Discuss the questions.
1 What have you read online today? How typical is this of your online reading?
2 Which of these headlines might you click on? Why?
- Celebrity plastic surgery revealed!
- Super-cute cat and canary
- Scientists uncover birth of the galaxy
- Art that makes your eyes sore
- Tornado demolishes seaside towns
- Spy on your kids online

b Read the blurb from the book *Rewire* by Ethan Zuckerman. Does he believe the Internet makes us more or less connected?

c What do the highlighted words in the blurb mean? Use the context and a dictionary to help you.

d The blurb suggests that shipping bottles of water is easier than sharing information between diverse cultures. Do you agree? Why / Why not?

e 07.11 Listen to a media expert, Zelda Freeman, talking about *Rewire*. Summarise the main point the book makes, according to Zelda.

f 07.11 Listen again and note down examples Zelda gives of …
1 our current online behaviour
2 ways the world is more connected these days
3 false *cosmopolitanism*
4 'bridge figures' and what they do.

g How similar is your online behaviour to your offline behaviour? Describe someone you know whose online and offline behaviour are different. What's your opinion of this?

We live in an age of connection, one that is accelerated by the Internet. This increasingly ubiquitous, immensely powerful technology often leads us to assume that as the number of people online grows, it inevitably leads to a smaller, more cosmopolitan world. We'll understand more, we think. We'll know more. We'll engage more and share more with people from other cultures. In reality, it is easier to ship bottles of water from Fiji to Atlanta than it is to get news from Tokyo to New York. In *Rewire*, media scholar and activist Ethan Zuckerman explains why the technological ability to communicate with someone does not inevitably lead to increased human connection.

REWIRE by Ethan Zuckerman

2 GRAMMAR Cleft sentences

a 07.12 Listen and match the sentence halves.
1 ☐ What's interesting is
2 ☐ The point he's making is,
3 ☐ The reason why it matters is,
4 ☐ The thing we really need to understand is
5 ☐ All we need to do is

a we're living in an age of economic and physical connection.
b 'disconnect' from our current way of thinking and 'rewire'.
c that we only think we're more connected.
d how other countries and cultures work.
e we're actually wrong.

b What information is being emphasised in each sentence in 2a?

c In 2a, the cleft part of the sentence is in **bold**. What verb joins the cleft to the rest of the sentence?

d 07.12 **Pronunciation** Listen to the examples in 2a again. Does the intonation of the phrases in **bold** … ?
- ↘ fall
- ↗ fall then rise

e Now go to Grammar Focus 7B on p. 151.

f 07.15 Change these sentences to cleft sentences that begin with the phrases in *italics*. Then listen and check.
1 We don't need free wi-fi all over town. *What we …*
2 I only use a landline at work. *It's only …*
3 We only have to unsubscribe from social media to help us reconnect. *All we …*
4 It's incredible just how liberating it is to go digital. *What's …*
5 It worries me because people end up living in virtual worlds and losing touch with reality. *The reason …*

g Use the phrases below to tell your partner about your own Internet use.

All I seem to do is …   The reason why I …   It's … that I find irritating.

83

UNIT 7

3 READING

a What differences are there between friendships that are mostly face-to-face and those that are mostly online?

b Do you think these ideas are true or false? Why?
1 Feeling colder improves our ability to understand other people.
2 Increasing the temperature of a room could help resolve an argument.
3 Some national and regional personality characteristics can be explained by climate.
4 Feeling warmer makes us feel more connected to other people.
5 Loneliness can affect your physical health.

c Read the article and check your answers in 3b.

d Read the article again and answer the questions.
1 How can cold make people more understanding?
2 What did the computer ball game tell researchers about loneliness? What two outcomes told researchers this?
3 What kind of research has 'been in the doghouse lately'? Why?
4 Why does the author think the findings will 'hold up'?
5 What's the writer's suggestion about the relationship between social media and the absence of heat?
6 Why does the writer suggest that having hot baths is a good idea?

e Discuss the questions.
1 In your experience, is the research about warmth and understanding the points of view of other people believable?
2 What other ways can you think of to help people who feel lonely?

Loneliness and temperature

Does coldness really make people feel lonely?

Oliver Burkeman

According to new research, people exposed to warmer temperatures find it harder to grasp viewpoints other than their own, while those exposed to colder ones find it easier. It seems that in order to take the heat out of a disagreement, you should literally take the heat out of the room. Since I've always preferred the cold, this was music to my ears. It's tempting to extrapolate: might this explain the affable tolerance of Canadians, say, or the history of prejudice in the southern states of the USA? Sadly, on closer reading, the study is only a partial victory for cold. We're better at seeing other perspectives when we're chilly, the researchers argue, because cold triggers a sense of social distance. It reminds us of our separateness, and thus the fact that others aren't like us. We gain perspective at the cost of intimacy.

So what looks, at first, like a surprising result turns out to reinforce one of the most intriguing psychological findings of recent years: that coldness makes people feel lonely. The opposite's also true: loneliness makes people feel cold. In one experiment, students played a computer game in which they threw a ball back and forth with other on-screen characters, each of whom they (wrongly) believed was controlled by another student, playing elsewhere. After a while, the others sometimes began to keep the ball to themselves.

Subsequently, players who'd been thus ostracised showed a marked preference for hot foods over cold ones; non-ostracised players didn't. In a recent rerun of the experiment, ostracism led to a drop in skin temperature. Other studies have found that hot baths relieve loneliness, and that merely being reminded of an experience of exclusion prompts people to judge a room's temperature as colder.

This kind of research – about how seemingly innocuous aspects of our surroundings can exert powerful effects – has been in the doghouse lately; several classic findings have proved difficult to replicate. It's no longer clear, for example, whether being exposed to words associated with old age ('grey', 'bingo') really does make people start walking more slowly. But there's reason to believe the link between loneliness and temperature will hold up. It's no mere matter of word association: temperature may be a crucial way our bodies keep track of whether we're getting the social contact we need. It's easy to see why natural selection might have given us a yearning to be near friendly fellow tribe members: they were crucial for food, security and relationships. People worry that social media is making us lonely and isolated, but what if that is exactly half-true? What if it is not making us isolated – online connections are real, after all – but *is* making us feel lonely, partly because those connections don't involve heat?

It sounds silly that hot baths and soup might be the answer to loneliness. Surely the only real answer to loneliness is real connection? But a feeling of isolation makes people try less hard to connect. So a nudge in the right direction – even a bath – can't hurt. (And severe loneliness really can hurt, physically: it's been found to exacerbate numerous serious diseases.) But I'm a cold lover. Does that mean I hate people? I hope not. When I really think about it, the thing I love most about cold weather is coming back into the warmth.

4 VOCABULARY Nouns with suffixes: society and relationships

a In pairs, try to find the meaning of the highlighted words in the article. Use a dictionary to check your answers.

b Can you remember which noun in the box completes these phrases in the article? Read the article again to check your answers.

intimacy   security   perspective (x2)   social contact   viewpoint

1 grasp a _____
2 see another _____
3 gain _____ at the cost of _____
4 get the _____ you need
5 food and _____

c Identify the noun forms of these words in the article.

cold   lonely   ostracise   exclude   isolate

d ▶ 07.16 Rewrite the words in each group 1–3 using one of the noun suffixes: -tion, -ism or -ness. Listen and check.
  1 material, optimistic, social, separate, capital
  2 nervous, rude, selfish, fair, close
  3 collaborate, distribute, liberate, innovate, separate
  Use a dictionary to check the meaning of any new words.

e Complete the rules with the correct suffix from 4d.

> • _____ nouns are states of emotion or being.
> • _____ nouns are often beliefs or ways of thinking or political systems.
> • _____ nouns are often single actions or general concepts.

💡 **Learning Tip**
While words that are formed from the same base word have a similar overall meaning, there can often be small and subtle differences in meaning when suffixes are added. It is easy to check the differences in a dictionary if you are unsure.

f What's the difference in meaning between *separation*, *separatism* and *separateness*?

5 SPEAKING

a Complete the sentences with abstract nouns from 4 or your own ideas. Add two more sentences with other *-ism/-ness* nouns.

1	For me, _____ is the most important quality in a friend/friendship.
2	The worst quality for a person to have is _____ because … .
3	_____ in a person sometimes irritates me.
4	_____ and _____ really help in teamwork.
5	_____ is worse than _____.
6	In social situations, _____ is a terrible experience.
7	…
8	…

b 💬 Explain your ideas in 5a to a partner. Together decide on five key qualities and kinds of behaviour that are important to social relationships.

c 💬 Choose one of the social situations below. What further problems might you have? How could you deal with them? Make a list of problems and suggestions.
  • You have to live in an unfamiliar country for six months. You don't speak the language, and very few people speak English or your native language.
  • You join a class and find that everybody there already knows each other.
  • You are doing an online course. During your classes, you sense that your teacher is not paying attention.
  • You meet someone you think is very interesting online, and you'd like to get to know them better.

d 💬 Have you or anyone you know ever been in any of the situations in 5c? How did you/they deal with it?

UNIT 7

85

7C EVERYDAY ENGLISH
I was out of line

Learn to apologise and admit fault
- Deal with a situation where you are at fault
- Sound and spelling: *ou* and *ough*

1 LISTENING

a Look at pictures a–d and discuss the questions.
1. Why do you think each character is saying sorry?
2. Do you use the same word for all the situations in your language?

b Look at pictures e and f. Who do you think is apologising for what?

c 07.17 Watch or listen to Part 1 and check your answers in 1b.

d 07.17 Watch or listen to Part 1 again and answer the questions.
1. What is Max's attitude towards his publisher?
2. How does Max react to Sara's suggestion?
3. How does Sara feel at the end of the conversation?

e Do you think Max's reaction is justified?

2 PRONUNCIATION Sound and spelling: *ou* and *ough*

a 07.18 Listen to the sentences from Part 1. Note down one word spelled with *ou* in each sentence. What do you notice about the sounds of the letters in the words?

b 07.19 Put the words in the box in the correct column below. Which sounds are short and which are long? Listen and check.

pron**ou**ncing sh**ou**ld consci**ou**s t**ou**gh en**ou**gh
th**ou**ght thr**ou**gh thor**ou**ghly th**ou**gh c**ou**gh
r**ou**gh **ou**ght p**ou**r s**ou**th s**ou**thern r**ou**te

1 /ʊ/	2 /uː/	3 /aʊ/	4 /əʊ/
could	soup	noun	

5 /ɔː/	6 /ʌ/	7 /ɒ/	8 /ə/
fourth	touch		jealous

c 07.20 Listen to the conversation. Then practise it in pairs. Pay attention to the words spelled with *ough*.

A I give up. I know it was supposed to be tough, but enough's enough.
B Have you thought it through thoroughly, though?
A Yes. I feel awful and I've got a terrible cough.
B Fair enough. You do look rough. You ought to take it easy.

3 LISTENING

a ▶ 07.21 Put events a–g in the order you think they will happen. Watch or listen to Part 2 and check.

- a ☐ Emma asks Max about his meeting with Sara.
- b ☐ Emma shows Max a house on a website.
- c ☐ Emma tries to boost Max's confidence.
- d ☐ Emma tells Max off.
- e ☐☐ Max calms down.
- f ☐☐ Max decides to make a phone call.
- g ☐☐ Max loses his temper.

b ▶ 07.21 Watch or listen to Part 2 again. Do Emma and Max agree that … ?

1 Max should move out
2 Alex's idea is good
3 Max should apologise to Sara

c **Language in context** *Challenging*
Paraphrase the two sentences Max says below.
1 Why don't you just come out with it?
2 Why doesn't everyone just get off my back?!

d 💬 What do you think of how Emma dealt with Max's … ?
- angry outburst
- fears

How do you think Max feels at the end of his conversation with Emma?

4 USEFUL LANGUAGE
Apologising and admitting fault

a 💬 Look at the picture below. Which part of the sentence is apologetic and which part admits fault?

I do apologise: it was my fault entirely.

b ▶ 07.22 Complete the expressions below with the words in the box. Listen and check.

| line tactful guess inexcusable came right |

1 It was _____ of me …
2 I was out of _____ / order.
3 I'm sorry. That wasn't very _____ of me …
4 I don't know what _____ over me.
5 I had no _____ to take it out on you …
6 I _____ I overreacted …

c Which expression(s) in 4b could you use if … ?
a you had done something you would never normally do
b you had been angry because you had a bad day
c you had said something that accidentally hurt somebody's feelings
d you had been more angry than you should about something small.

d 💬 Work in pairs. Plan the telephone conversation between Max and Sara. Use language from 4b. Role play your conversation for the class.

Hi Sara, it's Max Redwood here.
Hi Max. What can I do for you?
I'm phoning to apologise for earlier. I was completely out of line …

5 SPEAKING

Communication 7C Work in pairs. Student A: Go to p.137. Student B: Go to p.135.

UNIT PROGRESS TEST
→ CHECK YOUR PROGRESS
YOU CAN NOW DO THE UNIT PROGRESS TEST.

7D SKILLS FOR WRITING
It may result in improved cooperation

Learn to write a proposal

W Proposals; Linking: highlighting and giving examples

1 LISTENING AND SPEAKING

a Look at photos 1–4 of people working in teams. What kinds of teams are they? Which photo represents your idea of teamwork?

b Discuss the questions.
1 What teams have you been a part of?
2 Which of the teams worked well together? Which didn't?
3 What kinds of issues arose? Why? Think about:
 • productivity/achievements
 • disagreements
 • communication
 • energy and enthusiasm.

c ▶ 07.23 Listen to a team who work for an insurance company and answer the questions about each speaker.

• Claudio / Masha / Sam
 1 Which colleague does each speaker focus on?
 2 What problem(s) does each speaker mention?
 3 What positive qualities do they mention?
• Vicki
 4 What's her opinion of the team? What does she plan to do?

d ▶ 07.23 Complete the summaries below with the words and phrases in the box. Listen again and check.

> attention to detail   cynical smile
> beneath him   winds up   unsettles   drawback
> caught up in their own agenda   lighten up
> goes off on tangents

1 Masha _____ Claudio when they have meetings.
2 Claudio thinks Masha should _____ and see the funny side of things.
3 Masha admires Sam's _____, but at the same time thinks it's sometimes a _____.
4 Claudio's silence _____ Sam, and he doesn't like the _____ on his face.
5 Sam often _____ in team meetings.
6 The expression on Claudio's face gives the impression that everything is _____.
7 Each team member is _____ and they all communicate poorly.

e Order these personality attributes of an effective team member 1–6 (1 = most desirable; 6 = least desirable).

☐ pays a lot of attention to detail
☐ has a cynical smile
☐ is insincere
☐ goes off on tangents
☐ thinks most others are beneath them
☐ is caught up in their own agenda

Compare with a partner. Give reasons for your order.

2 READING

a Read the proposal Vicki wrote for a team-building programme for the consideration of senior management. Why has she chosen The Interpersonal Gym? How does she imagine the programme will help her team?

b 💬 Imagine you are on Vicki's team. What would your reaction be when you hear about the team-building programme?

3 WRITING SKILLS
Proposals; Linking: highlighting and giving examples

a Choose a word from the box to complete the headings in the proposal.

benefits	do	needs

b Underline the first person phrases in the proposal. Why does Vicki use these phrases? Tick (✓) all of the reasons.
- ☐ to introduce her opinions
- ☐ to sound more informal
- ☐ to be more persuasive

> **Writing Tip**
>
> It is always important to consider your audience and adjust the style of the language you use. Vicki's proposal is written for senior management, so a more formal style is appropriate. However, if she were writing to her team members, she would use a more relaxed style.

c Look at the highlighted words and phrases in the proposal. Which are used to … ?
1. give an example
2. give evidence
3. give more detailed information
4. highlight an individual thing, person, etc.

d Complete the paragraph below with the words in the box. Add the three words or phrases to the categories in 3c.

shown	such	especially

Group activities, ¹_____ problem-solving activities, are usually successful at building rapport among team members. An activity ²_____ **as** finding the way out of a maze uses both cognitive and practical skills. A very dysfunctional team did this and bonded as a result. They now work together extremely well **as** ³_____ **by** a 20% increase in their productivity.

e ▶▶ Now go to Writing Focus 7D on p. 173.

Introduction
The aim of this proposal is to outline plans to address training needs within my team.

Training _____
Recent team meetings have highlighted some breakdowns in communication in the team I currently manage. **Specifically**, the need for greater interpersonal awareness within a team framework has become apparent. I have identified one professional development day **in particular** that I believe is ideal.

The TIG programme – what they _____
The Interpersonal Gym (TIG) have been running personal development programmes for the past 12 years. **As detailed in** the attached brochure, TIG's speciality is team-building programmes. These involve games and problem-solving activities that are likely to appeal to all team members. **For instance**, there are simple but effective trust-building exercises in which team members have to help a partner negotiate a series of obstacles when blindfolded. The training places an emphasis on strategies to enhance active listening and collective decision-making.

_____ to our business
I believe the TIG programme will offer effective professional development. TIG has an excellent reputation, **as demonstrated by** their impressive range of testimonials from organisations similar to our own. Overall, the programme is likely to have a number of benefits for the business, **namely** increased sales and job satisfaction among team members, and therefore lower absenteeism and increased profits.

Conclusion
I hope you will agree that a training session run by TIG would be a practical and worthwhile way of addressing issues that are affecting the team's productivity.

4 WRITING

a 💬 Choose one of the teams below and imagine you are its team leader. What kind of training or team-building activities do you think would help?
1. an admin team who have absenteeism problems
2. a sales team who aren't selling very much
3. a student council who cannot agree on anything
4. a sports team lacking in motivation to do better

b ▶▶ **Communication 7D** Now go to p. 137 and choose a team-building programme for your team.

c Write a proposal to someone in authority for a team-building personal development day.
- Indicate which day you plan to go on and why.
- Describe how you think the team building will benefit the team.
- Remember to be gently persuasive and use formal language.

d 💬 Imagine you are the person in authority. Read another student's proposal. Will you accept it? Why / Why not?

UNIT 7
Review and extension

1 GRAMMAR

a Choose the correct options.
1. I'm sure the new version *may / will / should* work well.
2. I *couldn't / wouldn't / must not* have gone out last night; I was exhausted.
3. It's highly unlikely *for flying cars to / that flying cars will* appear.
4. There *may / can / must* be no such thing as paper money in 50 years.
5. Sorry, you did tell me. I *may / can / must* have forgotten.
6. This will be a good opportunity, and it *must / should / has got to* take you places.

b Complete the sentences with the words in the box.

not   happened   was   only   did   what   all   it

1. _____ interests me most is how stress affects relationships.
2. It was my youngest daughter who _____ the most affected.
3. What _____ was that Simon started spending less time at home.
4. _____ is Sue who needs to rethink her priorities, not me.
5. _____ that I am asking for is a little commitment.
6. It was _____ until the following day that Richard told his wife.
7. What I _____ was rearrange the seating plan.
8. It was _____ when I left home that I appreciated my parents.

2 VOCABULARY

a Correct the mistakes in the compound adjectives.
1. Sue is so hot-hearted that she'd do anything for anybody.
2. Cutting wood all day was really spine-breaking work.
3. Write it down for me because I'm getting rather absence-minded.
4. It's mind-wobbling what you can do with technology today.
5. The comedy is a light-headed look at what really goes on in hospitals.
6. To leave after all those years was heart-cracking.

b Replace the words in *italics* with the noun form of a word in the box.

collaborate   innovate   liberate   nervous
optimistic   rude   selfish

1. There was great *anxiety* among the crowd as they waited to find out the result.
2. What will be the next *new thing* in smartphone technology?
3. There is no excuse for *being impolite*.
4. We are proud to announce our *teamwork* on this project.
5. You can look to the future with some *positive feelings*.
6. *Only thinking about yourself* is common in society today.
7. The *freeing* of Paris in 1945 was an important event.

3 WORDPOWER self-

a ▶ 07.24 Replace the words in *italics* with the adjectives in the box. Listen and check.

self-sacrificing   self-centred   self-aware
self-confident   self-sufficient   self-satisfied

1. I'm sure she'll be a successful team leader. She's very *certain of her own abilities*.
2. Yoga is good for your health, and it also makes you more *able to notice your thoughts and feelings*.
3. He doesn't care about anyone else. I've never met anyone who's so *interested only in his own needs*.
4. She's so *pleased with herself* that it never occurs to her that other people don't like her.
5. She gave up her job so her husband could pursue a career in politics. Why is she always so *ready to give up things for other people*?
6. We've started growing our own vegetables, although I doubt we'll ever be *able to look after our own needs*.

b Complete the text with adjectives from 3a.

I have always thought of myself as a pretty successful person. I'm ¹_____ – for example, I don't get nervous if I have to give a presentation at work. I'm also ²_____ – I earn enough money to pay my bills and buy the things I want to. But then I went with a friend to a self-help course, and I realised that maybe I was wrong to be so pleased with myself. I was so concerned with my own life that I hadn't stopped to think about anyone else's. Maybe I was actually just ³_____? What if other people saw me as being just too pleased with myself – ⁴_____, even! This was such a horrible thought, I immediately decided to be more ⁵_____ and give up some of my time to help other people, and now I volunteer at a homeless shelter. This does make me feel quite good about myself, though, so maybe I haven't really changed at all? Well, at least I've started thinking about this, so hopefully I've become a little more ⁶_____.

c 💬 Use adjectives from 3a to describe:
- yourself
- people you know
- well-known people.

Discuss your ideas with a partner.

⟳ REVIEW YOUR PROGRESS

How well did you do in this unit? Write 3, 2 or 1 for each objective.
3 = very well   2 = well   1 = not so well

I CAN ...	
speculate about inventions and technology	☐
emphasise opinions about the digital age	☐
apologise and admit fault	☐
write a proposal.	☐

CAN DO OBJECTIVES

- Describe sleeping habits and routines
- Talk about lifestyles and life expectancy
- Negotiate the price of a product or service
- Write promotional material

UNIT 8

BODY AND HEALTH

GETTING STARTED

a Look at the picture and discuss the questions.
1. How old do you think the people in the photo are? What are they doing?
2. Why do you think they have chosen to do this activity? Do you think they are doing it for the first time or are they regulars at the class? Why?
3. What other activities might they enjoy? Make a list.

b Do you think it's more or less important to do physical activity as you get older? Why?

8A IT'S NO USE TRYING TO GO TO SLEEP

Learn to describe sleeping habits and routines

G Gerunds and infinitives
V Sleep

1 SPEAKING AND READING

a 💬 Do you know the answers to these questions? If not, guess with a partner.
1 Why do all animals (including humans) need sleep?
2 What proportion of their life does the average person spend asleep?
3 How long is it possible to go without sleep?
4 How many hours a night should adults sleep? What about newborn babies?

b ▶ 08.01 Listen to the radio interview and check your answers.

c 💬 Look at these headings for four tips for people who have problems getting to sleep. What do you think each tip involves?

> Acknowledge distractions   Everybody out!
> It is what it is   Compile a playlist

Read the article and match the headings with tips A–D.

d 💬 Do you think the tips would work for you? Why / Why not?

2 GRAMMAR Gerunds and infinitives

a Look at the highlighted phrases in the article. Which phrases are followed by … ?
  a to + infinitive: 1 too much
  b infinitive without to:
  c gerund (verb + -ing):

b Look at examples 1–4. Match the verb forms in **bold** with a–d.
1 Enjoy **being soothed** to sleep by music.
2 It's easy **to be distracted** by background noises.
3 Go to work tomorrow without **having had** eight hours' sleep.
4 Be pleasantly surprised **to have slept** all night long.

  a ☐ to + passive infinitive   c ☐ passive gerund
  b ☐ to + perfect infinitive   d ☐ perfect gerund

c ⏩ Now go to Grammar Focus 8A on p. 152.

d Look at these examples. What, if anything, is the difference in meaning between each pair?
1 a He got out of bed without saying a word.
  b He got out of bed without having said a word.
2 a He seems to sleep well.
  b He seems to have slept well.
3 a My daughter likes reading in bed.
  b My daughter likes being read to in bed.
4 a I'd like to wake up at 8:30.
  b I'd like to be woken up at 8:30.

TOP TIPS to help you sleep

Do you lie awake at night counting sheep? After a long day at work or university, do you find there's ¹too much to think about and your head is spinning?

Trying to get to sleep can be very frustrating. You might lie awake for hours until it gets to about five or six o'clock in the morning and then decide ²it's no use trying to go to sleep and you ³may as well get up. Here are four tips to help you get to sleep quickly:

A _____
If you enjoy being soothed to sleep by music, why not create the ultimate collection of soothing tracks? Choose songs with few or no lyrics and avoid anything with a catchy tune. When ⁴it's time to sleep, turn the volume down as low as possible.

B _____
When you're trying to fall asleep, it's very easy to become irritated by background noises. However, sometimes ⁵the best way to deal with them is by accepting them. Say to yourself, 'I can hear the clock, but it doesn't bother me', or 'I like the neighbour's music'. Soon they'll become less important.

C _____
Imagine your body is full of tiny people all working away with hammers. Announce that their shift is over so they ⁶'d better go home. Imagine them all putting their tools down and leaving your body one by one through your feet. This will make you relax, and you should soon drift off to sleep.

D _____
⁷There's no point in making judgements ('I should have been asleep hours ago') or indulging in catastrophic thinking ('If I go to work tomorrow without having had eight hours' sleep, I'll mess up that presentation, lose my job, and die tired and alone'). Make the night easier by accepting it for what it is, letting go of judgements and being gentle with yourself. The silver lining? You just might get to see a glorious sunrise.

So, for the chronic insomniacs out there, try some of these tips and by the time you wake up in the morning, you may be pleasantly surprised to have slept all night long!

e Think of possible endings for these sentences. Then compare with other students.

1 I've got to get up at 4:00 to go to the airport, so I may as well …
2 If you don't feel tired, there's no point …
3 You can't carry on sleeping only two hours a night. You'd better …
4 What a disaster! I went into the exam without having … (+ past participle)
5 When I feel tired, I really don't enjoy being … (+ past participle)
6 If you can't sleep, just accept it. It's no use …

3 READING

a Read the title of the article. What do you think the article will tell you about sleeping eight hours a night? Think of two possibilities. Read the article and check.

b Which of these are reasonable conclusions to draw from the article, and which aren't?

1 If undisturbed, most people would probably sleep in two segments.
2 In the 15th century, city streets probably would have been full of people at night.
3 The habit of sleeping for eight hours without waking up probably started in Europe.
4 People started going to bed later because the streets became less dangerous.
5 Stress in modern life is mainly a result of not sleeping well.

c Language in context *Cause, origin and effect*

1 What do the highlighted words and phrases mean? Match the expressions with the definitions.

1 be a factor in, contribute to
2 be because of (x2)
3 spread to
4 take from
5 say that the cause was

2 Why do you think the writer preferred each highlighted expression?

d Do you agree that 'lying awake could be good for you'? What arguments can you think of against Dr Jacobs' point of view?

THE MYTH OF THE EIGHT-HOUR SLEEP

We often worry about lying awake in the middle of the night – but it could be good for you. A growing body of evidence from both science and history suggests that the eight-hour sleep may be unnatural.

In the early 1990s, psychiatrist Thomas Wehr conducted an experiment in which a group of people were plunged into darkness for 14 hours every day for a month. It took some time for their sleep to regulate, but by the fourth week, the subjects had settled into a very distinct sleeping pattern. They slept first for four hours, then woke for one or two hours before falling into a second four-hour sleep. Though sleep scientists were impressed by the study, among the general public the idea that we must sleep for eight consecutive hours persisted.

In 2001, historian Roger Ekirch of Virginia Tech published a seminal paper, drawn from 16 years of research, revealing a wealth of historical evidence that humans used to sleep in two distinct chunks. His book *At Day's Close: Night in Times Past*, published four years later, unearths more than 500 references to a segmented sleeping pattern – in diaries, court records, medical books and literature.

During the waking period between sleeps people were quite active. They often got up, went to the toilet or smoked and some even visited neighbours. Most people stayed in bed, read, wrote and often prayed. Countless prayer manuals from the late 15th century offered special prayers for the hours in between sleeps.

Ekirch found that references to the first and second sleep started to disappear during the late 17th century. This started among the urban upper classes in northern Europe and, over the course of the next 200 years, filtered down to the rest of Western society. By the 1920s, the idea of a first and second sleep had receded entirely from our social consciousness. He attributes the initial shift to improvements in street lighting and domestic lighting and a surge in coffeehouses, which were sometimes open all night. As the night became a place for activity and as that activity increased, the length of time people could dedicate to rest dwindled.

Today, most people seem to have adapted quite well to the eight-hour sleep, but Ekirch believes many sleeping problems may have roots in the human body's natural preference for segmented sleep as well as the ubiquity of artificial light. This could be at the root of a condition called sleep maintenance insomnia, where people wake during the night and have trouble getting back to sleep, he suggests. The condition first appears in literature at the end of the 19th century, at the same time as accounts of segmented sleep disappear. 'For most of evolution we slept a certain way,' says sleep psychologist Dr Gregg Jacobs. 'Waking up during the night is part of normal human physiology.'

Jacobs suggests that the waking period between sleeps, when people were forced into periods of rest and relaxation, could have played an important part in the human capacity to regulate stress naturally. In many historic accounts, Ekirch found that people used the time to meditate on their dreams. 'Today we spend less time doing those things,' says Dr Jacobs. 'It's not a coincidence that, in modern life, the number of people who report anxiety, stress and depression has gone up.' So the next time you wake up in the middle of the night, think of your pre-industrial ancestors and relax. Lying awake could be good for you.

UNIT 8

4 LISTENING AND VOCABULARY Sleep

a 💬 You will hear four people talk about waking up at night. Look at the words below. What do you think each person is going to say?

ten or eleven – restless – photos – storm

1 Matt

yoga – studio – 20 other people – husband

2 Saba

artist – image – dream – therapeutic

3 Bernie

village – friends – sunset – fire – sweet potato

4 Iain

b ▶ 08.04 Listen to the radio programme. Were your ideas in 4a correct?

c Look at the expressions in the box from the recording. Which are about … ?
1 sleeping well or too long
2 not sleeping or not sleeping well
3 falling asleep
4 having a short sleep

have a nap   be fast asleep   feel wide awake
drift off to sleep   be a light sleeper   be restless
sleep like a log   not sleep a wink   toss and turn
oversleep   suffer from insomnia   drop off to sleep

d ▶ 08.05 **Pronunciation** Listen to this extract from the recording. Underline the stressed syllables in the fixed expressions in **bold**.

My wife used to force me to **get out of bed** 'cause I would lie there **tossing and turning** all night and I **couldn't sleep a wink**.

e ▶ 08.06 Underline the syllables you think will be stressed in the expressions in **bold**. Listen and check.

Sometimes I even get my husband to join us, if he's **having trouble sleeping**. But most of the time, **he's fast asleep** and doesn't even notice when I get up. He **sleeps like a log**!

f 💬 Talk about your sleeping habits using expressions from 4c. Use the questions below to help you plan what you are going to say.
1 Are they the same as people you live with? Why / Why not?
2 In what situations does your sleep pattern change? What can be different about it?
3 Do you know someone with particularly unusual sleeping habits?

5 SPEAKING

a 💬 Work in groups. Imagine that most people have segmented sleep patterns. What impact would it have on the way our lives are organised? How would society need to adapt? Consider these factors:
- travel and transport
- entertainment and socialising
- work
- leisure activities
- education
- mealtimes.

b 💬 Plan a typical day for a student who wants to start a segmented sleep pattern. How can they make the best use of their time? When should they … ?
- eat
- work
- relax
- learn
- exercise
- spend time with friends

c 💬 Choose one student from your group to explain your idea to the class.

d 💬 Decide which group's plan is:
- the most practical
- the most original.

8B SUPPOSE YOU COULD LIVE FOREVER

Learn to talk about lifestyles and life expectancy
- **G** Conditionals
- **V** Ageing and health

1 SPEAKING AND VOCABULARY
Ageing and health

a 💬 Look at the photos and read the quote. How do they make you feel?

> *Ageing is one of the most profitable fears of our time.*

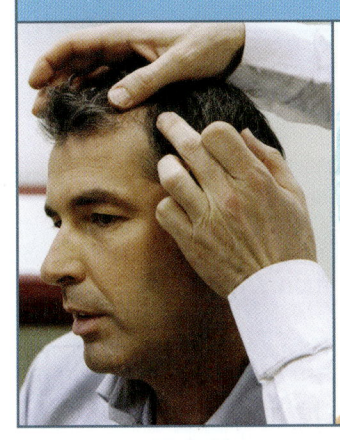

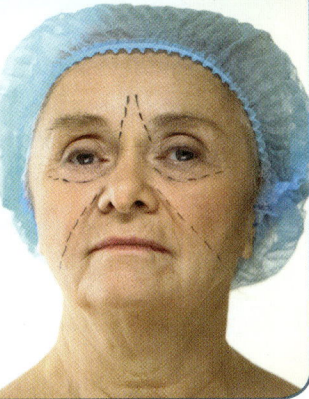

b 💬 Read about five treatments. Which do you think is the strangest? Which would you try?

c Match the highlighted words and phrases with the definitions.
1. _____ (adj.) of or on the face
2. _____ (adj.) clean and pleasant
3. _____ (n.) the movement of blood around the body
4. _____ (n.) lines on your face that you get when you grow old
5. _____ (n.) a temporary skin condition involving groups of small spots
6. _____ (n.) permanent marks left on the body from cuts or other injuries
7. _____ (adj.) not soft or loose, strong and healthy
8. _____ (n.) a beauty treatment involving gentle rubbing of creams into the face
9. _____ (n. phrase) the warm, healthy appearance of the skin on someone's face
10. _____ (n. phrase) the warm, healthy appearance of the skin typical of young people
11. _____ (adj.) hanging loosely, less tight than before

d ≫ Now go to Vocabulary Focus 8B on p. 165.

Anti-ageing treatments

Afraid of anti-ageing injections?
Try these alternative treatments to make you look younger!

Snail Slime Cream
Carefully collected snail's slime is a potent anti-ageing ingredient that helps reduce scars, acne and skin rashes, as well as smoothing out wrinkles.

Emu Oil
Rendered from the fat of an emu bird, emu oil is a lesser known anti-ageing oil that has been used for centuries in the Aboriginal communities for its healing powers. It leaves you with a glowing complexion.

Bee Sting Venom
The bee sting venom facial doesn't involve a swarm of bees stinging your face, but instead, the venom from the sting is transferred into a gel and then rubbed on the face as part of an intensive facial. It leaves your skin feeling fresh and renewed.

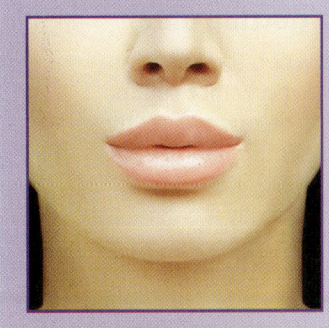

Anti-Sagging Lips
You can use a special rubbery mouthpiece to exercise your cheeks and lips. It is designed to keep the facial muscles firm by holding the cheeks and mouth stretched in a permanent 'trout pout' position. It will help bring back smooth, healthy-looking cheeks.

'Platza' Treatment
The 'platza' treatment involves the bare back being beaten with a 'broom' made of oak-leaf branches. It was first used in the *banyas* (saunas) of Russia and in Turkish baths. This alternative massage is designed to stimulate the blood circulation, creating a youthful glow.

UNIT 8

2 READING

a 💬 In the future, how likely do you think it is that medical science will keep people alive for much longer than today? Why do you think so?

b Read the interview with a scientist, Aubrey de Grey. How does he answer the question in 2a?

c Read the interview again. Summarise the main points made about these topics in paragraphs 2–7.

Paragraph 2: Diseases in old age
Paragraph 3: Attitudes towards the ageing process
Paragraph 4: The challenge our body faces
Paragraph 5: Aubrey de Grey and the medical profession
Paragraph 6: People who might benefit
Paragraph 7: Managing the population

d 💬 Would you like to live for a thousand years? Why / Why not?

We don't have to **get sick** as we get **older**

by Caspar Llewellyn Smith

Aubrey de Grey, expert in gerontology and Chief Science Officer, *SENS Research Foundation*

1 With his long beard and robust opinions, there's something of the philosopher about Aubrey de Grey. De Grey studied computer science at Cambridge University but became interested in the problem of ageing more than a decade ago.

2 What's so wrong with getting old?

It is simply that people get sick when they get older. I don't often meet people who want to suffer cardiovascular disease or whatever, and we get those things as a result of the lifelong accumulation of various types of molecular and cellular damage. This is harmless at low levels, but eventually it causes the diseases and disabilities of old age – which most people don't think are any fun.

3 Why does the world not recognise the problem of ageing?

People have been trying to claim that we can defeat ageing since the dawn of time, and they haven't been terribly successful; there is a tendency to think there is some sort of inevitability about ageing – it somehow transcends our technological abilities in principle, which is complete nonsense.

3 GRAMMAR Conditionals

a Read the web comments about longevity. Which ones reflect your opinion?

1. I would be a little more relaxed about my life goals if it were actually possible to live for a thousand years!
2. If medical science had been more advanced a hundred years ago, the world population would be out of control today.
3. Assuming what Aubrey de Grey says is correct, we probably don't need to worry so much about exercise and diet.
4. Supposing that we all were able to live for a very long time, people would just stop having children.
5. Had I been born 200 years ago, I would have been astounded to be told about life expectancies in the year 2000.
6. I won't care about living to a ripe old age as long as I feel I've had an interesting life.
7. Even if I only lived to a hundred, that'd be an amazing achievement.

REPLY ✉

b Which sentences in 3a refer to … ?
  a a real possibility
  b an imaginary or unreal situation
  c both the past and the present

c <u>Underline</u> the word or phrase in each example in 3a that introduces the condition.

d ≫ Now go to Grammar Focus 8B on p. 153.

e 💬 Use the phrases in the box to talk about yourself. Say one thing that isn't true or you don't really believe. Can you guess which of your partner's statements isn't true?

| Assuming that … | Had I … | Even if I only … |
| Supposing that … | If I hadn't … | As long as … |

Talk about:
- living for a long time
- life goals
- lifestyle and health
- the future of the planet.

4 Is it that our bodies just stop being so proactive about living?

Basically, the body does have a vast amount of inbuilt anti-ageing machinery; it's just not 100% comprehensive, so it allows a small number of different types of molecular and cellular damage to happen and accumulate. The body does try as hard as it can to fight these things, but it is a losing battle.

5 You say you want to enrich people's lives. Why is that?

The fact is, people don't want to get sick. I don't work on longevity; I work on keeping people healthy. The only difference between my work and the work of the whole medical profession is that I think we're within striking distance of keeping people so healthy that at 90 they'll carry on waking up in the same physical state as they were at the age of 30.

UNIT 8

4 LISTENING

a 💬 Why do people follow special diets? Talk about different reasons. Have you (or has someone you know) ever had to follow a diet? How was it?

b 💬 Read about a calorie-restricted (CR) diet. What kind of food do you think you can eat on this diet?

c ▶ 08.11 Listen to Peter Bowes talk to Martin Knight, who follows a CR diet. Answer the questions.
1 What does Martin do with the food in the photos below?
2 What does Martin's daily routine involve?

d ▶ 08.11 Listen again. Make notes on these topics.
1 eating out (discussed twice)
2 the look and taste of Martin's breakfast
3 Martin's lifestyle in general
4 Martin's reasons for following a CR diet
5 how Martin feels

e 💬 Do you think you could follow a CR diet? Why / Why not? If you did, what would the biggest sacrifice or challenge be in relation to your current lifestyle?

f ▶ 08.12 **Pronunciation** Listen to this extract.
1 Is the pitch lower or higher in the phrases in **bold**?

And then I have sprouted oats, **16 grams**, so that's at 70. Then this tomato paste here, **33 grams of that**, and almost done now. There we go. And then finally, add some olive oil, **that's 9.2**.

2 Does this happen because the speaker repeats information or adds extra information?

g 💬 Describe the process of preparing a typical breakfast, lunch or dinner to a partner. Vary your pitch as in the example above. Can you guess which meal your partner's describing?

Did you know

that a calorie-restricted (CR) diet will not only help you lose weight, it could increase your life expectancy by up to ten years? Research has shown that a CR diet reduces many of the health risks associated with ageing. All you need to do is eat less and eat smarter. Not only could you live longer, but you might feel years younger!

5 SPEAKING

a 💬 When have you or someone you know been told you were too young or too old to do something? Explain what happened.

b 💬 Work in small groups. What are your opinions of these statements? Talk about your own experiences.

1 How old someone feels depends entirely on their health.
2 TV adverts in my country represent older people in realistic ways.
3 It's easier for people under 40 to get a job than those over 40.
4 The longer you live, the more eccentric you become.
5 Companies that sell anti-ageing products don't want people to feel good about themselves.

c 💬 For each of the statements, choose one person in your group to tell the class their opinion and describe their experience. Take a class vote on who agrees and disagrees with each statement.

---

6 You've said you think the first person to live to 1,000 may already be alive. Could that person be you?

It's conceivable that people in my age bracket, their 40s, are young enough to benefit from these therapies. I'd give it a 30% or 40% chance. But that is not why I do this – I do this because I'm interested in saving 100,000 lives a day.

7 Can the planet cope with people living so long?

That's to do with the balance of birth and death rates. It didn't take us too long to lower the birth rate after we more or less eliminated infant mortality 100 or 150 years ago. I don't see that it's sensible to regard the risk of a population spike as a reason not to give people the best healthcare that we can.

chard

sprouted oats

kale

97

8C EVERYDAY ENGLISH
Is that your best offer?

Learn to negotiate
- S Negotiate the price of a product or service
- P Intonation in implied questions

1 LISTENING

a Discuss the questions.
1. What is the most memorable present you received as a child?
2. Who was it from?
3. What was the occasion?
4. Why is this present particularly memorable?

b You are going to hear about a present Max received as a child, which started his interest in life on other planets. What do you think it was?

c 08.13 Watch or listen to Part 1 and check your answer in 1b. Answer questions 2–4 in 1a about it too.

d What do you think Oscar will do next?

e 08.14 Watch or listen to Part 2 and answer the questions.
1. Why does Oscar call Miranda?
    a to tell her about a press conference
    b to find out what she knows about Max's new book
    c to sell her information
    d to arrange to meet
2. How would you describe the relationship between Oscar and Miranda?
    a old friends
    b business acquaintances
    c colleagues
    d they know each other only by name
3. Who do you think is the better negotiator?
    a Oscar
    b Miranda

f 08.14 Watch or listen to Part 2 again. Then write a possible *Why* question for each answer.
1. So that Miranda will understand that he's not calling on behalf of City FM.
2. So that Miranda will believe his information is from a reliable source.
3. Because she hasn't seen what Oscar is offering yet.
4. Because she's concerned that someone will announce Max's new book before she gets the chance.
5. Because he knows he could lose his job at City FM.

g Language in context *Expressions with* fair
Match the expressions a–c with meanings 1–3.
a ☐ it's fair to say   1 this is reasonable
b ☐ fair's fair   2 I understand this
c ☐ fair enough   3 this is true

h Discuss the questions.
1. Do you think Oscar is behaving fairly? What about Miranda?
2. How do you think these people would react if they knew what Oscar had done?
    • Sara • Nadia • Max

UNIT 8

2 USEFUL LANGUAGE Negotiating

a ▶08.15 Complete Oscar and Miranda's conversation. Listen and check.

M: There's just the ¹_____ of how much you would like for it.
O: Well, **how much would you be** ²_____ **to pay**?
M: Oh, I think **we'd be** ³_____ **to offer**, say, two fifty? Would that be a ⁴_____ suggestion?
O: Two fifty! Could you see your ⁵_____ to increasing that a little? I was kind of ⁶_____ for something more in the region of five hundred.
M: No, ⁷_____ of the question. What would you ⁸_____ to three fifty? In principle, of course. I'd need to see the article first.
O: Three fifty – **is that your** ⁹_____ **offer**?

b Add the expressions in **bold** in 2a to the correct column.

Opening negotiations	Making and accepting offers
I'm open to suggestions/discussion.	I'd be prepared to accept … I'm not in a position to offer more than …

Asking for more	Declining offers
It's worth much more than that. How flexible can you be on that?	I'm not authorised to accept anything less.

c 💬 Complete the conversation with words from the table. Practise it with a partner.

A How much would you like for it?
B I'm ¹_____ to suggestions.
A I think we could go to five.
B It's ²_____ much more than that. I'd be prepared to ³_____ seven.
A How ⁴_____ can you be on that? I'm not in a ⁵_____ to offer more than six.
B I'm not ⁶_____ to accept anything less than seven.

d 💬 Read the conversation below and answer the questions.
1 How is it the same / different from the conversation in Part 2?
2 Which conversation would be more successful in real life? Why?

A How much do you want?
B How much will you pay?
A 250.
B How about 500?
A No, 350.
B No more?
A No. And I need it by 1.
B What?
A OK, 2.

e 💬 Work in pairs. Cover 2a and use 2b and 2d to role play the conversation between Oscar and Miranda in Part 2.

3 PRONUNCIATION Intonation in implied questions

a ▶08.16 People often ask implied questions rather than direct questions in formal conversations. Listen to the implied questions below. What do you notice about their intonation?

Implied question	Direct question
1 I don't know if you remember?	Do you remember?
2 I've been doing a little freelance work?	Do you understand that the work I'm doing is not part of what I do for City FM?
3 Y'know, author of *Solar Wind*?	Do you know the author of *Solar Wind*?
4 We'd be prepared to offer, say, two fifty?	Would two fifty be acceptable?
5 And I need it by one o'clock?	Could you get it to me by one o'clock?

b ▶08.17 Listen to the statements below. Tick (✓) the implied questions.
1 ☐ I don't know if you've seen this item.
2 ☐ It's that well-known brand.
3 ☐ I'd be prepared to accept £50 for it.
4 ☐ I'm afraid I couldn't give you that much.
5 ☐ I could give you £30 for it.
6 ☐ I'd take £35.
7 ☐ Assuming it's available now.
8 ☐ It's yours today for £35.
9 ☐ We've got a deal.
10 ☐ Deal.

c 💬 Work in pairs. Practise the conversation in 3b.

4 SPEAKING

a Work alone. Think of an object or a service you could sell. Here are some ideas:
- an anti-ageing treatment
- a new-generation smartphone
- a homework service
- a car.

Make a list of selling points that might persuade someone to pay more for it.

b 💬 Work in pairs. Negotiate the price of your product or service and one other aspect. Use the language in 2c and implied questions.

✓ UNIT PROGRESS TEST

→ CHECK YOUR PROGRESS

YOU CAN NOW DO THE UNIT PROGRESS TEST.

8D SKILLS FOR WRITING
It's a unique dining experience

Learn to write promotional material

W Promotional material; Using persuasive language

1 LISTENING AND SPEAKING

a 💬 Think about occasions when you eat out and discuss the questions.
1. Do you think the food you eat out … ?
   - usually tastes better than what you eat at home
   - is usually healthier than what you eat at home
   In what ways?
2. When you eat out, what things are most important to you? Choose the five most important things from this list.
   - ☐ convenience
   - ☐ presentation
   - ☐ atmosphere
   - ☐ health
   - ☐ décor
   - ☐ service
   - ☐ value for money
   - ☐ difference from food at home
   - ☐ taste of the food
   - ☐ quality of ingredients
   - ☐ good reputation
   - ☐ type of cuisine (e.g., vegan, Chinese)

b 💬 You are going to listen to a restaurant chef talking about a 'Stone Age diet'. What do you think this might mean?

c ▶ 08.18 Listen to the interview and answer the questions.
1. Why was the Palaeolithic period significant in human development?
2. What foods does Julia believe are healthy, and why?
3. Why does Julia believe that dairy products, wheat and rice are unhealthy?
4. What are the similarities and differences between the food served at *Ancestors* restaurant and Palaeolithic food?
5. To what extent do you agree with Julia's views about food and health?

d 💬 Do you agree with each of these statements about diets? Why / Why not?
1. People are always thinking of new diets. It's just a way to make money.
2. The best diet is to eat whatever you feel like eating because your body knows what it needs.
3. It's better to think about changing your eating habits for life than to go on a short-term diet.

2 READING

a 💬 Quickly read the home page of *Ancestors* restaurant and answer the questions.
1. What new information not mentioned by Julia do you find out on the home page?
2. What kind of customer would go to *Ancestors*, and why? Would you go there yourself?

b 💬 What else do you think is on the menu at *Ancestors*? Imagine one starter, one main dish and one dessert. Then compare your answers.

ANCESTORS RESTAURANT

| Home | About | Menu | Contact |

ANCESTORS RESTAURANT

Our city-centre restaurant offers a unique dining experience. Lovingly prepared and exquisitely presented, our dishes contain only the purest ingredients, so you can be confident that our food is good for your body and your individual needs. So many people eat healthy food at home but then bend the rules when it comes to eating out. At *Ancestors*, we have a different concept. We serve you the foods you can eat, not the foods you can't!

THE STONE AGE DIET 🌿

For thousands of years, we humans were hunter-gatherers: we thrived on meat, seafood, seasonal vegetables, grains, fruit and nuts. Our bodies adapted to this diet, and it still suits our genetic makeup better than the recent additions of dairy products and processed foods. *[Find out more …]*

At *Ancestors*, we believe that eating is all about two things: health and enjoyment. So we've created a Stone Age menu fit for 21st-century living.

3 WRITING SKILLS Promotional material; Using persuasive language

a Which of these do you think is the main purpose of the home page in 2a?
- ☐ to give detailed information
- ☐ to give advice
- ☐ to promote the restaurant

b Why do you think the home page uses headings and short sections?

c Match the features of the home page 1–4 with their purposes a–d.
1. ☐ clear headings
2. ☐ short paragraphs
3. ☐ use of *we* and *you*
4. ☐ links

a to encourage the reader to browse the website
b to establish a personal relationship with the reader
c to show at a glance what the text is about
d to make it quick and easy to read

OUR MENU

The menu at *Ancestors* changes according to the seasons. Signature dishes from head chef Julia Dean include sweet potato and hazelnut soup, lamb with sesame seeds, and smoked salmon with wild leaves. We also offer a range of desserts made to the most exacting standards, using only wild fruits and natural sweeteners. *[Sample menu …]*

We take our drinks as seriously as our food. At *Ancestors* you'll find an exciting selection of natural fruit and vegetable juices from around the world, complemented by a range of teas, coffees and herbal drinks.

EARLY EVENING MENU

Based in the city centre, *Ancestors* is the ideal destination for a light and wholesome supper before you go to the theatre or the cinema. Tasty and fresh, the early evening menu offers a range of *Ancestors* dishes at a fixed price. Available 5:30 to 7:00 pm.

THE ANCESTORS COOKBOOK

So many of you have asked for our recipes that we've produced our own cookbook, using ingredients you can buy at any supermarket. Tried and tested by our team of cooks, our recipes will enable you to recreate the *Ancestors* experience in your own kitchen.
[View sample pages …]

d At the top of the *Ancestors* home page, there is a slogan missing. Which of these do you think would work best? Why?

> *Eat like our ancestors did*
>
> *Food that's good for you*
>
> *Pure enjoyment, pure health*
>
> *Only the best*

e The home page aims to give a positive message about the restaurant. Match phrases 1–4 from the first two sections with the messages a–d they convey.
1. ☐ a unique dining experience
2. ☐ Lovingly prepared and exquisitely presented
3. ☐ At *Ancestors*, we believe that
4. ☐ fit for 21st-century living

a The food is not at all old-fashioned.
b The food is made with care and looks good.
c *Ancestors* is not like other restaurants.
d What *Ancestors* is doing has a serious purpose.

f Compare these two sentences. Which emphasises the positive features of the dishes more strongly? How is the structure different?
1. Lovingly prepared and exquisitely presented, our dishes contain only the purest ingredients.
2. Our dishes are lovingly prepared and exquisitely presented, and they contain only the purest ingredients.

Find three more examples of description at the front of a sentence in the text.

g ≫ Now go to Writing Focus 8D on p. 174.

4 WRITING

a 💬 Work in pairs or groups. Think of a concept for a restaurant. You could either invent one or base it on a place you know. Note down ideas for a promotional text on a website. Consider:
- the underlying concept
- how it's different from other places
- what it offers customers
- what its positive features are
- food and drink, décor and atmosphere.

b Write a promotional text. Make sure you include clear headings, a name at the top and an appealing slogan.

c 💬 Read other groups' texts and decide which restaurant you'd most like to visit. Think of additional questions and ask the other group about their restaurant.

UNIT 8
Review and extension

1 GRAMMAR

a Choose the correct option.
1 *To wake / Waking / Having woken* up is easier in the summer.
2 *Being sent / Sending / Having sent* to boarding school is the best thing that ever happened to me.
3 I've always been a big fan of *to get / get / getting* up early.
4 Her refusal even *to listen / listening / for listening* to my idea really annoyed me.
5 There's no shame in *to have / having / being* lost to a team as good as theirs.
6 I was lucky enough *meeting / to have met / having met* Charles before he became famous.
7 Is there any hope of *to save / save / saving* the lost sailors?

b Complete the sentences with one word.
1 I wouldn't be in such good shape if I _____ look after myself.
2 If Steve had said it one more time, I would _____ walked out.
3 _____ I known the photo meant so much to you, I would have kept it.
4 I'm going to say yes if Dave _____ me to marry him.
5 The trip needs to be well planned, _____ it will be a nightmare.
6 _____ we to find out that Emily wasn't lying, would you apologise?

2 VOCABULARY

a Match 1–8 with a–h.
1 ☐ It wasn't until about three that I finally
2 ☐ Mark is a light
3 ☐ I couldn't sleep a
4 ☐ We thought the baby was fast asleep, but she was wide
5 ☐ Don't worry, I sleep like
6 ☐ It can help to have
7 ☐ Gradually my eyes closed, and I started to drift
8 ☐ About 10% of adults suffer

a wink with all that building work going on.
b a little nap in the afternoon.
c dropped off to sleep.
d from insomnia of some kind.
e awake and getting restless.
f off to sleep.
g a log on trains.
h sleeper, so don't make too much noise.

b Which word is different from the others? Why?
1 smooth, saggy, clear, firm
2 scars, acne, a rash, blotches
3 tighten, moisturise, strengthen
4 tooth loss, hair loss, weight loss
5 whitening, yellowing, toning
6 wrinkles, poor circulation, hair loss

3 WORDPOWER and

a ▶08.19 Match sentences 1–6 with pictures a–f. Listen and check.

1 ☐ There are still just a few **bits and pieces** to take away.
2 ☐ People came from **far and wide** to hear him talk.
3 ☐ It's **far and away** the best Italian restaurant in town.
4 ☐ I'm getting **sick and tired of** the noise.
5 ☐ It's just normal **wear and tear**.
6 ☐ It's just **part and parcel of** getting older, I suppose.

b Look at the phrases in **bold** in 3a. Replace each idiom with a non-idiomatic expression in the box.

easily   small things of different types
many places   annoyed by   a normal part of
damage caused by everyday use

c ▶08.20 Complete the sentences with the adjectives in the box. Listen and check.

tidy   safe   sweet   clear

1 'Can you hear me?'
   'Yes, I can hear you **loud and** _____.'
2 I'm almost afraid to touch anything in her room. She keeps it so **neat and** _____.
3 I don't want to have a long discussion over the phone, so let's keep it **short and** _____.
4 We got caught in a really bad blizzard, but fortunately we got home _____ **and sound**.

d Choose four expressions from 3a or 3c and write sentences but leave a gap for each expression.

e Read your sentences aloud. Can other students guess what goes in the gap?

REVIEW YOUR PROGRESS

How well did you do in this unit? Write 3, 2 or 1 for each objective.
3 = very well   2 = well   1 = not so well

I CAN ...	
describe sleeping habits and routines	☐
talk about lifestyles and life expectancy	☐
negotiate the price of a product or service	☐
write promotional material.	☐

CAN DO OBJECTIVES

- Talk about city life and urban space
- Describe architecture and buildings
- Deal with conflict
- Write a discussion essay

UNIT 9

CITIES

GETTING STARTED

a Describe the buildings you can see in the picture.

b Discuss the questions.
1. Why do you think the building in the centre of the picture hasn't been demolished?
2. How do you think the following people feel about this house?
   - the owners
   - the other buildings' owners
   - the local authorities
   - other local residents
3. What do you think will happen to the house in the future? What will happen to the homeowner?

c If there were a plan to demolish your family home, under what circumstances would you agree?

9A THEY JUST NEED TO RENOVATE IT

Learn to talk about city life and urban space

G Reflexive and reciprocal pronouns
V Verbs with *re-*

If you want to get close to nature, head into the city

Walk around in most cities and you see concrete buildings, paved squares and streets, and perhaps a few trees and well-tended parks. To find wild, natural habitats with a variety of birds, animals, fish, insects or wildflowers, you need to head out of the city into the countryside, or possibly even further afield.

5 But imagine a different kind of city. Along roadside verges, wildflowers and tall grasses grow, alive with the sound of bees. A river running through the city is allowed to follow its own natural course, the water unpolluted and full of fish. The walls of buildings are decked in luxuriant vegetation, providing a habitat for birds and insects, and some walls are covered with climbing crops which can be harvested for food. Roof spaces
10 are used for growing flowers, fruit and vegetables. Parks are not only spaces for recreation but are also wildlife reserves which support animal life. And as you look out of your window in the city centre, your view is not blocked by buildings but offers an unrestricted vista of trees and green spaces.

15 This may sound like science fiction, but many of these features actually exist in some cities around the world, as part of a movement called the Biophilic Cities Network. The aim of this project is to create cities which not only provide access to green spaces but where nature is incorporated into the urban design so that the residents of the city have continual contact with the natural world.

20 But why is this so important? Perhaps it's because, as human beings who have evolved over thousands of years to live in a natural environment, we feel at peace when we gaze out to sea or stroll through woodlands. This kind of contact with nature is essential for our mental well-being. Yet many people who live in cities – and that's 55% of the world's population – are largely cut off from nature, and
25 children often grow up with almost no knowledge or direct experience of the natural world. So, to re-establish this contact, it's important not just to make nature accessible but to recreate it as an integral part of city life.

1 READING

a 💬 Think about a city you know well and discuss the questions.
1 How would you describe the natural environment of these areas? Consider the number and variety of wildflowers, birds, animals, fish and insects you find there.
• the city centre, including inner-city areas
• outer suburbs
• the countryside around the city
2 In what ways have these areas changed over the last 50 years?

b 💬 Look at the definition of a 'biophilic city' in the panel. What features of biophilic cities do you think are shown in the photo above?

biophilic city a city where nature is integrated into the urban design.

c Read the article. What is the best summary of what it says?
1 Cities of the future will provide a better environment for the people who live there, so it won't be necessary to leave the city.
2 Because many people who live in cities are cut off from nature, it's important to design cities which provide a more natural environment.
3 People feel more at peace with themselves if they are in contact with the natural world in their everyday lives.

d 💬 Read the article again and the fact file about biophilic cities around the world. Answer the questions.
1 What action can be taken in biophilic cities to improve …?
 a roadsides b rivers c parks and green areas
2 What use can be made of …?
 a walls of buildings b roofs of buildings
3 How is human evolution connected to the idea of biophilic cities?
4 How would a biophilic city be different from a 'normal' city that has plenty of parks and green spaces?

Biophilic cities
Wellington, New Zealand – predator-free wildlife zones
Large areas have been fenced off and then allowed to develop naturally, creating predator-free wildlife zones within easy reach of the city centre.
Perth, Australia – natural river landscaping
City planners have restored a polluted industrial river and created natural wetlands which act as a wildlife corridor through the city.
Vitoria-Gasteiz, Spain – a natural green belt
A car-free green belt has been created all around the city, so you can walk and cycle through a natural landscape close to the city centre.
Singapore – 'vertical forests'
Walls and balconies are used to grow plants and trees, so the sides of buildings are covered in vegetation.
China – new 'forest cities'
There are plans to create complete new 'forest cities' in which several hundred buildings would have trees and plants growing on their facades.

e 💬 Choose the correct meaning (a or b) of the words in the article.

1	well-tended (*line 3*)	a	carefully looked after	b	popular and full of people
2	further afield (*line 5*)	a	in agricultural regions	b	in more distant places
3	luxuriant vegetation (*line 9*)	a	green and growing thickly	b	with rare and expensive plants
4	recreation (*line 11*)	a	leisure activities	b	creating new green areas
5	unrestricted (*line 13*)	a	in all directions	b	with nothing in the way
6	incorporated (*line 18*)	a	carefully thought about	b	included as part of
7	integral (*line 27*)	a	new and exciting	b	necessary and important

f 💬 Think again about the city you discussed in 1a. To what extent do you think it is already biophilic? What could be done to make it more so?

2 VOCABULARY Verbs with re-

a Look at the extracts from the article and the fact file. How are the words in **bold** similar in meaning?

So, to **re-establish** this contact, it's important not just to make nature accessible but to **recreate** it as an integral part of city life.

City planners have **restored** a polluted industrial river and created natural wetlands.

b ▶09.01 Complete the sentences with the correct forms of the verbs in the box that have the meaning shown in brackets. Then listen and check.

| recreate | redevelop | regain | regenerate |
| rejuvenate | renovate | | |

1 There are plans to _____ the port area of the city. (= improve it so that it becomes more active and productive)
2 It's a beautiful old building. They just need to _____ it. (= repair and modernise it)
3 It's good that students are moving into the area. It will help to _____ it. (= give a younger and livelier atmosphere)
4 In order to make the film, they _____ a medieval village, complete with cottages and a market square. (= built a copy of it)
5 They're moving the banks of the river so that it will _____ its natural character. (= get it back)
6 They are going to _____ an old industrial area to create parks and a wildlife zone. (= change it by building new streets and buildings)

c ▶09.02 Pronunciation

1 Listen to the pronunciation of *e* in *re-* in the verbs in the table.

1 /iː/	2 /ɪ/
redevelop	rejuvenate

2 ▶09.03 Add the other verbs in 2a and 2b to the table in question 1. Which verb has a different sound and can't be added to the table? Listen and check.

d 💬 What buildings do you know of that have recently been renovated or restored? Are there parts of your city that need redeveloping or regenerating, in your opinion?

3 READING AND SPEAKING

a 💬 What do you think is happening in each photo a–d? Why do you think it was worth taking a photo of it?

b ▶▶ **Communication 9A** Work in groups of four. Student A: Go to p. 135. Student B: Go to p. 136. Student C: Go to p. 136. Student D: Go to p. 137.

c 💬 Explain the idea you read about to the other students. Which idea do you think … ?
- provides the most benefit to the community
- provides the least benefit
- would work best in your own city

4 GRAMMAR Reflexive and reciprocal pronouns

a Read the comments about the events in photos a–d. Which could they refer to?

1 It's a great place to just sit **by yourself**, drink coffee and read the paper.
2 It just shows what local communities can do **for themselves**.
3 The place **itself** isn't very welcoming, but the people are.
4 People can sit and talk to **one another**.
5 It's a great neighbourhood because we all support **each other**.
6 It's nice to have somewhere people can make **themselves** comfortable while they wait for the bus.
7 Cars and pedestrians give way to **each other**. It really works.

b Look at the words and phrases in **bold** in 4a and answer the questions.

1 Which pronoun or phrase ending in *-self/-selves* … ?
   a ☐ shows that the object of the verb is the same as the subject
   b ☐ emphasises one thing in contrast to something else
   c ☐ means *alone* or *not with other people*
   d ☐ means *independently, without help*
2 What is the difference between … ?
   a *we support ourselves* and *we support each other*
   b *they talk to themselves* and *they talk to one another*

c ▶▶ Now go to Grammar Focus 9A on p. 154.

105

UNIT 9

5 LISTENING

a 💬 You are going to hear part of a podcast about how technology can improve life in cities. Look at the app in the picture. What do you think it is for?

b ▶ 09.06 Listen to the podcast and answer these questions.
1 How does the app work?
2 Why does Michelle think it's a good idea?
3 Do you agree with her? Would you use it? Why / Why not?

c ▶ 09.07 Listen to three more people talking about other ideas for 'smart' cities. Two of them really exist and one is invented. Which do you think is the invented one? Why?
• Frank   • Rita   • Nick

d ▶ 09.07 Listen to each description again. Which idea (or ideas) … ?
1 gives live information
2 is useful for forgetful or absent-minded people
3 probably uses GPS
4 could be useful when it's raining
5 would be popular with hypochondriacs
6 could help you make friends

e 💬 In groups, talk about the ideas. Which idea (or ideas) … ?
• would you use yourself
• would you be prepared to pay for
• would other people you know use

f 💬 Discuss the questions.
1 What other technology do you use or know of that makes city life easier?
2 To what extent do you think technology like that described makes people less self-reliant?

g **Language in context** *Colloquial expressions*

1 ▶ 09.08 Complete the expressions in **bold** below with the words in the box. Then listen and check.

keel   blow   place   whirl   neck
life   blend   dotted   smashed

a … a place where you're repeatedly having to **risk your** _____ to get across the road.
b We're going past a park, and there's a railing that**'s been** _____ **in** here.
c So I can get the map here, _____ it **up** a bit like that.
d They've got these screens all around the city; they're **all over the** _____.
e So let's **give it a** _____ … I put my finger on it.
f Let's see if I'm OK or whether I'm **about to** _____ **over**.
g These are artificial trees and they're _____ around the city.
h They're shaped like trees, so they _____ **in**.
i I'm always going out without charging my phone, so it's **a real** _____ **-saver** for me.

> 💡 **Learning Tip**
> A typical feature of colloquial English is the use of **multi-word verbs** rather than more formal, single-word verbs. When you come across a multi-word verb, notice if it has a single-verb equivalent and learn them both together.

2 Which multi-word verbs in 5g have the same meanings as *collapse* and *enlarge*?

6 SPEAKING

a 💬 Look at this list of ideas for making cities 'smarter' or better to live in. Do any of them already exist in the city you live in or one you know? If so, how useful are they? If not, would you use the app or facility if it were available?
1 an app giving information about new projects and impending legislation in the city
2 parking apps to show drivers the nearest available parking space and how much it costs
3 apps to let users 'adopt' city property, such as litter bins, trees and flower beds, and volunteer to maintain them
4 digital parking payment systems, allowing you to pay for parking by smartphone, without using coins or tickets
5 free wi-fi everywhere in the city, including on trains, buses and the metro
6 screens in public places that display traffic information, weather and local news

b 💬 Work in groups of three. Choose an idea in 6a or your own idea that does not exist where you live yet and prepare to sell your idea to the class. Make notes of some things you could say about it:
• how it would work
• what benefit it would bring to the city
• possible problems and solutions.

c 💬 Give a group presentation. Focus on one point in 6b each. Vote for the best idea in the class.

9B THEY WANTED A DRAMATIC SKYLINE AND THEY GOT ONE

Learn to describe architecture and buildings

- **G** Ellipsis and substitution
- **V** Describing buildings

Triumph Palace
Krzywy Domek (The Crooked House)
Casa Batlló
Torre Velasca
The United Nations Secretariat Building
Museo Soumaya

1 SPEAKING AND VOCABULARY
Describing buildings

a 💬 Have you seen these buildings before? What city and country do you think each is located in? What do you think they were built as? What do you think of each building?

b Which of the words and phrases in the box are positive? Which are negative? Check new words in a dictionary.

1 imposing	4 innovative	7 dated
2 nondescript	5 tasteless	8 out of place
3 graceful	6 over the top	9 stunning

c ▶ 09.09 **Pronunciation** Listen and underline the stressed syllable in each word or phrase in 1b.

d 💬 Use the words and phrases in 1b or other adjectives to describe the buildings in the pictures.

> The UN Building is fairly imposing, but it's a little nondescript.

> The Museo Soumaya is very graceful, but it's a bit over the top.

e ⟫ Now go to Vocabulary Focus 9B on p. 166.

f 💬 Take turns describing local or distinctive buildings that you think your partner will know about. Guess the building your partner is describing.

> It's an imposing building near the river. It used to be a warehouse.

> Is it the … ?

2 GRAMMAR Ellipsis and substitution

a 💬 Read sentences 1–6. Which of them are true for you or the place you live?

1 Most people dislike modern architecture. I know I **do**.
2 They don't consult residents about new buildings as often as they ought to ^.
3 They've put up that skyscraper and ^ ruined the skyline.
4 The old buildings are always being knocked down to make way for new **ones**.
5 The government promised they were going to build more houses, but they haven't ^ yet.
6 They haven't built anything new around here for ages. **Nor** are they likely to.

b Look at each sentence in 2a again. Which words have been omitted (^) or substituted with words in **bold**? Why?

c ⟫ Now go to Grammar Focus 9B on p. 155.

107

UNIT 9

3 READING

a Read the article about the architect Kazuyo Sejima. Choose the best summary.
  1 Kazuyo Sejima is an architect who has gradually gained an international reputation. Her buildings have a distinctive style, and aim to blend easily with the environment in which they sit.
  2 Kazuyo Sejima is one of a group of architects who have changed the approach to architecture in Japan. Her buildings allow people to move easily from one living space to another.

b Read the article again. Make notes on Sejima's:
  - background and personality
  - colleagues and architectural firms
  - architectural style
  - beliefs about architecture
  - design of a key building.

c Discuss the questions.
  1 Look at the photos of Sejima's buildings. What do/don't you like about them?
  2 To what extent does the environment in which a building is situated play a part in its success? Think of examples in your country where the environment has had a positive or negative impact on a building.
  3 In what ways can architects and builders help the environment?

d Language in context *Metaphorical phrases*
  1 Notice how forms of the words in **bold** in the phrases below are used in the text. Is the meaning exactly the same?
     a **walk** down the street
     b a tree **blossoms**
     c a **game** of tennis
     d **sparks** from a fire
     e heating **fuelled** by gas
     f the **hallmark** on a gold bracelet
  2 Match the highlighted expressions in the article with the definitions.
     a doing her best work
     b created her initial motivation
     c are examples of typical features
     d won a prize or award
     e a key event that causes a positive result
     f develop and become more successful
     g strongly increased her enthusiasm

> **Learning Tip** Many expressions include an indirect or metaphorical meaning. It can sometimes help to think about the literal meaning of key words as a way of understanding the expression. For example, *a tree that blossoms* suggests fresh and attractive new growth that will develop further.

KAZUYO SEJIMA: PASSION AND PRECISION

Quietly spoken and highly focused on her work, Kazuyo Sejima has slowly but surely become one of the world's best and most well-known architects. So good, in fact, that she has walked away with top architectural awards in Sweden, Germany, Mexico, the USA and her native Japan. Her work has an elegant simplicity, with buildings that create a sense of flow between inside and outside worlds.

In the field of architecture, where she is known simply by her surname, there is no doubt that Sejima is now at the top of her game. But her rise to prominence didn't happen overnight. It began as a child when she came across a photograph of an unusual, architecturally designed house. She found it beautiful and was immediately fascinated – this sparked her interest in architecture.

After graduating with a Master's in Architecture from Japan Women's University in 1981, Sejima went to work as an apprentice for another famous Japanese architect, Toyo Ito. Six years later, she set out on her own and established the firm Kazuyo Sejima and Associates. She quickly developed a distinctive style of neutral spaces with a light and spacious quality. In just five years, her design ability was recognised when she was awarded the Young Architect of the Year award in Japan.

However, the game-changer came in 1995 when Sejima joined forces with Ryue Nishizawa to create the firm SANAA (Sejima And Nishizawa And Associates). Previously, Ryue was Sejima's younger employee, but then their professional relationship blossomed into one of cooperation and intense creativity. They designed a series of spacious, airy buildings that almost seem to float above the ground. These include the New Museum in New York, the Institute of Modern Art in Valencia and the Rolex Learning Center in Lausanne.

One of Sejima's works in France shows all the hallmarks of a SANAA design. When the Louvre Museum in Paris decided to create a satellite museum in the northern city of Lens, SANAA was commissioned to design it. Attached to the central building of Louvre-Lens are two wings to match the design of the Louvre in Paris. However, unlike the Parisian museum, the Lens satellite is made up of glass walls and aluminium facades, which means it blends easily with the natural environment in which it sits.

Louvre-Lens, France

UNIT 9

4 LISTENING

a 💬 Look at the two photos of tourist attractions in Singapore. Which would you rather visit? Why?

b ▶ 09.18 Katie and Ryan are having a one-day stopover in Singapore. Who would prefer to see the following tourist attractions – Katie (*K*) or Ryan (*R*)?
1. ☐ Fort Canning Park
2. ☐ Marina Bay Sands
3. ☐ ArtScience Museum
4. ☐ SkyPark
5. ☐ Raffles Hotel
6. ☐ Botanic Gardens
7. ☐ Interlace

c ▶ 09.18 Listen again and make notes on what Katie and Ryan say about the tourist attractions in 4a.

d 💬 When you are on holiday, which of these types of tourist attractions do you prefer to visit? Why?
- mostly older, historical ones
- mostly modern ones
- an equal balance of historical and contemporary ones

The interplay between interior and exterior worlds fuels Sejima's strong interest in a fluid architectural style. She doesn't believe that these two worlds need to be completely separate. Nor does she think that a building is a kind of a barrier between inside and outside. This means that Sejima often takes her inspiration from the natural surroundings in which her buildings will be situated because she wants the building to be a reflection of its location. This awareness also determines the materials she uses for each building.

While her buildings suggest an architect with a light touch, Sejima is very passionate about her work. She maintains that her only interest in life is in making architecture. She works slowly, and she carefully thinks through every decision she makes. She is famous for her dedication and hard work. This has inspired and attracted staff from around the world wanting to work at SANAA. Employees are often there until two or three in the morning, but they aren't forced to work with such intensity. Rather, they are driven by the same passion and commitment that Sejima herself displays.

When she was a child, she imagined only that she would grow old and become a grandmother leading a quiet life. Instead, she has become one of the foremost architects in the world. Her vision, dedication and impeccable taste have all helped her achieve fame and recognition in a field traditionally dominated by men.

21st Century Museum of Contemporary Art, Kanazawa, Japan

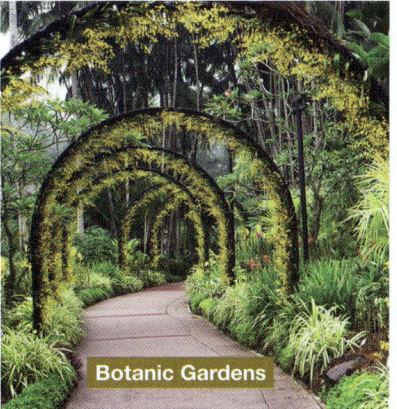

Botanic Gardens

Marina Bay Sands

5 SPEAKING

a 💬 Read the scenario, talk about your ideas and come up with a proposal and a reason for it.

There is a derelict warehouse in your community that was built in the early 20th century. You are a member of the city council, and you have to help make a decision about how the warehouse or the land itself could be repurposed.

Consider:
- the needs of your community
- demolition and rebuilding
- the benefits of a new, distinctive building
- a high-profile architect
- your community's architectural heritage
- the warehouse's architectural features.

b 💬 Work in groups of four. Present your proposals to each other. Agree on one proposal and tell the class.

New Serpentine Gallery Pavilion, London, UK

109

9C EVERYDAY ENGLISH
Let's not jump to conclusions

Learn to deal with conflict
- S Complain and respond to complaints
- P Sound and spelling: foreign words in English

1 LISTENING

a How would you feel if, without your permission, ... ?
- you saw yourself in a documentary about learning English
- your picture appeared on Google Earth
- a radio station phoned you live on air to offer you the chance to win a prize

b Look at the picture. What do you think is happening?

c 09.19 Watch or listen to Part 1 and check your answer to 1b.

d 09.19 Read these phrases from Part 1. Who or what do the words in **bold** refer to? Watch or listen to Part 1 again and check.
1 Max: I really think **it**'s going to work.
2 Emma: **That**'s brilliant!
3 Max: **This** is outrageous!
4 Emma: But **it**'s true.
5 Max: How dare **she**?!
6 Max: I'm ringing **them** right now.

e **Language in context** *Animal idioms*
1 09.20 Correct the idioms from Part 1. Listen and check.
   a Night rat, Max Redwood
   b There's something horsey about this.
   c I smell an owl.
   d Hold your fish, Max.
2 What do you think the idioms mean? Use a dictionary if necessary.

f 09.21 Watch or listen to Part 2 and answer the questions.
1 How does Nadia respond to Max's complaint? Does she ... ?
   a pass on the blame to someone else
   b accept responsibility and apologise
   c promise to take action and try to arrange a meeting
2 How do you think Max feels after the phone call?
3 What do you think Nadia will do next?

2 USEFUL LANGUAGE
Dealing with conflict

a 09.19 09.21 Watch or listen to Parts 1 and 2 again and complete the expressions.

Expressing disbelief
1 This is _____ belief!
2 Where on _____ did they get this from?!
3 I'm lost for _____!

Expressing anger
4 It's d_____!
5 I'm calling to express my _____.
6 Words cannot express my _____.
7 It's totally _____!

b Which two expressions does Max decide not to use? Why not, do you think? Would either of these expressions need to change for use in writing?

c 09.22 Complete the expressions from Parts 1 and 2 with the words or phrases in the box. Add *to* where necessary. Listen and check.

explanation   jump   fulfil your responsibility   raise   take full responsibility   right

Commenting on the behaviour of others
1 Let's not _____ conclusions.
2 There's no need _____ your voice.
3 They've got no _____!
4 You owe me an _____.
5 Don't you think you should _____ ... ?
6 You've failed _____ ...

d Which of these comments were on Max's behaviour and which were comments on Breaking News Online / City FM's behaviour?

e 09.23 Complete the sentences with words from Part 2. Listen and check.

Taking action
Offering
1 I have every _____ of investigating the matter.
2 I _____ you, there will be consequences.
Responding to offers
3 _____ **not**. And **I'd** _____ **it if** you didn't try to contact me again.

f Work in pairs. Role-play the conversation between Max and Nadia using the language in 2a, c and e. This time Max should respond positively to Nadia's invitation.

UNIT 9

3 LISTENING

a ▶ 09.24 Watch or listen to Part 3. What two reasons does Nadia have for believing Oscar sold Sara's information to Breaking News Online? What does she want from Oscar?

b ▶ 09.24 Watch or listen to Part 3 again and answer the questions.
1. Why does Nadia say the article gave her a sense of déjà vu?
2. What does Nadia suspect happened between Oscar and Miranda?
3. What does Nadia think would happen if Oscar took her to court?

c 💬 Do you think Nadia has done the right thing? Why / Why not?

4 PRONUNCIATION Sound and spelling: foreign words in English

a ▶ 09.25 Listen to these words. Are they from Spanish, Italian or French? Which four were in Parts 1–3?
1. avant-garde
2. nada
3. déjà vu
4. cappuccino
5. finito
6. tête-à-tête
7. rendezvous
8. pronto

b Match the words 1–8 in 4a with their meanings a–h.
a ☐ a strange feeling that you have experienced the same thing before
b ☐ an arrangement to meet, usually secret
c ☐ coffee made with heated, bubbly milk
d ☐ finished
e ☐ nothing
f ☐ different and modern
g ☐ private conversation between two people
h ☐ quickly and without delay

c ▶ 09.25 Listen to the words in 4a again. Underline the consonant sounds which are pronounced in a way which is untypical of English.

d Look at the words in the box. Answer the questions below and then check in a dictionary.

c'est la vie	kaput	aficionado	faux pas
kindergarten	tsunami	paparazzi
Schadenfreude	typhoon	karaoke	siesta

1. What languages do you think these words come from?
2. What do they mean?
3. How are they pronounced by British English speakers?

e ▶ 09.26 Listen and practise saying the words in 4d.

5 SPEAKING

a Work alone. Think of a situation you wish to complain about. Here are some ideas:
- planning permission to build a multi-storey car park opposite your house has been granted
- the luxury spa holiday you booked and paid for turned out to be in a hostel
- your private medical information has been accidentally posted on your doctor's website

b 💬 Work in pairs. Take turns to be A and B. Use your ideas in 5a and the language in 2.

Student A: Explain your situation and complain.
- Express anger and disbelief.
- Comment on B's behaviour.
- Respond to B's offer to take action.

Student B: Respond to A's complaint.
- Express understanding of A's situation.
- Comment on A's behaviour.
- Offer to take action.

✓ UNIT PROGRESS TEST

→ CHECK YOUR PROGRESS

YOU CAN NOW DO THE UNIT PROGRESS TEST.

9D SKILLS FOR WRITING
The impact on cities is plain to see

Learn to write a discussion essay
- Discussion essays; Linking: reason and result

1 LISTENING AND SPEAKING

a Which city in your country has the fastest-growing population? Why do people want to live there?

b Look at the photos of rural and urban New Zealand. Which environment would you prefer to live in? Why?

c 09.27 Listen to Lizzie and Ron talking about life in a rural community in New Zealand compared to life in Auckland, the largest city. Answer the questions.

1. What's Lizzie's news? How is she feeling about it?
2. What point does Ron make about his own and Lizzie's children?
3. What makes it difficult for their children to return to their home town?
4. Why are Lizzie and Ron better off living where they do?
5. What does Lizzie worry about for the future of their town?

d What do you think Lizzie, Ron and their partners should do? Should they stay where they are or follow their children to Auckland? Why?

2 READING

a Read the essay about urban migration. Put these points in the order they are mentioned (1–6).

Urban migration …
- [ ] has a negative effect on communities in small towns.
- [ ] is a problem that requires a political solution.
- [ ] impacts living standards in both cities and small towns.
- [ ] is driven by work and study needs.
- [ ] is happening all over the world.
- [ ] has a negative impact on the supply of city housing.

b What challenges are there for people who move from small towns or the country to a large city?

Document1

Urban migration is an international phenomenon. In recent years, *there has been increasing awareness* of issues associated with the migration of people from small towns and rural communities to larger cities. This essay looks at the impact of urban migration on both large cities and rural communities.

Why do people decide to move to a large city? One key factor is that there are often more employment opportunities in urban areas. Secondly, younger people may need to go to a city in order to attend university or other educational programmes. Beyond this, others are drawn to cities because of the increased stimulation offered by an urban environment.

The impact on cities [1] *is plain to see*. An increase in population leads to greater demand for housing, causing house prices and rents to rise. As a result, both existing residents and new arrivals in the city are required to spend more of their income on accommodation or are forced to live in substandard conditions.

However, [2] *it could be argued* that the impact on small towns and rural areas is perhaps even greater. A dramatic decrease in the population of rural communities is often due to the number of young people leaving in search of work and study opportunities. This exodus results in the closure of businesses and cutbacks in social services. And those who remain in rural communities suffer a decline in living standards which, in turn, means small communities are seen as even less attractive places to live. As a consequence, towns serving rural communities begin to look like ghost towns.

[3]*By examining* the way urban migration affects both rural and urban communities, [4] *it is evident that* the phenomenon can lead to a decline in living standards for all concerned. [5]*It would seem that* there is a role for governments to play in the way that the movement of population is managed. Intervention such as business incentives and subsidies can ensure small communities continue to offer inhabitants employment opportunities and a good standard of living.

Page 1 of 1   334 words

112

3 WRITING SKILLS Discussion essays; Linking: reason and result

a What is the purpose of each paragraph in the essay?

b Notice the phrase in *italics* in the introduction. Does this express the writer's point of view directly or indirectly? Match the phrases in *italics* (1–5) in the essay with the meanings below.

- ☐☐ you can clearly see
- ☐☐ I think
- ☐ I've looked at

> **Writing Tip**
> When you present a balanced discussion in a formal essay, you should avoid using personal pronouns *I* and *you* and use pronouns like *we*, *it* and *there*.

c Use the words in the box to complete the formal equivalents; a and b in each pair mean the same thing.

| outcome | outlining | noticeable | claimed | appear |

1 a I've noticed a slow decline …
   b There has been a slow but _____ decline …
2 a I think it's hard to predict what will happen …
   b The _____ is difficult to predict …
3 a What I'd say is that most residents …
   b It would _____ that most residents …
4 a Now that I've described the issues here …
   b By _____ the issues here …
5 a In my opinion, it's likely …
   b It could be _____ …

d Look at the highlighted examples in the essay in 2a. Which introduce a reason? Which indicate a result? Make two lists.

e Underline the reason or result language in these examples.
1 Urban migration has decreased owing to an increase in grants to rural businesses.
2 There are now many more unemployed people in the city. Consequently, there has been a noticeable increase in small crimes.
3 A drop in living standards causes problems for those at the lower end of the socioeconomic scale.
4 There has been a population increase of 12%. Hence, there has been an increase in new building projects in suburban areas.
5 Some rural workers have returned to the countryside as a direct consequence of the loneliness and isolation of urban life.

f Which expressions in 3e can be used in the same way as these examples?
1 lead to, result in
2 due to, because of
3 As a consequence, As a result

g Choose the correct word in *italics* in these sentences.
1 The increase in new residents in some areas of the city has seen a rise in the number of potential customers for businesses, thereby *creating / create* many new business opportunities.
2 Enrolment in local primary schools has fallen dramatically. *Thus / Thereby*, many have been closed.
3 Certain local students have gained scholarships to the city's university, *thereby / therefore* freeing their parents from a significant economic burden.

h ⟫ Now go to Writing Focus 9D on p. 175.

4 WRITING

a 💬 Think about some kind of social change in your country that is of interest to you, for example:
- demand for university places
- involvement in community organisations
- your own idea.

What are the reasons for this change? What are the results? Tell a partner.

b Write a discussion essay about the social change you have chosen. Follow these steps.
- Outline the issue in the introduction.
- Describe reasons for the change and their results.
- Avoid using personal language.
- Hypothesise about the future.
- State whether anything can/should be done about the issue.

c Work with a new partner. Read each other's essays. What kind of social change does your partner's essay discuss? How aware were you of this issue?

UNIT 9
Review and extension

1 GRAMMAR

a Complete the sentences with a reflexive or reciprocal pronoun.
1 I washed the car _myself_ because the car wash was closed.
2 I can see Grandad is getting old. He seems to talk to _____ all the time.
3 While Simon was in hospital, his mother was absolutely beside _____.
4 While I'm on holiday, my secretary and I still send _____ several messages a day.
5 We call _____ 'The Pirates' because we have a stadium on the coast.
6 Rita and I sat down next to _____ and we looked into _____'s eyes.
7 No one helped us with our house. We built it all by _____.

b Correct one mistake in each sentence or exchange.
1 Kate wanted to put in new windows, but I didn't want.
2 'I'll never listen to her advice again.' 'So will I.'
3 It was a beautiful morning, although was rather cool outside.
4 He living nearby, Frank had no problem getting in early.
5 So they wouldn't get bored, were listening to the radio.
6 'Kelly hasn't read the contract properly.' 'I don't suspect.'
7 She became a famous actress, as her mother.
8 Take the clean mug, not the dirty.

2 VOCABULARY

a Complete the sentences with the words in the box.

| recreate   redevelop   regain |
| rejuvenate   renovate   restore |

1 The city council plan to _____ the wasteland near the port.
2 A few cafés and independent shops would _____ this run-down area.
3 The picture was badly damaged, but they managed to _____ it.
4 The aim of *The Oscars* restaurant is to _____ the atmosphere of Hollywood.
5 The town has long been in decline, and I doubt it will ever _____ its former prestige.
6 It took years to _____ the old hotel and modernise all the facilities.

b Choose the best phrase to complete each sentence.
1 ☐ I grew up on a
2 ☐ The nature walk took us to a
3 ☐ Our new office is in a
4 ☐ I work at a
5 ☐ I know a millionaire who owns a
6 ☐ Every city needs an

a power station on the coast.
b housing estate near Hamburg.
c mansion in the Caribbean.
d log cabin in the woods.
e iconic skyscraper or two.
f tower block overlooking the river.

3 WORDPOWER build

a Look at these multi-word verb collocations with *build*. Match multi-word verbs 1–6 with meanings a–f.
1 **build up** savings / stamina / a following / a reputation
2 **build** an event / an argument **up into** something
3 traffic / problems / dirt / pressure **build(s) up**
4 **build on** our success / strengths / relationship
5 **build in** features (to a product) / activities (to a schedule)
6 **build** something **around** a concept / people

a ☐ use as a basis for the future
b ☐ make an effort to increase
c ☐ use as the main principle/idea
d ☐ include, incorporate
e ☐ increase naturally over time
f ☐ talk or think a lot about something so it becomes more important

b ▶09.28 Complete the sentences with the words in the box. Listen and check.

| up (×4)   on   around   in |

1 He's **built** this day _____ so much I'm afraid he'll be disappointed.
2 They forgot to **build** _____ auto-locking on this phone.
3 He's **built** _____ a huge fan base over the years.
4 I'm looking for ways to **build** _____ last year's sales.
5 Our business is **built** _____ the idea that people want coffee with their books.
6 She really needs to **build** _____ her confidence if she wants to get a job.
7 When the pressure **builds** _____ at work, you need a good, long break.

c Complete each statement with your own idea. Check the meaning of the expressions in **bold** in a dictionary if necessary.
1 People sometimes **build up a tolerance** to _____.
2 I had to **build up the courage** to ask _____.
3 I once **built my hopes up about** _____ but was disappointed.
4 I think **building up a business** would be _____.

d 💬 Compare your answers to 3c with a partner.

⟳ REVIEW YOUR PROGRESS

How well did you do in this unit? Write 3, 2 or 1 for each objective.
3 = very well   2 = well   1 = not so well

| I CAN ... |
| talk about city life and urban space ☐ |
| describe architecture and buildings ☐ |
| deal with conflict ☐ |
| write a discussion essay. ☐ |

114

CAN DO OBJECTIVES

- Give a presentation or a speech
- Talk about superstitions and rituals
- Take turns in more formal conversations
- Write a film review

UNIT 10

OCCASIONS

GETTING STARTED

a ⃞ Look at the picture and answer the questions.
1 Where are these people? What are they doing? How do you think they feel?
2 Why do you think they chose this venue?
3 What do you think happened in the 15 minutes before this picture was taken? What do you think happened afterward?

b ⃞ Discuss the questions.
1 What's the most memorable wedding you've been to? Why?
2 For you, what are the most important parts of wedding day celebrations?
3 If you could hold a ceremony – such as a wedding – in a unique way, what would you do? Why?

115

10A I REALLY WISH I'D BEEN ON TIME

Learn to give a presentation or a speech
- **G** Regret and criticism structures
- **V** Communication verbs

> If you're not comfortable with public speaking – and nobody starts out comfortable; you have to learn how to be comfortable – practise. I cannot overstate the importance of practising. Get some close friends or family members to help evaluate you, or somebody at work that you trust.
>
> *Hillary Clinton, politician*

> Words mean more than what is set down on paper. It takes the human voice to infuse them with deeper meaning.
>
> *Maya Angelou, poet and civil rights activist*

> If you have the opportunity to use your voice, you should use it.
>
> *Samuel L. Jackson, actor*

> Being introverted, it doesn't mean necessarily being shy or being afraid of public speaking; it just means that it's hard for me to interact with people for too long.
>
> *Amy Schumer, comedian and actor*

1 SPEAKING AND VOCABULARY
Communication verbs

a Have you ever had to give a speech or presentation? What was the experience like? If not, how would you feel about doing this?

b Read the quotes. What does each quote tell you about the person's attitude towards giving speeches? Which quotes do you agree with or relate to?

c What makes a good presentation? What kinds of things can go wrong?

d Read sentences 1–5. Do they mention your ideas in 1c?
1. He kept **making** comments under his breath when he was supposed to be **addressing** the audience.
2. She lost her place whenever she **moved on to** her next point!
3. She **went into** far too much detail and **presented** the information in a confusing way.
4. He **demonstrated** their new approach, but it was all a bit boring.
5. He used lots of anecdotes to **illustrate** his points. It was brilliant!

e 🔊 10.01 Find the verbs or verb phrases in **bold** in 1d that collocate with phrases 1–7 below. Listen and check your answers.
1. _____ the results
2. _____ her understanding
3. _____ a conference
4. _____ a different topic
5. _____ the finer points
6. _____ the concept with examples
7. _____ throwaway remarks

f Now go to Vocabulary Focus 10A on p. 167.

2 READING

a Read Scott Berkun's advice and survival tips on giving presentations and speeches. Which of the four mottos below do you think Berkun would agree with?
1. Take care how you prepare.
2. Feel the fear, go through it and keep on going.
3. Aim for perfection.
4. Keep explaining again and again until they get it.

b Read the advice and survival tips again. Write notes under the following headings. Compare your ideas with a partner.
1. People's fear of public speaking
2. How fear can help
3. Communicating your ideas effectively
4. Coping with delivery problems
5. Ways to prepare well
6. Understanding your audience

c Imagine you have to give a talk or presentation. Which piece of Scott Berkun's advice is most relevant for you? Why?

Don't Be BORING!

How to feel the fear but speak well in public

You've either seen it or you've experienced it yourself: a person standing up in front of a large group. There's no microphone or, if there is, it makes a terrible feedback noise. The person can't be heard, and they say 'um' and 'er' after what seems like every second word. Then they click through their slides too fast and then go back and get themselves in a state of total confusion. Or maybe the projector just gives up the ghost and there are no slides at all.

If this happens to you, you probably feel like you just want to vanish into thin air. If you watch it happen to someone else, you either fall asleep or you desperately want to run out of the room. Public speaking can be one of the most terrifying things you have to do in life. But people have to do it all the time – when they study, in their job and at important events with friends and family.

The fear factor

So, how can you make it better? How can you get over the fear? Scott Berkun, author of *Confessions of a Public Speaker*, suggests that we don't. He thinks we should just own the fear and try and use it to our advantage. There's no doubt that standing up alone in front of a group is never a fun thing to do. It's a little like being in the middle of an open field when you know there are all sorts of dangerous animals nearby. It triggers a classic fear-response scenario that's as old as humankind. Our natural instinct is to run. But, at the same time, our body is pumping adrenalin and this can give us energy and help us focus. Adrenalin can help us do a good job.

A little narrative goes a long way

Berkun is also a great believer in making sure you have prepared by honing your ideas so that you get them across as effectively as you can. What are the key points you want to make? Work out the most direct way of conveying these to your audience. It's worth remembering that if you wrap your message up in a story, it'll probably have more impact. Storytelling is a very old skill, and audiences usually have a positive response to a message inside a narrative.

Scott Berkun is a writer and public speaker who's interested in a wide range of topics associated with creativity, culture and business. He studied computer science and philosophy at university and then worked at Microsoft. He now makes his living from his writing and speaking and is the author of the best-selling *Confessions of a Public Speaker*.

Just moving on, folks …

But how do you respond when things go wrong? Berkun suggests that disaster often invites more disaster. So when you get up to speak, don't apologise for all the things that you don't think are perfect. This starts you off on the wrong foot and doesn't motivate the audience to pay attention to you.

Once you get underway, the trick is just to keep going no matter what happens. If you say you're going to make four points but actually end up making just three, it's likely that almost no one will notice. And if a couple of slides are in the wrong order, just apologise and move on. No one will care that much. Well, you will, but what counts here is what the audience thinks, and they're probably nowhere near as critical as you are.

Even the most accomplished public speakers have good and bad days. And most speakers feel some degree of fear or anxiety at some time. But if you've done your preparation and you greet your audience with confidence, half the battle is won, and your speech will probably be OK!

Scott Berkun's Survival Tips

Berkun's book has a lot of other commonsense tips on how to survive the ordeal of public speaking. Here are some really useful ones:

- Remember the big *R*: research. Make sure that the content of your presentation is thoroughly researched and well planned. This gets you off to a good start.
- Practise, practise, practise. If you practise, you'll be better equipped to deal with unforeseen events while you're speaking – unexpected comments and problems with equipment.
- Don't be boring! This should go without saying, but Berkun continues, 'If you are, the worst you'll do is meet expectations.' This is great advice because it's so reassuring – you don't have to be exceptional, just good enough.
- Arrive early and sit in one of the chairs that your audience will be in. This will help you empathise with the people you're talking to. They will sense it and like you more as a result.
- Find out what they think: don't forget to ask for feedback after your speech or presentation. Talk to someone who you know will be honest and listen to what they have to say. This will help you the next time around.

UNIT 10

3 LISTENING

a Which of these, 1 or 2, would you feel more comfortable doing? Why?
1 a presentation for work/school/university
2 a speech for a relative's or friend's birthday/anniversary/wedding

b ▶10.03 Listen to three people talk about giving a speech or presentation. Answer the questions.
1 Why were they giving a speech?
2 What went wrong?
3 What was the outcome?

Rob   Chantal   Milos

c Discuss the questions.
1 Do you think Rob should have refused to be best man? Why / Why not? What's your opinion of Jessica's reaction?
2 What are Chantal's suspicions about the missing file? How likely is it they are correct? How would you react in this situation?
3 How do you think Milos could have regained control when he got distracted during his talk?

d Language in context *Idioms: plans into action*
1 ▶10.04 Complete the idioms in **bold** with the words in the box. Then listen and check.

good   went   threw   recipe
yourself   made   out   words

1 I just _____ **myself into** it.
2 They make me **feel right** _____ **of my depth**.
3 I thought I'd **made a** _____ **job of it**.
4 Always make a copy; otherwise it's **a** _____ **for disaster**.
5 I just explained the whole project, and **it** _____ **like clockwork**.
6 The managers were all impressed, and I really _____ **my mark**.
7 I couldn't go on; I was completely **lost for** _____.
8 I was sort of saying to myself, 'C'mon, **get a grip on** _____!'

2 Match the idioms in 1 with the meanings below.
a ☐ likely to cause serious problems
b ☐ not know what to say
c ☐ do something well
d ☐ regain some self-control when upset or stressed
e ☐ get fully involved in something new
f ☐ go very smoothly without problems
g ☐ impress somebody
h ☐ feel it's too difficult for you

4 GRAMMAR Regret and criticism structures

a Read sentences 1–8. Which sentence does not show a regret?
1 ☐ I should never have agreed to be best man.
2 ☐ If only I'd checked those cards.
3 ☐ Part of me wishes that Dan hadn't asked me to be best man.
4 ☐ I really wish I'd copied the presentation onto my hard drive.
5 ☐ Had he been less underhand, I might not have the job I've got now.
6 ☐ She wasn't my girlfriend, but I used to wish she were.
7 ☐ If I had listened to Teresa's advice, I might have been OK.
8 ☐ If it wasn't for my stupidity, we could have raised more money that day.

b Underline the part of each example in 4a that shows regret. Which examples are unreal conditionals?

c ▶10.05 **Pronunciation** Mark the word groups and underline the main stress in these two sentences. Listen and check. Practise saying the sentences.
1 If I had listened to Teresa's advice, I might have been OK.
2 If it wasn't for my stupidity, we could have raised more money that day.

d ⇒ Now go to Grammar Focus 10A on p. 156.

e What regrets have you had? Talk about one of these past situations.
- a decision to study the wrong subject at school/university
- losing touch with an old friend
- something unfortunate you said to a relative or friend
- a bad decision associated with some kind of social activity

I wish I hadn't mentioned the family holiday home to my cousin.

I really regret not replying to her emails.

5 SPEAKING

a Plan a one-minute speech with the title *Learning from my mistakes*. Talk about a personal experience of some kind. You could develop ideas that you talked about in 4e.

Follow Scott Berkun's advice:
- include an anecdote about your experience to get your point across
- practise your speech several times
- keep going, even if things go wrong.

b Work in small groups. Deliver your speeches.
Speakers
- Maintain eye contact with group members.
Listeners
- Think of a question you can ask each speaker about their experiences.

10B HE IS KNOWN TO HAVE AN UNUSUAL RITUAL BEFORE HE PLAYS

Learn to talk about superstitions and rituals

G Passive reporting verbs
V Superstitions, customs and beliefs

Horseshoe

Ba gua mirror

Maneki-neko

Wish bracelets

1 SPEAKING AND VOCABULARY
Superstitions, customs and beliefs

a Look at the objects in the photos above.
1 What do you think they all have in common?
2 What part of the world do you think they are from?

b Which of the objects in 1a do you think these sentences describe?
1 You **make a wish** with every knot you tie.
2 They were **traditionally** nailed above doorways.
3 They stop bad luck entering the house, and they protect it against **magic spells**.
4 It is **customary** to hang them above the front door.
5 It invites **good fortune** and brings wealth to the owner.
6 They are worn as a **good luck charm**.
7 They always face outwards so they can **ward off evil**.

c ▶10.10 Listen and check your answers.

d Look at the words and phrases in **bold** in 1b. Which are connected with … ?
- luck and magic
- customs

e ≫ Now go to Vocabulary Focus 10B on p. 168.

f Look at the idiomatic expressions connected with good luck in the box. When do people say them?
1 when they hope something good will happen
2 to warn someone of danger
3 when they're taking extra precautions

fingers crossed   to be on the safe side   touch wood
third time lucky   you're tempting fate

g ▶10.13 Complete the sentences with the expressions in 1f. Listen and check.
1 They've agreed to sell the house, so this time next week it'll be ours – _____.
2 I've failed the driving test twice now. Ah well, _____.
3 'I do hope Lisa passes her English exam.'
   'Yes, I'll keep my _____.'
4 You should wear a motorbike helmet. You've been lucky so far, but _____.
5 I know it's not raining, but take an umbrella just _____.

h ▶10.14 **Pronunciation** Underline the consonant clusters in the words in the box in 1f. Remember that these can be across words. Listen and check. Practise saying the expressions.

i Work in pairs. Take turns being A and B.

Student A: Tell your partner something you're planning to do. Choose from this list.
- go rock climbing
- take an exam
- apply for a new job
- travel across Africa by bus

Student B: Respond using a suitable expression from 1f.

> I'm going to climb the Matterhorn.

> Take a guide with you to be on the safe side.

> Good luck. I'll keep my fingers crossed.

j Discuss the questions.
1 Do you know of other things that traditionally bring good luck or ward off evil (in either your own country or another country you know)?
2 How seriously do you think most people believe in charms of this kind? What about you?

119

UNIT 10

2 READING

a 💬 Without reading the text, look only at the headings. What rituals do you think sports people might perform before a match? Do you know of any sportspeople who do this?

b Read the first part of the article and check your answers. What appear to be the main reasons for this behaviour? How effective is it?

c Read the rest of the article and find examples of the rituals 1–8 below. Who performs these rituals? Which ritual is not mentioned?
1 touching their face
2 touching objects
3 doing things in a particular sequence
4 things that also involve other players
5 lucky objects or clothes
6 particular ways of putting on clothes
7 things people do on their way to a match or event
8 things that involve family or friends

d 💬 Which of the rituals do you think is the most unusual?

3 GRAMMAR Passive reporting verbs

a Look at the verb forms in **bold**.
1 **It's thought that** performing a 'lucky' routine reduces anxiety.
2 Thibaut Courtois **is known to have** an unusual ritual before he plays in an international match.
3 **It is reported that** he has a whole series of rituals which he goes through before every major game.
4 Then he **is believed to send** a selfie to four of his friends in Belgium.
5 **It is said that** he always puts his left skate on before his right skate.
6 He **is** also **thought to be** quite superstitious.
7 Before the Olympics, she **is believed to have worn** a pair of 'lucky' socks.

Why does the writer use passive reporting structures? Two of these answers are correct.
☐ to show that they believe the information
☐ to show that the information comes from someone else
☐ to show that this is not necessarily what they believe

b The sentences in 3a show two structures for reporting information:
  a it + passive + that clause …
  b subject + passive + to + infinitive …
1 Which structure is shown in **bold** in each sentence in 3a, a or b?
2 Which structures in **bold** … ?
  a refer to the present
  b refer to the past
3 How could you express each idea in 3a 1–7 using the other structure?
  Performing a 'lucky' routine is thought to reduce anxiety.

THE GAME BEFORE THE GAME

From British cyclist LAURA KENNY, who always treads on a wet cloth before she starts a race, to Serbian tennis champion Novak Djokovic, who eats a blade of grass from the court after every win at Wimbledon – many of the biggest sports stars believe in the power of rituals to bring them luck.

Despite the hours spent training and developing winning strategies, players still go through superstitious rituals just before a big event. It seems nonsensical that such players would give credit for their own success or failure to rituals. However, sports psychologists suggest that these beliefs can actually help players, and in highly competitive sports this small advantage may mean the difference between winning and losing.

Rituals usually come about when we repeat something we did in the past which seemed to bring us success, even if there's no rational explanation for it. It's no different for sports players. It's thought that performing a 'lucky' routine reduces anxiety by giving them an illusion of control and a way to contribute to their own success on the day.

Top Belgian goalkeeper THIBAUT COURTOIS is known to have an unusual ritual before he plays in an international match. While the Belgian national anthem is being played, he always touches his chin. But that's not all. In fact, it is reported that he has a whole series of rituals which he goes through before every major game, not all of them in public. He always enters the stadium corridors at a fixed time. Then he is believed to send a selfie to four of his friends in Belgium. Before going onto the pitch, he always wets the tip of his gloves, and when reaching the goal, he gives the goalpost one kick and then punches the middle of the net. Why does he go through this unusual ritual? He claims that it makes him enter a kind of trance and he can no longer be distracted during the game.

c 💬 The sentences in 3a are typical of news reports and factual writing. How could you say them in a more conversational style?

(People say …)   (I've heard …)

(Many people think …)

d ▶ Now go to Grammar Focus 10B on p. 157.

The incredible rituals that top athletes perform before an event

Japanese figure skater YUZURU HANYU is famous for going through exactly the same routines before he skates. It is said that he always puts his left skate on before his right one and that before practice sessions he always touches the ice to say 'hello' to it. At the start of competitions, he bends down and places his hands on the boards at the side of the rink, then slaps the boards with both hands. Then, when he stands up in order to start skating, he always pushes off backwards with his left leg. He is also thought to be quite superstitious: for example, he always carries a 'lucky' bear with him when he enters competitions. Yuzuru Hanyu is certainly successful, having become an Olympic champion, but it's not known how much the bear helped him achieve this.

The secrets of KAYLA HARRISON's phenomenal success are her rigorous approach to training and a stubborn determination to win. But the US judo Olympic gold medallist also admits to being superstitious and says it's important for her to have rituals and patterns to give her the confidence she needs to win. Before the Olympics, she is believed to have worn a pair of 'lucky' socks that were knitted for her by her grandmother, and she decided not to wear a judo outfit that had previously failed to deliver her a win. But there was more than just superstition at play – she combined this with the power of positive thinking. For weeks before the tournament, she visualised herself winning and went meticulously through every step she needed to take on the day of the tournament in order to win.

e Look at these comments about well-known people. Change them so their style would be suitable for a news report using passive reporting structures like those in 3a.
1 They say the goalkeeper is retiring next season.
2 Apparently the manager of the company has resigned.
3 People say she's the best tennis player of all time.
4 The team captain has had eye surgery – or so some people believe.
5 There are rumours that he pulled a muscle in his ankle.

f Think of a well-known person. Write a sentence from a news report about him or her using a passive reporting structure. Then read your sentence aloud. Can other students guess the person?

4 LISTENING

a Work in groups. Discuss the questions and note down your ideas.
1 Why do you think players go through the rituals described in the article?
2 In what ways do you think rituals might help them?

b 10.16 Listen to an interview with Sandy Hearst, a sport psychologist. Does she mention any of the points that you noted?

c What is the main point she makes in the interview? Choose 1, 2 or 3.
1 Athletes feel helpless just before a match because they can't influence events, so they need something to make them feel better.
2 Rituals boost athletes' confidence by making them feel more in control, and this makes them perform better.
3 Pre-match rituals have a kind of 'magical' effect which can't be explained rationally but which seems to work.

d 10.16 Listen to the interview again. Here are some of the things Sandy Hearst says. What do you think she means by the expressions in *italics*?
1 Their behaviour may seem *eccentric*.
2 This kind of behaviour *makes total sense*.
3 Before a match they get very *hyped up*.
4 Rituals keep their anxiety *at bay*.
5 It's not a *magical effect*.
6 It's like a kind of *placebo effect*.
7 The experiment was *quite telling*.

5 SPEAKING

a Think about people you know (or yourself) and write a few notes to answer the questions.
1 Do they do anything you would consider a 'ritual'? Think about:
   - routine activities (e.g., getting up, going to work or school)
   - communal activities (e.g., meals, meetings)
   - situations where they need both ability and luck (e.g., taking an exam, sport events).
2 How do you think these 'rituals' help them, and why are they important?

b Work in groups. Use your notes to tell other students about the people you chose.

10C EVERYDAY ENGLISH
Before we move on

Learn to take turns in more formal conversations
- S Take turns in an interview
- P Intonation in question tags

1 LISTENING

a 💬 Look at picture a below. Who do you think is calling Max?

b 🎥▶ 10.17 Watch or listen to Part 1. What are the two main reasons for Nadia's call?

c 🎥▶ 10.17 Watch or listen to Part 1 again and answer these questions.
1 Why does Max say that Nadia's 'got a nerve'?
2 What does Nadia say Sara *wasn't* doing?
3 What word does Nadia use to describe the potential interview? What does it mean?

d 💬 Look at picture b. Why do you think Max changed his mind about doing the interview?

e 🎥▶ 10.18 Watch or listen to Part 2 and put the things in the order they're mentioned.
- a ☐ Max's father
- b ☐ Max's insomnia
- c ☐ Max's inspirations
- d ☐ Max's home town

f 🎥▶ 10.18 Watch or listen to Part 2 again and make notes on the points in 1e.

g 💬 Do you think the interview has been successful? Why / Why not?

2 USEFUL LANGUAGE Turn-taking

a Match the expressions in **bold** with their uses a–c. Some expressions have more than one use.
1 **Sorry, if I could just finish** what I was saying, Max!
2 **Sorry to interrupt, but** Sara wasn't idly gossiping.
3 **Speaking of which,** you grew up here in Brighton, didn't you?
4 **Please, after you.**
5 **As I was saying,** I never forgot those worlds.
6 **If you don't mind me coming in here,** you had trouble sleeping as a child, didn't you?

a interrupt someone and take a turn speaking
b encourage someone else to speak
c continue speaking about the same subject

b When would you use these phrases in a conversation?
1 **Go on.**
2 **Before we get started …**
3 **Before we move on …**

c ▶ 10.19 Complete the conversation with suitable expressions from 2a and b. There may be more than one correct answer. Listen and check.

A So, I understand you're a motivational speaker.
B That's right. Basically I go to company conferences and give talks on …
A ¹_____ where are these conferences?
B Oh, all over the country. Overseas sometimes, too. But, ²_____, companies employ me to talk about my mountaineering adventures to share a message of drive and ambition.
A And I don't suppose you imagined when you started mountaineering that you would end up doing this.
B No, I …
A I mean, did you think …
B Sorry?
A No, I'm sorry. ³_____.
B Well, no. I never imagined I would be going around speaking at conferences …
A ⁴_____ you have some really exciting stories of your mountaineering days, don't you?
B ⁵_____ what I was saying. I never imagined speaking at conferences, but I'd just like to say that I've been amazed at the warm welcome I've received in the business world.
A That's good to hear. Now, …

d 💬 Practise the interview in 2c with a partner, but change the profession of the interviewee.

3 LISTENING

a ▶ 10.20 Watch or listen to Part 3 and choose the best answer to each question.

1 Why is Sara pleased?
  a She did a great interview with a difficult interviewee.
  b She's finally getting the credit she is due.
  c She feels exhilarated after a successful broadcast.
  d Nadia is going to promote her to a full-time position.
2 What does Alex suggest Nadia said?
  a that Sara's a better interviewer than Oscar
  b that Sara's performed well
  c that Sara's job's safe
  d that Sara should celebrate
3 What are Max, Sara, Emma and Alex going to do together?
  a have a party at Emma's flat
  b watch *Moon Station X* at the cinema
  c go to a dance club
  d spend time at Max's flat

b 💬 How do you celebrate your achievements?

c ▶ 10.21 *Language in context* Praising idioms
Match the two halves of the idioms. Listen and check.

1 ☐ Hats off   a your praises this morning.
2 ☐ Well, credit where   b to you both!
3 ☐ I overheard Nadia singing   c best thing since sliced bread!
4 ☐ Thinks you're the   d credit's due.

4 PRONUNCIATION Intonation in question tags

a ▶ 10.22 Listen to the sentences from Parts 1, 2 and 3. Does the intonation rise (↗) or fall (↘) on each question tag in **bold**?

1 I asked you not to contact me again, **didn't I?**
2 You grew up here in Brighton, **didn't you?**
3 You had trouble sleeping as a child, **didn't you?**
4 You were so different this time, **weren't you?**
5 It's massive, **isn't it**, Max?

b Complete the rules with *rising* or *falling*.

- If you're not sure what you've said is correct, use _____ intonation on the question tag.
- If you know what you've said is correct and you want the other person to confirm it, use _____ intonation on the question tag.

c ▶ 10.23 Listen to these questions and say which intonation you hear – A (↗) or B (↘).

1 ☐ You did, didn't you?   4 ☐ They do, don't they?
2 ☐ You can't, can you?   5 ☐ I should, shouldn't I?
3 ☐ She hasn't, has she?   6 ☐ It will, won't it?

d 💬 Work in pairs. Take turns to say a sentence from 4c, using different intonation for the question tag. Your partner says A or B.

e 💬 We often use a question tag with falling intonation after giving an opinion to elicit agreement from the person we are speaking to. Give your opinions on the topics below and elicit your partner's agreement using a question tag.

- a strange superstition
- a great sportsperson
- a good TV documentary

5 SPEAKING

a Work on your own. Invent a fictitious sportsperson. Answer the questions.

1 What's your name and nationality?
2 What's your sporting background and what team/country do you play for / who is your sponsor?
3 What bizarre superstitious rituals do you have (think of three)? Here are some ideas:
   - lucky charms   • pre-match routine   • particular clothing

b You are going to interview your partner in their role as a sportsperson. Think of some questions to ask them.

c 💬 Work with a partner. Take turns to interview each other. Think of answers to your partner's questions. Use expressions for turn-taking and question tags.

✓ **UNIT PROGRESS TEST**

→ **CHECK YOUR PROGRESS**

YOU CAN NOW DO THE UNIT PROGRESS TEST.

10D SKILLS FOR WRITING
The film is a visual feast

Learn to write a film review

W Film reviews; Concise description

1 SPEAKING AND LISTENING

a 💬 What makes you want to see a film? Choose one or more from the following or your own idea.

> seeing a trailer   reading a plot synopsis
> reading a review   having read the book
> hearing a friend's recommendation

b Read the four descriptions of the film *Knives Out* A–D and match them to the places you would read them.
1. ☐ on a film download website
2. ☐ on a review blog
3. ☐ on a sign outside a cinema
4. ☐ in a critic's review online

c 💬 How much are you influenced by reviews? Is there a reviewer whose judgement you trust? What are the reasons for and against reading reviews?

d ▶10.24 Listen to four people talking about how they use reviews. Take notes to answer the questions.
1. What kind of film reviews do they read? Why?
2. When do they read them?
3. Do they read any other kinds of reviews?

Which person's opinions are closest to your own?

e 💬 What other kinds of reviews do you find useful? What kinds of reviews have you written yourself?

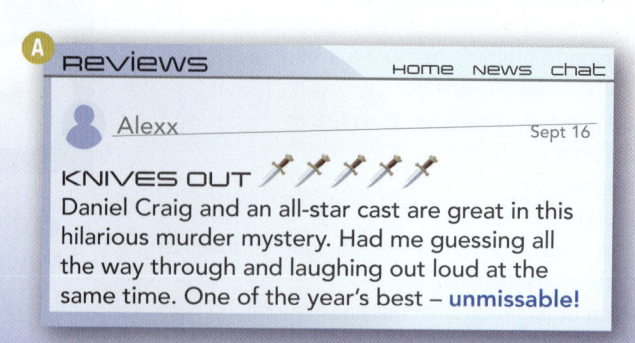

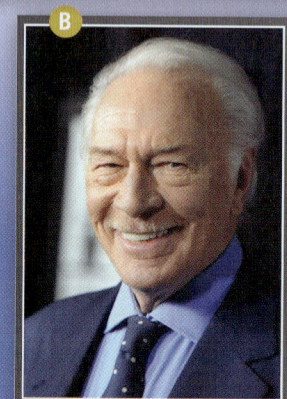

A Reviews — Home News Chat

Alexx — Sept 16

KNIVES OUT 🗡🗡🗡🗡🗡

Daniel Craig and an all-star cast are great in this hilarious murder mystery. Had me guessing all the way through and laughing out loud at the same time. One of the year's best – **unmissable!**

B **Knives Out** 2019

Mystery surrounds the death of wealthy crime novelist Harlan Thrombey, played by Christopher Plummer (left). As his family gather for Harlan's memorial, gentleman detective Benoit Blanc investigates his death. Did someone murder him? And who hired Benoit Blanc? Everyone has a motive for murder. And they all have secrets they don't want to tell.

Buy film £10.99   Rent film £4.49

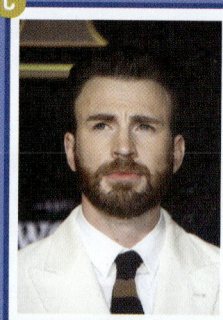

C **Review**

Daniel Craig is not the only actor making a change in direction. Chris Evans (left) detours from his Captain America role to play bad-boy grandson, Ransom. It's good to see both these actors widen their range and have such fun doing so.

Read More

D **NOW SHOWING**

KNIVES OUT

'**Gripping** and **hilarious**.

It's ages since I've had this much fun at the cinema.'

– Cinema Review Magazine

Daniel Craig plays detective Benoit Blanc in Knives Out

UNIT 10

2 READING

a Read two reviews of *Knives Out*. Which reviewer is more positive? What negative points does the less positive reviewer make?

b 💬 Based on these two reviews alone, would you want to see the film? Why / Why not?

Review — Knives Out

After completing two highly successful sci-fi films, director Rian Johnson switches genre to come up with a classic whodunnit, *Knives Out*. And it's a brilliant move. *Knives Out* is one of the most entertaining films to be released this year – and one of the funniest.

Having celebrated his 85th birthday, veteran crime novelist Harlan Thrombey (Christopher Plummer) dies in suspicious circumstances. He leaves behind him a huge fortune and a family of three dysfunctional children who are keen to find out what's in his will. And then there's Harlan's nurse, Marta (Ana de Armas) – did she make a mistake or not? Detectives are called in to establish the real cause of Harlan's death. They are helped by a mysterious gentleman sleuth, Benoit Balance (Daniel Craig). No one seems to know who hired him.

The twists and turns in the plot of *Knives Out* will keep you guessing until the end. It looks like everyone has a motive to murder Harlan. The witty script will also keep you laughing with joke after joke. The cast is terrific. Johnson has assembled a great line-up of stars, but no one is trying to outshine anyone else – this is classic ensemble acting at its best. However, Daniel Craig's performance as a gentleman from America's Deep South shows how far his range extends beyond James Bond.

I really can't recommend *Knives Out* highly enough. It feels like Agatha Christine brought into the 21st century. And while it is hugely entertaining, there are subtle observations on the theme of belonging – to a family, to a society – that boil quietly away beneath the jokes. Rian Johnson has shown he can triumph in another genre and give us a great night at the cinema at the same time.

KNIVES OUT — Review

Knives Out, the latest film directed by Rian Johnson, has a stellar cast. Daniel Craig is joined by Chris Evans, Jamie Lee Curtis, Toni Collette and Michael Shannon – and they all have a whole lot of fun in this classic murder mystery.

Craig plays Benoit Blanc, a mysterious gentleman detective helping two hapless detectives. **Suspecting foul play**, they're trying to unravel the sudden death of multi-millionaire mystery writer, Harlan Thrombey (Christopher Plummer). We discover that Harlan settled personal scores with all three of his children, and the only person who he seemed to like was his nurse Marta (Ana de Armas). She has a mysterious habit of throwing up whenever she tells a lie. Just about everyone has got a motive to kill Harlan off.

There's a compelling array of characters in *Knives Out*, and the plot is in the tradition of all good murder mysteries with unexpected revelations and narrative zigzags. Jamie Lee Curtis, Toni Collette and Michael Shannon stand out as Harlan's three desperate children. Daniel Craig, in a noticeable change from his 007 role, conveys a menacing charm, but his American accent doesn't always convince.

The actors are working from director Rian Johnson's script. It's very funny with lots of jokes, but just occasionally it feels a bit wordy, and the action needs to get a move on. Nonetheless, Johnson shows he knows how to master the murder mystery genre. *Knives Out* is delightfully old-fashioned but with a contemporary touch that feels just right.

At just over two hours long, I found *Knives Out* highly enjoyable. This film will appeal to just about everyone – crime buffs, comedy lovers and those who love character-driven plot. I couldn't work out whodunnit until the very end – always a good sign.

3 WRITING SKILLS
Film reviews; Concise description

a Tick (✓) the elements that are included in the reviews. Are they included in the same order in both reviews?

1 ☐ when and where the writer saw the film
2 ☐ the names of the director and actors
3 ☐ outline of the plot
4 ☐ how the film ends
5 ☐ strong points of the film
6 ☐ weak points of the film
7 ☐ short summarising statement
8 ☐ recommendation – whether to see it or not

Should the elements you didn't tick be included in a review? Why / Why not?

b Which reviewer mentions strengths or weaknesses in the following areas? Write A, B or *both*.

1 plot 3 acting 5 themes/messages
2 characters 4 pace 6 success of the film

c <u>Underline</u> three expressions the writers use to write about films that you would find useful to learn. Compare with other students. Did you choose the same ones?

d Compare the sentences below with the phrases in **bold** in the two reviews. How are the words in *italics* different in the reviews? Why do you think the writers chose to do this? Choose 1 or 2.

1 to make the meaning clearer
2 to give the information more concisely

After he has celebrated his 85th birthday, veteran crime novelist Harlan Thrombey (Christopher Plummer) dies in suspicious circumstances.
Because they suspect foul play, they're trying to unravel the sudden death of multi-millionaire mystery writer, Harlan Thrombey (Christopher Plummer).

e ⟫ Now go to Writing Focus 10D on p. 175.

4 WRITING

a Choose a film or TV series you know and plan a review of 220–260 words. Think about:
- describing the film or TV series for someone who hasn't seen it
- main strengths and weaknesses
- how to structure your review into four paragraphs.

b Write the review. Try to:
- use adjectives to give an intense description
- make the information as concise as possible.

c Read another student's review. Do you know the film or TV series? If so, decide if you agree with what it says. If not, decide whether you'd like to see it based on the review.

125

UNIT 10
Review and extension

1 GRAMMAR

a Complete the sentences with the words in the box.

have   it   needn't   only   ought to   rather   wish

1 You could _____ asked me before getting involved.
2 I would _____ you spoke to Jean about it.
3 _____ was revealed that the manager had resigned.
4 If _____ everyone were as generous as you.
5 I _____ you would behave when my friends come round.
6 You _____ look at me with a face like that.
7 Harriet _____ feel ashamed of herself.

b Rewrite the sentences using the words in brackets.

1 Why didn't you call me? (should)
2 It wasn't necessary for you to meet me. (needn't)
3 They say that the president owns a private zoo. (said)
4 It's a shame we don't live closer. (wish)
5 There's no way that Alex was on time. (couldn't)
6 It was a bad idea for Sarah to lose her temper. (If only)
7 People think that she died in a car crash. (thought)

2 VOCABULARY

a Match the sentence halves 1–6 with endings a–f.

1 ☐ The president concluded
2 ☐ It is important to back
3 ☐ I would also like to pay
4 ☐ There's no time to go into
5 ☐ Before we move on to
6 ☐ You also need to sell

a tribute to a dear friend, Carlos Sanchez.
b the idea to your audience.
c up arguments with solid facts.
d the finer points, so I'll leave it there.
e her speech with some words of thanks.
f a different topic, let me summarise.

b Complete the missing words.

1 Good luck in the race. I'll keep my f_____ crossed.
2 We've lost twice already. Third t_____ lucky!
3 That might be t_____ fate.
4 I find Tracey's story c_____ and will support her.
5 To be on the safe s_____, let's go by taxi.
6 Blow out the candles and m_____ a wish.

3 WORDPOWER *luck* and *chance*

a ▶10.25 Replace the words in *italics* with the correct phrases in the box. Listen and check.

a fighting chance   blow my chances   on the off chance
don't stand a chance   it's tough luck   're in luck
count yourself lucky

1 I can't believe what you said in that meeting! You should *be relieved* that nobody was listening.
2 We're inviting you *because there's a small possibility* that you're free that night.
3 The treatment is essential to give him *a possibility of recovering*.
4 I'm sorry you don't like the situation, Mark, but *you'll have to put up with it*, I'm afraid.
5 I always *destroy any possibility of success* in interviews because I get so nervous.
6 You know that book you wanted to borrow? Well, you *can do that now*! I found it under the bed.
7 Their top player is out with an injury, and without him they *have no possibility of winning*.

b ▶10.26 Complete the exchanges using the correct forms of the phrases in 3a. Use one word in each gap. Listen and check.

1 **A** I can't believe I missed the entry date for applications. I've really _____ my chances there.
   B Why don't you send it in anyway, _____ the _____ chance they're still recruiting?
2 **A** Do you have the notes from yesterday's lecture?
   B You're _____ luck. That's the first lecture I've taken notes at this year. Here you go.
3 **A** It's six o'clock already. I don't _____ a chance of getting this homework finished tonight.
   B _____ luck, I'm afraid. I'm not helping you.
4 **A** I'm worried about how badly I did in those exams.
   B Well, _____ yourself lucky that everyone else did badly, too. At least you have a _____ chance of getting in.

c 💬 What could you say to these people using the expressions in 3a? (There is more than one answer.)

- a friend who missed the bus
- a busy person you'd like to meet with
- someone who wants to borrow some money from you
- a friend who should go to bed because they have a test the next day
- a friend who lost their wallet but got it back

🔄 REVIEW YOUR PROGRESS

How well did you do in this unit? Write 3, 2 or 1 for each objective.
3 = very well   2 = well   1 = not so well

I CAN ...
give a presentation or a speech ☐
talk about superstitions and rituals ☐
take turns in more formal conversations ☐
write a film review. ☐

COMMUNICATION PLUS

1B STUDENT A

a Read about two more language changes. How does each heading represent the change?

1 To be or not to be?

Verbs that are followed by *to* + infinitive or verb + *-ing* give us a choice of form with no real difference in meaning. In the last century, there was a steady shift towards more frequent use of the verb + *-ing* after verbs like *begin*, *start*, *like*, *love* and *hate*, and these are still on the increase.

A *I like getting up late and eating a big breakfast.*

B *I like to get up late and eat a big breakfast.*

The more modern of these two speakers is Speaker A, although they're unlikely to be aware of it.

2 Are you being serious?

English is getting more and more progressive. Constructions such as *I must be going now* and *I'm being cleverer about my choices* wouldn't have sounded correct 150 years ago, but nowadays are fairly high frequency. The use of continuous passive verb forms has also seen a rapid rise. And what*'s being done* about it? Nothing.

b ⟫ Now go back to p. 11.

2C STUDENT A

a Read about this problem you have and think about what you want to say.

- You live in a shared flat. While your flatmate was away, you borrowed an item belonging to them without asking. (*Decide what you borrowed.*)
- Unfortunately, you broke the item. (*Decide what you were doing when this happened.*)
- You go to the shops to buy a replacement. You can't find anything exactly the same, but there's something very similar and you don't think your flatmate will notice.

b Student B also has a problem. Listen carefully and talk about some solutions to the problem. Make three suggestions using the language for giving advice on p. 27.

c Now present your problem to Student B and ask for advice.

2A

a Answer the questions with a partner. Do you feel the same about the different types of sound? Who do you think is more sensitive to noise?

HOW SENSITIVE ARE YOU TO SOUND?

1 Do you find it difficult to read a book if someone is having a conversation in the same room?

2 When a colleague types loudly on their computer at work, do you have problems concentrating?

3 Does the sound of household appliances like vacuum cleaners irritate you?

4 Does constant traffic noise drive you mad?

5 Does the sound of excited children playing together annoy you?

6 Do unexpected sounds at night spook you?

7 Do you find it impossible to sleep if you can hear your neighbours having a party?

b Ask and answer the questions.
 1 Are there any other sounds that drive you mad? Which ones?
 2 What can you do if you feel apprehensive about going to noisy places?
 3 What can you do to improve your tolerance of background noise?

c ⟫ Now go to p. 128 for suggestions on how to manage noise.

4C STUDENT A

a Read your card. Think about what you might say, using the language on p. 50.

> You're an employee. You have produced a report for your boss. You think it's good, but your boss has some criticisms. Make these points tactfully:
> - You weren't given a clear brief about what was required, so you had to use your initiative.
> - You were only asked to write a report a week ago, so you had very little time to do it.
> - Your boss is often out of the office, so you couldn't ask for help.

b Listen to Student B and respond. Try to agree on a way forward.

127

2A

a Read and talk about each suggestion about managing noise. Can you think of any practical problems with each suggestion? Are any of these things … ?
- already part of your routine
- something you'd like to try

DON'T APOLOGISE!
If you are sensitive to noise, don't worry about it too much. It's not a weakness in your character; it's just who you are. You don't need to apologise for this.

SPEAK UP!
If you're in an environment where another person is making unnecessary noise, don't be afraid to ask them politely to be a little quieter.

REST AND RELAX.
Make sure you get plenty of sleep and rest. If you are sensitive to noise, feeling tired will only make the problem worse. If you start the day feeling rested and relaxed, you'll be able to cope better.

FIND THE RIGHT PLACE.
Work out which sounds and which noisy environments are particularly annoying or stressful for you. Try to avoid these places as much as possible.

BE PREPARED.
Plan activities so you can avoid noise. For example, it might be a good idea to avoid going to the cinema on a Saturday evening when it's busy and noisy – choose another night of the week to go.

FIND YOUR OWN SOLUTIONS.
Think of ways to help you manage noisy environments. For example, if you find the sounds of public transport make you feel apprehensive, try using noise-cancelling headphones to reduce the noise.

HAVE A BREAK.
Find a place near your workplace or home that you know is always quiet. During the day, take a break and go there to enjoy some relaxing quiet. This will help you manage the rest of the day.

b ⟫ Now go back to p. 20.

5C STUDENT A

a **Conversation 1** Read your first card. Think about what you want to say, using the language on p. 63. Then start the conversation with Student B.

> **1** You're the manager of a _____ company (*decide what kind of company*) and you're interviewing Student B. Unfortunately, you haven't had time to read Student B's application, and you've forgotten to bring it with you. You don't want Student B to know this. Refer to your 'memory' of the application and try to find out about:
> - the job Student B has applied for (Administrative Assistant / Marketing Executive / Assistant Manager) (*guess which job*)
> - Student B's education/training
> - Student B's experience
> - Student B's hobbies.

b **Conversation 2** Now look at your second card. Listen to Student B and reply.

> **2** You've bumped into Student B by chance. You recognised Student B instantly: you used to use the same gym / catch the same train into town every morning / live next door to one another (*decide which*). Prepare to talk about:
> - what job you did then and still do (defence lawyer / psychiatrist / surgeon) (*decide which job*)
> - how many years it's been since you last saw each other
> - what happened the last time you saw each other.

5B STUDENT A

a Read the text and prepare to tell your partner about the main points in each section.

ETHICAL HACKER

TYPICAL SALARY: £60,000 to £90,000 at the team leader level, while a newly qualified hacker can expect a minimum salary of £35,000 to £50,000.

THE JOB: A company will pay an ethical hacker to hack into its computer system to see how well it might stand up to a real attack.

QUALIFICATIONS: For government work, ethical hackers must hold a relevant degree. In the financial services sector, these qualifications are a mandatory requirement for some types of specialist work. However, you don't necessarily need a degree in computer science, says Ian Glover, president of Crest. 'The industry accepts individuals with a very wide range of academic backgrounds and skills. Often, people have not come the traditional route through education because the "system" did not necessarily match their way of working and learning.'

TO SUCCEED AS AN ETHICAL HACKER, YOU NEED ... a passion for technology and detail. You should also have a very good analytical mind, enjoy solving difficult problems, and be able to articulate your observations to senior management.

WORST THING ABOUT THE JOB: 'When we're called in to test the security of a new customer's network, only to discover that they have already been the victim of a data breach,' says Matthew Gough from cyber security consulting firm Nettitude, 'we have to explain that sensitive data belonging to the company's customers has been compromised by hackers. It's not pleasant.' To stay on top of the latest threats, you have to constantly update your knowledge in your spare time. Specialist consulting firms will also expect you to be flexible and willing to travel.

'A passion for technology and a keen eye for detail is required.'

b ⟫ Now go back to p. 61.

3C

a Read conversations 1–4. Complete the sentences with your own ideas. Think about how you will describe your experiences.

1.
   - I wouldn't travel by _____ to _____ if I were you.
   - Why not?
   - In a nutshell ... (*summarise what's wrong with it*)

2.
   - I had a terrible time when I went to _____.
   - What happened?
   - Well, to cut a long story short ... (*summarise what happened*)

3.
   - I shouldn't have said _____ about _____.
   - Why not?
   - Well, what I meant by that was ... (*paraphrase what you intended to say*)

4.
   - I think that _____ is absolutely perfect!
   - Really?
   - That is to say ... (*rephrase your opinion, giving your evidence*)

b Student A: Use the yellow speech bubbles. Start conversation 1 with Student B. Student B: Use the grey bubbles. Have conversations 1 to 4. Then swap roles.

4B 1 STUDENT B

a Study these photos for one minute.

b Think about the words you learned in this lesson. Use as many as you can to write a description of the scene.

c ⟫ Now go to p. 132.

STUDENT A

a Test your partner. Ask Student B to describe the crime you can see in the photos above. You can question your partner on any details they have forgotten. Is Student B a good eyewitness?

b ⟫ Now go back to p. 49.

5B STUDENT B

a Read the text and prepare to tell your partner about the main points in each section.

'We aren't the bad guys, but we attempt to mimic them.'

SOCIAL ENGINEER

TYPICAL SALARY: Between £84,000 and £135,000 on average. Graduates start at £42,000, but salaries increase rapidly with qualifications and experience.

THE JOB: A social engineer is paid by a company to try to trick its employees into divulging confidential information that allows the engineer to access sensitive company data on the company's computer network. 'We aren't the bad guys, but we attempt to mimic them in order to help our clients understand how and why such attacks work, and how to prevent them from being successful,' says Tom Roberts, a social engineer at Pen Test Partners. 'You have to understand the psychology and technical elements involved in phishing, telephone manipulation, letter writing and the design and production of security tokens and devices used in the day-to-day access of modern buildings and workplaces.'

QUALIFICATIONS: Typically, social engineers have a degree in IT, although an understanding of psychology is useful, as is a background in marketing, teaching and customer service.

TO SUCCEED AS A SOCIAL ENGINEER, YOU NEED ... the confidence to lie convincingly and the ability to fit in almost anywhere without looking too out of place. Good social engineers can also speed-read facial expressions and body language and understand the nuances of written and spoken English. But most importantly, says Roberts, you need a strong sense of personal ethics and an understanding of the law.

WORST THING ABOUT THE JOB: 'Once you start to read people with ease, it can make life outside work tricky, and it can make you cynical,' says Roberts. 'And other people will misunderstand your job: social engineers are not spies, nor do they work in that manner, but most people will label us that way.'

b ⟫ Now go back to p. 61.

Communication Plus

5C STUDENT B

a **Conversation 1** Read your first card. Then listen to Student A and reply.

> **1** You've applied for the role of Administrative Assistant / Marketing Executive / Assistant Manager (*decide which job*) and Student A is interviewing you. Prepare to talk about:
> - your education/training
> - your experience
> - your hobbies.

b **Conversation 2** Now look at your second card. Think about what you want to say, using the language on p. 63. Then start the conversation with Student A.

> **2** You've bumped into Student A by chance. Student A has recognised you instantly, but unfortunately, although Student A looks vaguely familiar, you can't remember how you know each other. You don't want Student A to know this. Try to find out about:
> - what job Student A did then and still does (defence lawyer / psychiatrist / surgeon) (*guess which job*)
> - how you know each other
> - how many years it's been since you last saw each other
> - what happened the last time you saw each other.

1B STUDENT B

a Read about two more language changes. How does each heading represent the change?

> **3 Do you want to dance with me?**
>
> Modal verbs are gradually giving way to other less formal expressions – stiff, formal words like *shall* and *ought* are on the way out, and words which cover the same ground, such as *going to*, *have to*, *need to* and *want to*, are taking over.
>
> This modernisation process is far from efficient. Compare:
>
> *You ought to see a doctor.*
>
> *You are going to want to get that looked at by a doctor.*
>
> But why use three words where ten will do?

> **4 I got fired, but I still got paid!**
>
> The verb *to be* has lost its grip on the passive in recent years, and the use of *get* passives has grown substantially. These days you *get fired*, *get robbed* and *get married*, and buildings *get built* and *get knocked down* again. Whether it's good or bad news for the subject, these days there's a *get* passive for any occasion.

b ≫ Now go back to p. 11.

2C STUDENT B

a Read about this problem you have and think about what you want to say.

> - As a reward for meeting your targets, your thrill-seeking boss wants your whole team to go out for the day to do a dangerous sport (*decide which sport*).
> - You are absolutely terrified of doing the sport for a specific reason (*decide what*) but don't want your boss or colleagues to know.
> - There is a promotion coming up, and you don't want your boss to judge you on your sport performance.

b Present your problem to your partner and ask for advice.

c Now listen to your partner's problem carefully and talk about some solutions to it. Make three suggestions using the language for giving advice on p. 27.

5B

Average annual salaries in the UK.

nurse	£35,000
primary school teacher	£27,000
investment banker	£51,000
Premier League footballer	£3 million
police officer	£30,000

💬 Do you think the differences in pay would be similar in your country?

4A

a Add up your score: 2 for each A answer and 1 for each B answer. Then mark your position on the line and read your results. Are you surprised by them?

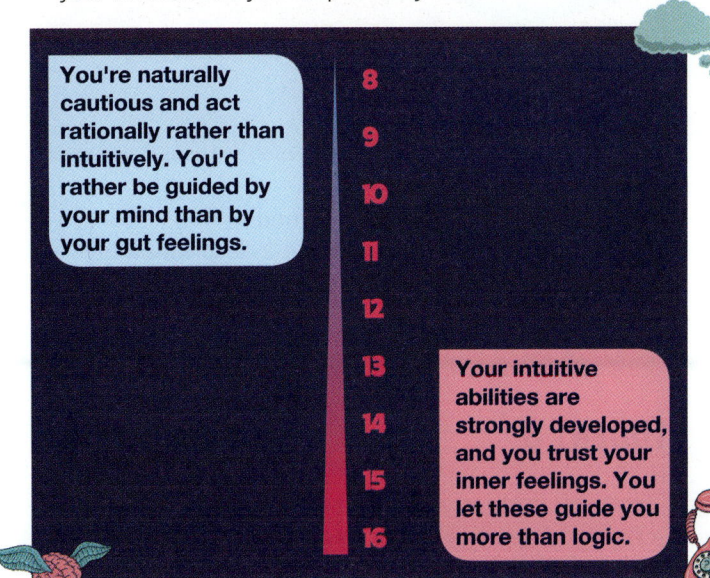

> You're naturally cautious and act rationally rather than intuitively. You'd rather be guided by your mind than by your gut feelings.

8
9
10
11
12
13
14
15
16

> Your intuitive abilities are strongly developed, and you trust your inner feelings. You let these guide you more than logic.

b ≫ Now go back to p. 44.

4B 1 STUDENT A

a Study these photos for one minute.

b Think about the words you learned in this lesson. Use as many as you can to write a description of the scene.

c ⟫ Now go to p. 130.

STUDENT B

a Test your partner. Ask Student A to describe the crime you can see in the photos above. You can question your partner on any details they have forgotten. Is Student A a good eyewitness?

b ⟫ Now go back to p. 49.

2B

a Read Andy's blog post. What's Andy's job, and who do you think he's writing to? Were you right about his reasons for moving to the place in the photo?

ANDY'S BLOG

HOME   POSTS   LINKS   CONTACT

Hi everyone!

Sorry I've been quiet for a while, but a lot's been happening. Here I am in Canada, and I'm planning to travel even further north and live alone for a year in the wild. It can't be worse than insurance claims!

I'm renting a cabin by a lake, and I'll be staying there through the winter. I'm going to stock up on food to keep me going, but I'm also planning to catch fish – I've brought my fishing gear along.

Well, think of me when you're on the 7:30 train to work! I hope to be back in the spring and will post again then.

Wish me luck!

b Work in pairs. Imagine you are about to do one of these things:
- stay in a remote place
- travel somewhere adventurous
- completely change your lifestyle
- live in a new country.

Write a blog post like Andy's about your plans. Then swap posts with another pair.

c Read the post you received. Think of some questions to ask when you next meet and add comments on the post.

d You meet a year later. Talk about your experience and answer questions. Read the comments on your post and respond to them.

Communication Plus

4B 2

a Read the information in the fact file. How similar is it to the list you made?

FACT FILE

Refreshing your MEMORY...

1. **FOOD** fresh vegetables and healthy oil (e.g., fish oil) – cut down on sugar and grain carbohydrates; drinking green tea can also help
2. **EXERCISE** a good balance of cardio and strength training
3. **SLEEP** a good night's sleep refreshes the brain
4. **MULTI-TASKING** avoid it – be fully focused on one thing at a time
5. **BRAIN GAMES** fun activities to stimulate your brain, but don't play them for too long at a time
6. **NEW SKILLS** learn a new skill that is stimulating and interesting for you
7. **MNEMONIC DEVICES** techniques to help you remember information, e.g., a doctor's appointment: imagine a stethoscope and a number for the day of the week, or remember an acronym like *DAT = Doctor's Appointment Thursday*
8. **VISUALISING** make a connection between new information you want to learn and the visual memory of a place you know well, e.g., a room or an object

b ▶▶ Now go back to p. 49.

4C STUDENT B

a Read your card. Think about what you might say, using the language on p. 50.

> You're a boss. A member of your team has produced a report that you don't think is very good. Make these points tactfully:
> - The report doesn't include all the relevant information it should include.
> - You offered to help the person, but they insisted they could do the report themselves.
> - They left writing the report until the last minute, rather than working on it in advance.

b Start the conversation with Student A. Try to agree on a way forward.

133

6A

a Look at the photos from a photography competition. Why do you think each photo won a prize? Use the adverbs and adjectives from the box and your own ideas to talk about the photos with a partner.

Adverbs

truly   utterly   incredibly   completely   absolutely
extremely   rather   a bit   pretty   quite   gently
wonderfully   very

Adjectives

well-composed   powerful   meaningful   gritty
raw   playful   humorous   evocative   exotic   iconic
nonsensical   sensational   bleak   flawless   ironic
elaborate   cluttered

> This is an utterly sensational image. It really draws you in.

> Yes, it's quite evocative. It makes me think of …

b Which photo do you think should be the overall winner of the competition? Why? Agree on one image with your partner.

c ⟫ Now go to p. 70.

7C STUDENT B

a Conversation 1 Read your first card. Think about what you might say, using the language on p. 87. Then listen to Student A and reply.

1
- You had arranged to meet Student A at the cinema to see a film you'd been wanting to see.
- The appointment slipped your mind completely.
- You went out with another friend to a restaurant instead. Your phone had died.
- On your way out of the restaurant, you saw Student A across the street. You suddenly remembered your appointment and decided to pretend you hadn't seen them.
- When you got home and recharged your battery, you received an angry text from Student A.
- You realise that you were in the wrong and feel very ashamed. You hope you can still be friends.

b Conversation 2 Now look at your second card. Think about what you want to say. Then start the conversation with Student A.

2
- You requested a promotion at work. Anxious about it, you told one of your colleagues, Student A, in confidence.
- You got the promotion!
- While congratulating you, another colleague let slip that they'd known for some time that you'd requested the promotion.
- You realise that Student A must have told her, but it doesn't matter now anyway.

9B STUDENT A

a Start a conversation with Student B. Listen to Student B and reply using the ideas below in order. Use ellipsis and substitution to make the conversation natural.

1. I don't like our neighbourhood any more.
3. I'm glad you agree. They're knocking down all the lovely old buildings, and they're putting up ugly new buildings.
5. It's terrible, isn't it? And they said they were going to restore the old town hall, but they haven't restored the old town hall yet.
7. It's all a big mess. I really want to do something, but it's hard to know what to do.
9. Yes, starting an online petition to save the town hall is a good idea. And we could hold a protest.
11. You're right. It probably would be taking things a little too far. We'll start with the petition.

b ⟫ Now go to p. 108.

9A STUDENT A

a Read the fact file and prepare to tell other students about the situation.

EXHIBITION ROAD, LONDON, UK
- A busy street turned into 'shared space'
- Street is shared between vehicles and pedestrians
- Traffic signs, safety barriers removed; trees and benches added

AIMS AND ACHIEVEMENTS
- Traffic is reduced and moves more slowly
- Drivers take more responsibility and drive more carefully because there are no signs telling them what to do
- Drivers and pedestrians make eye contact with each other
- Safety is improved and pedestrians have more space to move

b ⟫ Now go back to p. 105.

9A STUDENT B

a Read the fact file and prepare to tell other students about the event.

BANKJESCOLLECTIEF (BENCHES COLLECTIVE),
MONTHLY EVENT IN WARMER MONTHS, AMSTERDAM, THE NETHERLANDS

- Residents and businesses bring a bench to the street from which they offer food or other activities
- Visitors to the bench pay what they think the offering is worth

AIMS AND ACHIEVEMENTS

- To transform Amsterdam into the biggest outdoor café in the world
- People get the opportunity to meet their neighbours and enter into spontaneous interactions
- People become comfortable in the city as a place they own and influence, like their living room
- Beyond food and drink, benches have included: story-telling, salsa classes, knitting workshops and clothes swap sessions

b ⟫ Now go back to p. 105.

9B STUDENT B

a Student A will start a conversation with you. Listen and reply using the ideas below. Use ellipsis and substitution to make the conversation natural.

> 2 I don't like our neighbourhood any more. A lot of people think it's OK, but I don't think it's OK.
> 4 That's right. They've just gone ahead and they have built that horrible new supermarket and they have put up the ugly new sports centre.
> 6 They'll probably knock it down, but they shouldn't knock it down.
> 8 We could start an online petition to save the town hall.
> 10 Do you think we ought to hold a protest? It might be taking things a bit too far.

b ⟫ Now go to p. 108.

9A STUDENT C

a Read the fact file and prepare to tell other students about the situation.

Suburban bus stop makeover, Pittsburgh, USA

- Revamp a bus stop on a busy road

Aims and achievements

- Long-term, provide a bus stop where people would actually want to sit
- Create shelter from unpleasant weather
- Increase the distance from the road so pedestrians feel safe
- Reduce the risk of crime by lighting the surrounding area
- For the opening, colourful soft furnishings were used to decorate the bus stop

b ⟫ Now go back to p. 105.

Communication Plus

9A STUDENT D

a Read the fact file and prepare to tell other students about the situation.

CONGRESS SQUARE PARK, PORTLAND, USA
- Community organisation formed to save a public space

AIMS AND ACHIEVEMENTS
- Restore public faith in the safety of the area
- Repopularise the square
- Local residents cleaned up the area
- People brought furniture and street food stalls, free wi-fi
- More and more people used the square
- Protected land from being sold to developers

b ⟫ Now go back to p. 105.

7D

a Read about two different team-building programmes. Which one would be more appropriate for your team? Why?

Adventure team building

We will take your team hiking in the great outdoors.
Our activities develop:
- real-life survival skills
- cooperation and communication skills
- self-awareness and mutual respect.

Ideal for building a really strong team.

Personal Adventures

Action team building

We have a fantastic range of action games that develop better team dynamics. The games are chosen to foster problem-solving abilities and promote active listening and effective, positive communication among team members.

These physical activities are great fun and really safe – no special abilities are necessary!

Let your team remember the joy of being a child while learning how to work together.

Action Stations Development

b ⟫ Now go back to p. 89.

7C STUDENT A

a **Conversation 1** Read your first card. Think about what you want to say. Then start the conversation with Student B.

1
- You had arranged to meet Student B at the cinema to see a film you'd been wanting to see.
- As Student B has a reputation for being late, you had bought the tickets in advance for yourself and Student B.
- You waited for a long time, but Student B didn't turn up, despite the fact that you texted and called.
- You went to see what was left of the film on your own, and on your way home you saw Student B leaving a restaurant.
- You shouted and waved, but Student B seemed to be ignoring you. You now feel very hurt and angry, and don't think your friendship has much future.

b **Conversation 2** Now look at your second card. Think about what you want to say, using the language on p. 87. Listen to Student B and reply.

2
- A colleague, Student B, had confided in you about a promotion they'd asked for.
- Another colleague also told you that she had requested a promotion and that she was absolutely certain she'd get it because there was no one else in the office with her skills and capabilities.
- In the heat of the moment, you told her that Student B had also requested a promotion and that, in your opinion, Student B was the stronger candidate.
- Afterwards, you realised that you shouldn't have betrayed Student B's confidence, and you feel terrible.

137

GRAMMAR FOCUS

1A Adverbs and adverbial phrases

There are three main positions for adverbials in relation to a main clause: front, middle and end:
Obviously, I **usually** study **after work**.
Adverbials include single-word **adverbs**, e.g., *obviously*, and **adverbial phrases**, e.g., *after work*.

▶ 01.01 **End position**
In spoken English, adverbials of manner, place and time usually go at the end of the clause, after the verb and the object:
I write **very slowly**. NOT *I very slowly write*.
I live **nearby**, *so we'll be* **there soon**.
Adverbial phrases of frequency usually go in the end position. Some single-word frequency adverbs take this position too: *sometimes, occasionally, regularly* …
We have a test **every couple of weeks**.
I go there **regularly**.
Don't place adverbs between the verb and the direct object:
She did **the work too quickly**. NOT *She did too quickly the work*.
I'm sure I'll meet **her someday**. NOT *I'm sure I'll meet someday her*.
The usual order for adverbs at the end of a sentence is manner, place, time:
We didn't sleep **well on those airbeds last night**.
However, when an adverb of place is necessary to complete the meaning of the verb, this order can change:
I came **here on foot**. NOT *I came on foot here*.
Where there are two verbs, adverbs of manner go before the first verb or after the second verb, depending which verb the adverb modifies:
I **quickly** *decided to take the job*.
She made the effort to drive **carefully**.

> **Tip** For emphasis in written texts such as narratives, adverbs of manner can go in the front or middle position:
> **Hesitantly**, *she* **carefully** *unwrapped the package*.

▶ 01.02 **Middle position**
Adverbial phrases are very rare in the middle position:
At last *I got home. I got home* **at last**. NOT *I at last got home*.

In the middle position, the adverb goes before the main verb, usually after the first auxiliary or modal verb, or after *be*. Adverbs of probability, certainty, frequency and focus often take the middle position:
Good exam results **don't inevitably mean** *success in later life*.
Grammar **is usually** *my weakest point*.
Many adverbs of frequency (*never, always, ever*) and certain time adverbs (*just, still*) can only go in the middle position:
She **still** *practises her Japanese*. NOT *Still she practises* … / *… practises her Japanese still*.
Adverbs of certainty usually go after auxiliaries, but they go before contracted negative auxiliaries:
I'll **probably** *see you soon*. NOT *I probably will* …
She **probably/definitely can't** *hear you*. NOT *She can't probably* …
Be careful with the word order of contracted negative auxiliaries:
I **don't really** *care*. (= not much) *I* **definitely won't** *come*. (= no chance)
I **really don't** *care*. (= not at all) *I* **won't definitely** *come*. (= not sure)

▶ 01.03 **Front position**
Comment and linking adverbs usually go at the front of the clause, followed by a comma:
Obviously, *he knows his grammar*. **However**, *he isn't as fluent as he'd like to be*.
Adverbials of time, place and frequency can also go at the front, when we want to set the scene or change the focus:
In London *there are plenty of jobs*.
Every so often *I forget the word for 'window' in French*.

▶ 01.04 **Modifying adverbs and adjectives**
Adverbials of degree go directly before the word(s) they modify:
Laura speaks German **reasonably** *well, but her French is* **a bit** *basic*.
Adverbs can be modified by phrases with prepositions:
I drove here **slowly by my standards**.
Luckily for you, *I'm in a good mood*.

> **Tip** Some adverbs have different meanings in different positions: *amazingly, strangely, naturally, clearly, fairly, reasonably*, etc.:
> **Strangely**, *Kate speaks Chinese*. (= surprisingly)
> *Kate speaks Chinese* **strangely**. (= badly)

---

a Tick (✓) the correct sentences. Correct the incorrect sentences. More than one answer may be possible.

1 ✓ I am definitely thinking of going abroad, by the way.
2 ☐ The secretary put abruptly the phone down.
  The secretary (abruptly) put the phone down (abruptly).
3 ☐ Presumably, your wife knows you've sold the car.
4 ☐ At the end of the walk, I was exhausted utterly.
5 ☐ The ambulance arrived on the scene within minutes.
6 ☐ I beforehand had had a nasty feeling.
7 ☐ That was the certainly best game so far.
8 ☐ You will find the bathroom downstairs on the left.
9 ☐ You have ignored repeatedly all my warnings.
10 ☐ She definitely won't resign.
11 ☐ He wasn't behaving reasonably at all.
12 ☐ We decided to go by taxi home.

b Add the words and phrases in brackets to each sentence. More than one answer may be possible.

1 So where did language *first* come from? (first)
2 Well, funnily enough, we can't answer this question. (still)
3 Some of the theories are ridiculous. (simply)
4 It has been said that we copied the animal sounds. (even)
5 Language developed for a variety of reasons. (no doubt)
6 Our brains increased in size, and we became more intelligent. (dramatically, a great deal)
7 Also, unfortunately, we started working in groups to get more food. (for other animals)
8 Group behaviour would have made the need for language essential. (undoubtedly, absolutely)
9 We won't know the exact causes with any certainty. (probably, ever)
10 What we can say is that the origins of language will fascinate us. (always)

c ▶▶ Now go back to p. 9.

138

Grammar Focus

1B The perfect aspect

▶ 01.12 **Simple tenses**
Perfect simple tenses describe actions which take place before or up to a particular time in the past, present or future.

- We use the **present perfect** to describe actions that are complete now, or which took place at some (unspecified) time before the present:
  Linguists **have invented** a new language with only 200 words.
  I**'ve done** all I can. You'll have to finish the project on your own.
- We use the **past perfect** to describe actions that were complete or that took place before a particular time in the past. The past perfect can often be used in the same sentence as another past form (e.g., the past simple):
  When she**'d finished** putting the decorations up, the room looked wonderful.
  At long last the war **had ended**; we couldn't believe it.
- We use the **future perfect** to describe actions that will be complete or will take place before a particular time in the future:
  I **will have finished** the book by tomorrow, so I can give it back to you. I'm on the last chapter.
  I can't meet you at 7:00. I **won't have left** the office by then.

▶ 01.13 **Continuous tenses**
Perfect continuous tenses refer to activities continuing up to or just before a certain time in the past, present or future.

- We use the **present perfect continuous** to describe activities continuing up to or just before now:
  We**'ve been waiting** to see the doctor all morning.
  Your eyes are red. **Have you been crying**?
- We use the **past perfect continuous** to describe activities continuing up to or just before a particular time in the past. It can often be used in the same sentence as another past form (e.g., the past simple):
  Everything was wet because it **had been raining** all night.
  Something **had been worrying** her at work, so she spoke to her boss.

- We use the **future perfect continuous** to describe activities continuing up to or just before a particular time in the future:
  He **will have been driving** all night, so he'll need to go to bed.
- Compare the present perfect and the present perfect continuous:
  I**'ve made** dinner! Let's sit down and eat. (focus on the action being completed)
  I**'ve been making** dinner. The kitchen is in a bit of a mess. (focus on doing the activity)
  I was beginning to get worried. I**'d been calling** him all morning. (focus on the activity)
  I**'d called** him five times, but I'd failed to get through. (focus on individual actions that can be quantified)

▶ 01.14 **Unfinished states**
Perfect verb forms can also describe states still continuing up to a certain time in the past, present or future. Because state verbs have no continuous form, they use a simple tense instead of a continuous one.
  They**'ve been sad** since their old teacher left.
  They **had known** for several months that the company was in difficulties, so the news came as no surprise.
  In February, I **will have had** my car for a year.

- With certain verbs we can use both perfect simple and perfect continuous tenses with little difference in meaning (they can be regarded as a state or an activity):
  How long **have you worked** / **been working** in the language department?
  This June I **will have lived** / **been living** here for five years.

> 💡 **Tip** We can use the past perfect with stress on *had* to express dissatisfaction:
> We **had hoped** Sheila would be out of hospital by now. = Sheila is still in the hospital, and we are disappointed.

---

a Choose the best verb form in each sentence.
1 I *lived* / *have lived* in the same place my whole life.
2 I can't join you for dinner – I *won't finish* / *won't have finished* the report by then.
3 Have you ever *tried* / *been trying* to drive in the snow?
4 This is the third time I have *told* / *been telling* you to be quiet!
5 Don't sit there! I've *painted* / *been painting* and the paint is wet.
6 As soon as I got home, I *went* / *had gone* straight to bed.
7 Eve had *read* / *been reading* most of the book before she saw the film.
8 Luke *has* / *had* been thinking about leaving college, but in the end he decided to stay.
9 The train *has* / *had* just left when we got to the station.
10 They might have *finished* / *been finishing* the decorating by the time we get home.

b Complete the sentences with a correct perfect form of the verbs in brackets. Sometimes more than one answer is possible.
1 It's been a long time since I _____ anything as nice as this. (eat)
2 I really couldn't tell you how long I _____ in Bangkok. (live)
3 I missed the match because I _____ a ticket in time. (not buy)
4 I was so good at dancing everyone thought I _____ it my whole life. (do)

5 If every question takes this long to answer, I _____ before midnight. (not finish)
6 This coming January, I _____ here for three years. (live)
7 I'm exhausted because I _____ around all day. (run)
8 This is the first time I _____ you so angry. (see)

c Complete the text with the correct perfect form of the verbs in brackets.

People ¹ *have been complaining* (complain) about English spelling for centuries because certain sounds can be written in several different ways. For example, you will have noticed that /ɪ/ is the sound in s*i*t, carp*e*t and w*o*men. Linguists ² _____ (suggest) several reasons for our difficult spelling. First, English ³ _____ (accept) a lot of foreign words into its vocabulary, so the *ch* in *ch*orus /k/, a Greek word, and *ch*auffeur /ʃ/, a French word, sounds different. Second, early printers often weren't certain of the spelling of a word – no official spelling ⁴ _____ (be established) – so they generally spelled a word pretty much as they liked. The spelling of English ⁵ _____ (become) a bit of a joke today, but who knows, by the time our grandchildren go to school maybe someone ⁶ _____ (invent) a spelling system that is logical and easy to remember.

d ⟫ Now go back to p. 12.

2A Comparison

02.02 Comparative patterns
We use comparative adjectives to describe a difference between two people, things or activities. We use double comparatives with adjectives and adverbs to say that somebody or something is changing:
These exams are getting **harder and harder**.
Time seemed to go **more and more slowly**. NOT ~~more slowly and more slowly~~.
We use *the … the …* with comparatives or *more/less* to say that things change together because they depend on each other:
The harder you train, **the longer** you can run.
The more I think about it, **the more** I realise it was a mistake.
The more hours I work, **the less** time I have for my family.

02.03 Superlative patterns
We usually use superlatives to highlight something exceptional. We often limit the range of superlatives with relative clauses or adverbs:
She's **the most talkative** person **I know**. / **ever**! / **in the world**. / **of all**.
I did **the best I possibly could**.
We can modify the strength of a superlative with adverbs like *by far, easily, (not) nearly, almost, not quite*.
That was **by far the best** lesson this year.
He's **easily the happiest** I've ever seen him these days.
It was**n't quite the most difficult** test I've ever had, but it was close!

02.04
Modifying comparisons with *than*

A big difference: *a good/ great deal, a lot, considerably, decidedly, far, infinitely, miles (informal), much, significantly, three/four/many times (etc.), way (informal)*
A small difference: *a (little) bit, barely any, fractionally, marginally, slightly*
No difference: *no, not any*

The total silence was **a lot worse than** any sound could ever be.
There's **considerably more noise** when you get inside the venue.
I listen to live music **far more frequently than** I used to.
Tickets are **slightly more expensive** this year.
I'm **no happier than** I was in my last job.

Modifying comparisons with *as … as …*

A big difference: *not nearly, nowhere near, twice/three times (etc.)*
A small difference: *almost, nearly, not quite*
No difference: *equally, just*

The smell was **not nearly as bad as** we thought it would be.
Stella knows **almost as much about cars as** I do.
There are **just as many people** who want to study French.

---

a Complete the text with the words in the box. Use each expression once.

> not way and considerably
> nowhere the far slightly louder

Last year, I went to Glastonbury Festival. It was a real eye-opener. The festival takes place in a remote valley, and after you come off the motorway, the roads get smaller ¹_____ smaller. The closer you get to the site, ²_____ more cars full of festival-goers you see. Then, when you finally get into a car park, you have to get through the gates and find a place to camp. This is ³_____ harder than it sounds because you're basically going hiking while carrying a tent and bedding and clothes and all your food and drink for the next few days. The site is ⁴_____ bigger than any other festival I've ever been to. As you sit by your tent on the first night, these huge cheers roll towards you across the valley and get ⁵_____ and louder until they're all around you and it's your turn to cheer. Tickets are ⁶_____ more expensive than other festivals, but when you consider that there are ⁷_____ nearly as many acts and installations and ⁸_____ near as many people at other festivals, Glastonbury is by ⁹_____ the greatest party on the planet.

b Write sentences using the prompts to make comparisons.
1 pizza / considerably / small / box
   The pizza was considerably smaller than the box.
2 plant / grew / not nearly / fast / expected
   The plant didn't grow nearly as fast as expected.
3 he / strong / not enough / control / horse
   He wasn't strong enough to control the horse.
4 kilo / iron / heavier / kilo / feathers
   _____
5 sales / marginally / better / last June
   _____
6 harder / rain / fell / more difficult / game / became
   _____
7 new car / not / nearly / expensive / we thought
   _____
8 they / made money / three times / much / last year
   _____

c Now go back to p. 21.

Grammar Focus

2B Intentions and arrangements

● 02.14 *will*, *going to* and present continuous

We use *will* + infinitive for decisions we make at the time of speaking:
OK, I**'ll come** to the meeting, but I **won't say** anything.
We use *going to* for things in the future that we have decided or are planning to do (but may not have arranged definitely):
I'm **going to have** lunch with Terry this afternoon. (I've decided to have lunch with him.)
What **are** you **going to do** after you leave university? (What are your plans?)
We use the present continuous for things in the future that are already arranged with someone else, or which we think of as being fixed:
I'm **having** lunch with Terry this afternoon. (Either it's actually arranged – we've already fixed a time and place – or it's a definite arrangement in my own mind.)
To talk about future plans (not arrangements), we can also use the phrases *be planning to, be aiming to, be intending to, be thinking of* + verb + *-ing*:
Kevin **is planning to walk** across America.
He**'s aiming to do** it in under 100 days.
I'm **thinking of applying** for a job as an aid worker.
We can also use *will* and *going to* to make predictions. To make predictions we normally use *will*:
I think there **will be** a colony on the moon by 2060.
We use *going to* to make predictions when we can already see evidence of what will happen:
I think I**'m going to be** sick. (I feel sick already.)
The prime minister is probably **going to resign**. (People are already talking about this.)

● 02.15 Future continuous

We use the future continuous, *will* + *be* + verb + *-ing* to talk about things that have been arranged for the future, with almost the same meaning as the present continuous:
I**'ll be going** to the meeting, so I can pass on your apologies.
We often use the future continuous to talk about arrangements in the future which are routines or things we normally do:
I**'ll be catching** the 6:30 train. (I usually do this.)
Compare *going to*, present continuous and future continuous:
Are you **going to see** your grandmother this weekend? (Have you planned this?)
Are you **seeing** your grandmother this weekend? (Have you arranged to do this?)
Will you **be seeing** your grandmother this weekend? (Have you arranged to do this – as you normally do?)
We can also use the future continuous to make predictions, to say that something will be in progress at a time in the future:
While you're enjoying yourself, I**'ll be working**.

● 02.16 Present simple

We use the present simple for scheduled activities:
The first race **begins** at noon.
What time **do** you **get** back tomorrow?
We can use *will* with the same meaning in official situations:
The president **will meet** with business leaders next week.

● 02.17 Expressions with *be*

We use *be about to* to say something will happen very soon:
Hurry up! The bus **is about to leave**!
We use *not be about to* + infinitive to emphasise negative intentions:
I've never smoked, and I**'m not about to start** now!
We use *be due to* to say something should happen or is expected very soon, often at a certain time:
I**'m due to meet** her secretary this afternoon.
We**'re due to get** a pay rise.

---

a Complete the sentences with the correct future form.

Interviewer So Rudy, you ¹*'re going to go* / *'ll be going* on your first wing walk.
Rudy That's right, yep. We're ²*going* / *about* to take off approximately half an hour from now.
I And what ³*are you* / *will you be* doing exactly? You're ⁴*due* / *going* to stand on the wing, right?
R That's right. Well, my instructor said I ⁵*'ll be standing* / *stand* on top of the plane, between the wings. I'll be strapped into a kind of frame, so I don't have to do anything. I'll just stand there, admiring the view … I'm not ⁶*about* / *planning* to panic. I'm just going to enjoy it.
I So it'll be pretty windy.
R Yes, we're ⁷*due* / *going* to be flying at about 120 km an hour, so it will be windy, sure. But I ⁸*'ll be wearing* / *wear* a padded suit, so I shouldn't get too cold.
I OK, well, good luck!

'I'm not going to look down.'

b Cross out the one future form that is NOT possible in 1–10.

1 I *will let* / *am going to let* / *am letting* you know soon.
2 'The pipe needs to be fixed now.' 'I*'ll be doing* / *'ll do* / *'m going to do* it.'
3 I *won't see* / *don't see* / *won't be seeing* Sharon anytime soon.
4 When Annie leaves school, she *will look* / *is going to look* / *is looking* for a job.
5 Serena *is going to wear* / *is wearing* / *wears* her new dress for the party.
6 'Did you take the necklace?' 'I*'m not aiming to answer* / *won't be answering* / *am not about to answer* that.'
7 He *will repay* / *is going to repay* / *repays* the full amount.
8 The meeting *aims* / *is about to* / *is due to* begin, so sit down everyone.
9 I'm not *about* / *going* / *due* to learn French at my age. I'm far too old!
10 We *are planning to become* / *are becoming* / *are aiming to become* millionaires one day.

c Complete each sentence with one word or contraction.

1 I'm about ___to___ leave, so hurry up.
2 I _____ bring a torch in case it gets dark.
3 Adelia is _____ of writing a book about her experiences.
4 A taxi is _____ to pick us up from the airport when we arrive.
5 Where will you _____ staying in New York?
6 Mark is _____ to get a warning for his lateness.
7 Don't worry. I'm _____ about to spend all our money.
8 You can trust me. I _____ say anything.
9 Sorry, I can't come because I _____ be working.
10 The president _____ open the new airport.

d ⇒ Now go back to p. 25.

141

3A Inversion

▶ 03.01 Inversion after negative or restrictive adverbials

When we want to emphasise an event because it is new, rare, unexpected, sudden, impossible, etc., we can use negative or restrictive adverbials followed by inverted word order:
I had never been there before. > **Never before had I been** there.
They didn't try to help me. > **Not once did they try** to help me.
When the journey ended, we felt we could relax. > **Not until the end of the journey did we feel** we could relax.
Inversion structures are usually very formal. We use them more in written texts such as narratives and in formal speech such as presentations.

Never again would Lofty travel without researching his destination first.

Negative or restrictive adverbials

None	Too much / (not) enough	One place/time/person, etc.	Unusual
Not a penny would they give to charity. **Not one bite** did he eat. **Not a single person** did they meet that day.	**Too often** do we see people struggling to make ends meet. **Too long** have we waited for a change.	**Only in the capital** did we feel truly welcome. **Only in the summer** was it possible to open the windows.	**Rarely do you find** someone like that. **Seldom do we stop** to think about people in poorer countries.
Never / Not any more	***Immediately / Only just**	**Only after/at a certain time**	**Impossible/Prohibited**
At no time did we think the project would fail. **Never** (**before**) have I felt so angry. **No longer** can we ignore the problem. **Not in a thousand years** will I go back there again. (informal) **Not once** did they offer any help. **Never** (**again**) will we attempt to intervene.	**No sooner** had one game finished **than** another was begun. **Barely** had we got over the flu **when** we were struck down with a stomach bug. **Hardly** had the policy been announced **than** the government came up with a new and better idea. **Scarcely** had we had time to meet the villagers **than** we were hustled back onto the bus.	**Not until his return** did we appreciate how much we had missed him. **Only at the end of the dance** did people start to go home. **Only then** did people start to go home.	**Under no circumstances** should you buy products from companies that exploit workers. **On no account** can drinks be taken outside. **No way** can I forget what I saw there. (informal)
		Addition	**Unexpected**
		Not only is she young, she's also inexperienced.	**Little** did she know that trouble was coming.

💡 **Tip**
Do not overuse emphatic inversion as it will sound unnatural.

*We use the conjunctions *than* or *when* after *barely*, *hardly*, *scarcely* and *no sooner*:
Barely had we stepped off the plane than …   **Scarcely had we fallen asleep** when …

---

a Choose the best answer, 1 or 2, to follow a and b in each pair.

1 a ☑2 Under no circumstances should you drink cola.
  b ☑1 Not once did they drink cola.
    1 It was difficult to find.
    2 It is bad for your teeth.

2 a ☑2 At no time can you walk on the ice
  b ☑1 Barely had he stepped onto the ice
    1 than it gave way under his feet.
    2 because it is too thin.

3 a ☑1 On no account should visitors to the zoo feed the animals.
  b ☑2 No way am I feeding the animals.
    1 They can't digest the food people give them.
    2 Some have been known to bite.

4 a ☑1 No way did they score –
  b ☑2 Only then did they score,
    1 that's unbelievable.
    2 which was way too late.

5 a ☑2 Too late did I learn
  b ☑1 No sooner did I learn
    1 that than I apologised profusely.
    2 that they had only the best intentions.

b Rewrite the sentences with inversion and an adverb or adverbial phrase.

1 She doesn't often refuse. Not often does she refuse.
2 We only felt relaxed in the evenings. Only in the evenings did we feel relaxed
3 I had barely got home when the phone rang. Barely had I gotten
4 Rita seldom takes responsibility for her actions. Seldom does Rita take...
5 We didn't find a single shop. Not a single shop did we find
6 I'm not going to accept on any account. On no account am I going... will I accept.

c Complete the sentences in the first person using the words and phrases in the box. Use the pronoun *I* each time.

~~little / know~~   ~~not a single person / see~~   ²no sooner / arrive
³~~not in a million years / think~~   ⁴~~not until 9 pm / find~~   ~~rarely / be~~

1 _Little did I know_ what was waiting for me when I arrived.
2 _2 had I_ than there was a terrible rain storm and I was completely soaked through.
3 I'd thought I might have a few adventures, but _3 did I_ it would start as badly as this.
4 _4 did I_ my way back to the bus stop.
5 The place was empty – _1 did I_.
6 _5 had I_ so happy to get home!
  have

d ▶▶▶ Now go back to p. 33.

3B Future in the past; Narrative tenses

03.09 Future in the past
We use past tenses of future forms to say what plans, intentions or predictions we had at a point in the past.

be to / be about to / be set to	Grace **was about to get** on the plane when she got an urgent text message.
be going to	Last summer I **was going to visit** my sister, but I went to Italy instead.
be + verb + -ing	I **was leaving** for Mexico that morning and I was worried about the long flight.
modal + be + verb + -ing	I knew I **might be staying** there for a while, so I made myself comfortable.
would / might / could	One day I **would find out** the truth, although I didn't know it yet.

Tip
We use be + to + infinitive for events or situations that came true:
I had to leave France and I **was never to return**.
We use be + to + have + past participle when things did not happen as planned:
The present **was to have been** a surprise but Sandra knew all about it.

Tip
There are different meanings of would in the past:
She **would** not discuss the matter. = refused to
She**'d** generally keep her ideas to herself. = habit
One day he **would** be famous. = future in the past
But for a lack of talent he **would** have been famous. = hypothetical past

Narrative tenses
- **Setting the scene**
  We use the past perfect, past perfect continuous and past continuous to give the background to events in the past:
  We set off at dawn. Everyone **had slept well**, despite the unfamiliar environment.
  The sun **had just been creeping** over the horizon when we packed up camp.
  We **were** all **looking forward to** what the day ahead might hold. Or so I thought at the time …
  We use the past perfect or past perfect continuous to say how long something continued until a time in the past:
  By the time we got to Rio, we **had been travelling** for 16 hours. NOT were travelling

- **Sequence of events**
  We use the past simple for actions in sequence in a narrative. We use the past continuous for background actions or actions that are interrupted:
  By the time we **reached** the top of the mountain, the sun **was sinking** fast. I **started** to panic. I **was looking around** hopefully for a place we could set up camp when somebody **screamed**.
  We use the past perfect to refer back to an earlier time in the sequence:
  Sarah **fell** ill and **was taken** to hospital. She **had started** feeling dizzy the evening before.
  Past perfect and past perfect continuous often explain the main action or give relevant background:
  There was a large swelling where he**'d been bitten**.
  I**'d been hearing** noises off to the left of the path, so I decided to investigate.
  Nobody **had warned me** of the dangers I was now facing.

*The children **had been going to tell** their father, but they left it too late.*

a Choose the more appropriate verb form in each sentence.
1 Graham *was / is* going to meet me at the airport, but I got a taxi.
2 I thought Karen *had been getting / would be getting* first prize, but I was wrong.
3 That money *was to have paid / might pay* for our daughter's education. Now it's all gone.
4 I *made / had been about to make* lunch when you suggested going out to eat.
5 I *wondered / was about to wonder* who could have done it.
6 Tony *was driving / had driven* to work when he heard the news on his car radio.
7 By the time we left the office we *were working / had been working* for 12 hours without a break.
8 After I *had been getting / got* home, I rushed to check the papers in the safe.
9 We *had been going to give / would be giving* up, but suddenly we saw the peak of the mountain.
10 In those days, Simon *would / was about to* get up at 6:00 and go for a run.

b Complete the text with a possible form of the verb in brackets.

I thought it ¹ _would be_ (be) the holiday of a lifetime, but it was a nightmare!
We ² _____ (not / go) on holiday for ages, so I was really excited about our trip, but I didn't check out the facts that the nice man from the travel agency ³ _____ (tell) me. All of which ⁴ _____ (turn) out to be untrue! For a start, the 'luxury' hotel was a building site. The workers ⁵ _____ (still prepare) the bedrooms when we arrived, so we had to sleep in the lobby the first night! I ⁶ _____ (bring) my swimming things, as I ⁷ _____ (hope) for a nice refreshing swim each morning, but there was no water in the pool. I'll tell you, I ⁸ _____ (plan) to get us all on the first plane home, but my wife persuaded me to stay.
Nothing ⁹ _____ (get) any better as the holiday went on.
I ¹⁰ _____ (lose) five kilos in weight by the time I got home.
I called the company to find out if they ¹¹ _____ (give) me some money back and told them I ¹² _____ (sue). They ¹³ _____ (apologise) profusely, but I'm still waiting for my refund.

c Tick (✓) the correct sentences. Correct the mistakes you found in the remaining sentences.
1 ☐ I always thought I'd get married, but it was never to be.
2 ☐ By the time the flight was cancelled, we waited for four hours to board the plane.
3 ☐ The children felt sick because they'd been eating sweets all day.
4 ☐ Tom had sent the details to me before the meeting had started.
5 ☐ The boat was supposed to have left at 3 pm, but it was delayed until 5 pm.
6 ☐ Zara had always believed she'll be famous one day.

d ≫ Now go back to p. 37.

143

4A Noun phrases

Structure of noun phrases
Combining information into noun phrases results in the clearer and more concise expression of both abstract and concrete ideas. Compare:
She's an author. She wrote a book. It's on psychology. I read it recently. It's very interesting.
*She's the author of **a very interesting psychology book that I read recently**.*
All complex noun phrases have a head noun; in the example above it is *book*. It can be preceded by determiners (*a, my, this*, etc.) and adjective phrases, and can be followed by clauses or prepositional phrases.
More complex noun phrases are common in written language. They tend to be more formal and they are frequently used in academic language. Complex noun phrases develop ideas and group them efficiently. Compare:
In some countries, people often touch foreheads when they greet each other, and this is acceptable in those places.
*Touching foreheads is **a commonly accepted form of greeting** in some countries.*

Compound nouns
Compound nouns are the most efficient way of showing the subject or purpose of something, for example, a lecture about maths = *a maths lecture*, a machine which makes bread = *a bread maker*.
Compare:
There were prints from her fingers all over the vase. → *Her **fingerprints** were all over the vase.*
A person who was passing by found the wallet. → *A **passer-by** found the wallet.*

Adverbs and adjectives
An adjective phrase (two or more adjectives together or an adverb and adjective(s)) can be used before nouns instead of clauses after nouns. There is often a hyphen when compound adjectives are used. Compare:
An artefact has recently been discovered and has caused a sensation. → *A **recently-discovered artefact** has caused a sensation.*

We put adjectives before the indefinite pronoun *one(s)*, but after other indefinite pronouns:
*Don't get the **expensive ones**.*
*Let's go **somewhere romantic** for our holiday.*

Clauses and prepositional phrases
We use clauses and prepositional phrases after the head noun for ideas that cannot be easily expressed before the noun.
Relative clauses: *He gave a speech **which inspired millions**.* NOT ~~a millions inspiring speech~~.
***that* clauses:** *I get the feeling **that he never cared**.* NOT ~~the he never cared feeling~~
Prepositional phrases: *I'd like a house **in a quiet area**.* NOT ~~a quiet area's house~~
Noun + *to* + infinitive: We can use *to* and an infinitive after certain nouns (e.g., *plan, decision, choice*):
*There's a plan **to redevelop the town centre**.* NOT ~~a redevelop the town centre plan~~

Possessives
To show that there is a relationship between two nouns, we use either a possessive *'s* or an *of* phrase:
*The **company's** decision / decision **of the company** to make staff redundant was unpopular.*
We prefer the possessive *'s* when the possessor is a person, group of people or an animal:
*The **cat's bowl** is the yellow one over there.*
We prefer an *of* phrase when the possessor is an item:
*The roof **of the house** needs repairing.* NOT ~~The house's roof~~
Location, measuring, quantifying and qualitative words like *back, piece, cup, kind* and *sort* are always followed by an *of* phrase:
*Get in the back **of the car**.* NOT ~~the car's back~~
*Have a piece **of chocolate**.* NOT ~~chocolate's piece~~

> **Tip**
> Very long noun phrases for people usually aren't followed by the possessive *'s*:
> *The children **of the man who lives opposite** are staying with me.*
> NOT ~~The man who lives opposite's~~ *children are staying with me.*

---

a In the text, underline all words before and after the head nouns in **bold** that make a noun phrase.

<u>One memorable summer</u> **day** I was coming home after an exhausting **day** at work when I met an old **friend** who I hadn't seen for ages. I don't know why but I had the strong **feeling** that this was no mere coincidence. In fact, she had a **proposition** to make to me which was about to change my life. She said that she was looking for a reliable **partner** who she could trust because she wanted to invest in a **project** that had been started by a few friends of hers. I made a few phone **calls** to the bank and I had the money needed to get involved. My boring **days** of sitting behind a desk were behind me.

b Improve the noun phrases in *italics*.

1 Let's climb to the *hill's top*.   the top of the hill
2 We arrived early at *the station for the train*.
3 'My Beautiful Friend' is *a book written brilliantly*.
4 Their 25th anniversary is *an occasion that is awaited eagerly*.
5 It won't take long – it's *a meeting which lasts one hour*.
6 A skiing accident can cause *an injury that can change your life*.
7 I think we should vote on *the bright idea of Ed*.
8 Zoe is *the girl that I introduced you to yesterday's aunt*.

c Improve the noun phrases in *italics* without significantly changing their meanings.

Human resources experts
~~Experts who work in the field of human resources~~ say that interviewers make *decisions about who to hire* within the first minute of an interview. Of course, *mistakes which cost a lot* can be made, and sometimes the wrong people are hired. Nevertheless, companies have to rely on their managers' *skills in being able to make decisions*. Most of us have experienced at least one *interview which was a nightmare*, perhaps conducted by a *manager who has relatively little experience*. In a situation like this, your options are limited: plough on through the interview, or walk out after the first minute!

*You never get a **second chance** to make a **first impression**.*

(speech bubble: "I've got a feeling you won't really fit in here, Mr Lloyd.")

d Now go to p. 46.

Grammar Focus

4B Structures with *have* and *get*

Causative *have/get*
Causative *have/get* structures have the form *have/get* + object + past participle. We use them to talk about things we ask another person to do:
We **got our windows cleaned** last week.
He **has his teeth cleaned** every month.
Alternatively, we use them to talk about things that happen to you:
I **had my bike stolen** outside the gym.
They **had their house destroyed** in the bush fires.
We can use *have/get* + object + past participle in two ways:
1) where the subject has initiated the action;
2) where someone else has initiated the action.

▶ 04.07

Initiated by the subject	
We'll **have the window fixed** by the time you come back.	= We'll arrange for somebody else to fix it **or** we'll do it ourselves.
He **gets his house cleaned** every Friday.	= He pays a cleaner to clean for him.
I'm going to **have my ears pierced**.	= The subject has organised someone to do this.
Not initiated by the subject	
I **got my bag searched** at the airport.	= Somebody searched my bag.
Baby Alice **had her first photo taken** today.	= Somebody, probably a professional, took a photograph of the baby.
We **had our flight cancelled** when we checked in.	= The airline cancelled the flight.

We can also use *get* + object + past participle to talk about completing an activity:
I haven't managed to **get the paperwork finished**.
We can't go until we've **got the kids dressed**.

get + reflexive pronoun + past participle
A variation of the causatives with *get* is to use a reflexive pronoun as the object. While the action is performed by another person, the use of the reflexive pronoun suggests that the subject is, in some way, responsible for what happened to them:

He tried to use a fake passport and **got himself arrested** again.
Stop that! Are you trying to **get yourself killed**?!
She's managed to **get herself promoted** for the third time in two years.

> **Tip**
> In informal speech we can leave out *to* + *have/get* after *need*, *want*, *would like*, etc.:
> I **would like** (to get) **my hair cut** soon.
> I **need** (to have) **my bike mended**.

get passives
Get can be used with a past participle to create a passive structure in the same way as *be*:
Sandra **got kicked** by a horse. = Sandra **was kicked** by a horse.
Get passives tend to be less formal and often describe unfortunate events:
I **got fired** yesterday. They **got mugged** in broad daylight.

> **Tip**
> *Get* passives are different from *get* causative structures. Compare:
> They **got Roberts freed** from prison. = Roberts was in prison and a group of people, 'they', worked to free him.
> They **got freed** from prison. = 'They' were in prison and for some reason were allowed to go free.

▶ 04.08

Other patterns	
have/get + object + verb + *-ing* = cause someone/something to do something	Grandma's story really **had/got me thinking**. The music soon **had/got everyone dancing away**.
have + object + infinitive = give instructions or orders	Our teacher **has us call** him 'Sir'. The boss **had us clean** our desks.
get + object + *to* + infinitive = persuade someone to do something	My mother-in-law **got me to take** her to the station. Advertising is the art of **getting people to buy** things they don't want.

---

a Choose the correct options.

1 Two people *got injured* / *had themselves injured* when the roof collapsed.
2 I'm going to *get him measuring me* / *get myself measured* for a new suit.
3 My blood pressure is really high. I *was checked* / *had it checked* this morning.
4 *Selling your house* / *Getting your house sold* online is much cheaper because there are no agents' fees.
5 We're trying to get more people *to give* / *giving* to our charity.
6 Jenkins, *have* / *get* the first candidate come in, please.
7 The news *had everyone shouting* / *got everyone to shout* with anger.

b Rewrite these sentences using the words in brackets.

1 Someone needs to repair our car. (have)
 We need to have our car repaired.
2 Tina worked hard and was promoted. (herself)
3 Someone stole my bike. (got)
4 Arrange for someone to test your eyes. (have)
5 The news made everyone panic. (got)
6 It wasn't easy to calm the children down. (get)
7 Our teacher told us to write an essay. (had)
8 Alex talked me into going with him. (got)

c Complete the conversation with the correct form of the verbs in brackets.

Ryan That podcast about the generation gap really got me ¹ *thinking* (think). Are we that different from our kids?
Olivia I haven't listened to it yet …
Last week I got ² _____ (hand) a load of work to do by my boss, and I've just had no time. She has me ³ _____ (work) all hours at the moment.
R Well, listen when you manage to get everything ⁴ _____ (do). The thing is, I think a lot of this generation gap stuff is exaggerated. Like, we think that parents are too lenient today, kids are used to having everything ⁵ _____ (do) for them, and that goes to their head.
O That sounds true enough. You know my youngest, Tessa? I got her ⁶ _____ (make) her own bed, and you should have seen the look on her face! When I was that age my parents had us ⁷ _____ (work) from six o'clock in the morning.
R Oh, come on! You delivered newspapers twice a week. This is just what I mean – the generation gap is something we've imagined, and we have been fooled into believing it.

d ≫ Now go back to p. 47.

145

5A Relative clauses

▶ **05.01** **Defining and non-defining relative clauses**
Defining relative clauses are essential to the meaning of a sentence because they make it clear who / which noun phrase we're referring to:
The law **that was recently passed** makes no sense.
The man (**who**) **he attacked** is recovering in hospital.
Non-defining relative clauses are not essential; they give us additional information about nouns. In non-defining relative clauses, we cannot use the relative pronoun *that* or leave out object pronouns:
German law, **which is based on Roman law**, is quite different.
NOT ~~that is based~~
The victim, **who we cannot name for security reasons**, is recovering in hospital. NOT ~~The victim, we~~
Non-defining relative clauses are separated by commas in writing and pauses in speech.

▶ **05.02** **Relative pronouns**

- **when / where / why**
With nouns that refer to time like *time* and *day*, and after *place* or *somewhere*, we can use *that* instead of *when/where* or no pronoun in informal language:
The 1930s was the time (**when/that**) organised crime flourished.
Take me somewhere (**where/that**) I can relax for a few days.
After *reason*, we can use *why/that* or no pronoun:
Does anyone know the reason (**why/that**) crime is so high?

- **which**
In non-defining relative clauses we can use *which* to talk about a whole clause, not just a noun phrase:
She lied on her interview form, **which** was a bad sign.
We all get on well, **which** is fantastic.
We can use *which* after prepositions and before nouns in fixed phrases like *in which case*, *the chance of which*, (neutral) *at which time*, *the result/outcome of which*, *the likelihood of which* (formal):
It would seem that the guilty person has been found, **in which case** you are free to go.
A major police operation started, **the result of which** was that six people were arrested.

- **who / whom / whose**
We usually use *who* as subject and object in relative clauses, but we can use *whom* as an object in formal written language. We use *whom* (not *who*) after prepositions. In defining relative clauses we can also use *that* instead of *who* or *whom*:
The woman **that** I met at the party is a famous scientist. (neutral)
The woman **who** I met at the party is a famous scientist. (neutral)
The woman **whom** I met at the party is a famous scientist. (formal)
We use *whom* (not *who*) after prepositions:
Mr White, **to whom** the police gave a caution, was held overnight.
NOT ~~to who the police gave a caution~~
We use *whose* as a possessive of people and animals:
The elderly woman **whose** bag was taken was really upset.

- **none of whom / all of which / some of whose**
We can use quantifiers like *some*, *none* and *few* with *of whom*, *of which* and *of whose* in non-defining relative clauses:
Three suspects were interviewed, **all of whom** were released without charge.
Carter is accused of three crimes, **none of which** he admits to.

- **whoever / whatever / wherever / whenever**
We use the indefinite pronouns *whoever*, *whatever*, *wherever* and *whenever*, to mean 'the person', 'the thing that', etc.:
Whoever stole my yoghurt from the fridge is in big trouble!

> **Tip**
> *What* is not a relative pronoun. We use it as a noun to mean 'the thing which': *Young people today don't know* **what** *they want*.

Prepositions in relative clauses
We usually put prepositions at the end of relative clauses, but we can put them before the relative pronoun in formal language:
Prison is not the kind of place **that** you would want to spend time **in**.
Prison is not the kind of place **in which** you would want to spend time.
We keep the particles with the verb with multi-word verbs:
The children who I **look after** at the day centre are very naughty.
NOT ~~The children after whom I look~~
Stealing from the kitchen is something which we will not **put up with**.
NOT ~~with which we will not put up~~

He tried to make a getaway, the chances of which were very slim.

a Put a relative pronoun in the gaps if necessary.
1 I don't want to stay anywhere ___that___ doesn't have decent facilities.
2 Give me one good reason _____ I should believe you.
3 The letter took a week to arrive, _____ is far too long.
4 I might have made the mistake, in _____ case I'll apologise.
5 Ten people agreed to take part, some of _____ later dropped out.
6 It was a long and confusing story, little of _____ was true.
7 That was the best excuse _____ she could come up with.
8 We should not give up our rights, for _____ people have made great sacrifices.

b Choose the correct options.
1 The emergency number is 999, *that* / *which* is easy to remember.
2 Mrs Jackson, to *who* / *whom* we are very grateful, has kindly agreed to speak.
3 Florida is the only place *that* / *wherever* I want to live.
4 It's up to the person *what* / *whose* job it is to sort out the transport.
5 The police arrived half an hour later, *by which time* / *by that time* the gang had escaped.
6 We recruited some younger staff, *few of whom* / *few of who* had any experience.
7 Most graduates lack the skills for *whom* / *which* there is the most demand.

c Use relative clauses to join the sentences. Replace the words in **bold** and change the punctuation and word order as necessary.
1 Two criminals wanted to escape from the prison. They had been held **in it** for two years.
Two criminals wanted to escape from the prison, in which they had been held for two years.
2 The criminals shared a prison cell. **The floor of the cell** was over the city drainage system.
3 **They** were desperate for freedom. The prisoners built a tunnel. They could escape **through it**.
4 One night, they went down the tunnel. There was a full moon **then**.
5 The two criminals came out into a street. **The street** looked familiar.
6 They had come up outside the local police station. They had first been charged **at this police station**.
7 **All of them** knew the criminals by sight. The local police arrested them.
8 They took them back to the prison. They never tried to escape **from it** again.

d ▶▶ Now go to p. 57.

5B Obligation, necessity and permission

Strong obligation and necessity
We use *must* and *have to* to say what is necessary. We use *must* to impose obligation (setting the rules) and *have to* to talk about obligation (describing the rules). For negative obligation, we use *mustn't* and *can't / not allowed to*:

	Imposing obligation	Describing obligation
+	(Doctor to patient) You **must** stay in bed till your temperature goes down.	(Patient to friend) I **have to** stay in bed till my temperature goes down.
–	You **mustn't** tell anyone I'm being promoted. (= Please don't tell anyone.)	You **can't/aren't allowed to** eat sandwiches in the office. (= That's the rule.)

Instead of *have to*, we can use *have got to* or *need to*:
I**'ve got to** be in the office by 8:00 tomorrow as there's a meeting.
We also **need to** consider how the employees feel about the reorganisation.

Must and *mustn't* are very strong and it's often better to use *need to* or a different expression:
You must come to the meeting on time. → **Make sure** you come to the meeting on time.

Must is commonly used after *I* (to impose obligation on yourself):
I really **must** organise my time more effectively.

Must only refers to the present or future. To talk about the past, we use *had to*:
I'll **have to** / I **must get** some more qualifications soon.
Irene **had to** go on a business trip, so I took her to the airport. NOT ~~must have gone~~

Mild obligation
We use *should(n't)* and *ought (not) to* to say what is the right or wrong thing to do and to give advice. *Ought (not) to* is slightly more formal:
You **shouldn't do** unpaid overtime.
The company **ought to do** more to ensure equal opportunities for women.

We use *had better* + infinitive to give urgent advice or a warning:
She**'d better** see a doctor before it's too late.
You**'d better** be early tomorrow!

We can use *be supposed to* to say what is necessary according to certain rules or instructions:
The Finance Director **is supposed to authorise** all major expenditures.
I **was supposed to** read the report by today, but I didn't have time.

Lack of obligation
We use *don't have to*, *needn't* and *don't need to* to say what is not necessary or that there is no obligation:
You **don't need to** tell me how the accident happened. I was there.
She **doesn't have to work** on Thursdays. It's her day off.

▶ **05.12** Other phrases for obligation / lack of obligation and permission / lack of permission
These phrases are all followed by the infinitive:

be obliged to obligation (formal)	In our contract we **are obliged to start** work at 8:00.
be required to obligation (formal)	At first, I **was required to put** in very long hours.
have no choice but to strong, unwelcome obligation	Well, I **have no choice but to quit**, then.
be expected to mild obligation	How can she **be expected to be** in two places at the same time?
be under no obligation to lack of obligation (formal)	I **am under no obligation to meet** your demands.
(not) be allowed to permission, lack of permission	We**'re not allowed to wear** jeans to work.
be free to lack of obligation, permission	You**'re free to choose** whatever position you want.
(not) be permitted to permission / lack of permission (formal or official)	We **are not permitted to** discuss company policy with reporters.
be forbidden to lack of permission (formal or official)	Visitors **are forbidden to** bring food into the building.

In formal language, e.g., official notices, obligation and permission can also be expressed by impersonal phrases beginning with *It*: *It is advisable to, It is (not) permitted to, It is forbidden to, It is essential to*:
It is advisable to wear protective clothing.
It is not permitted to enter the laboratory when the red light is showing.

> 💡 **Tip**
> We can use *It's up to* + person + *whether* to say somebody is not obliged to do something in informal language:
> **It's up to you whether** you take this job, but I think it's a great offer.

---

a Choose the correct options.
1 Maria *must / will / should* keep her promotion a secret until it's officially announced.
2 You *mustn't / needn't / can't* bring a towel for the swimming pool. They provide them free of charge.
3 Pilots are *essential / required / obligatory* to get a medical exam every six months.
4 When we lived in the village, we *must / were alllowed to / had to* drive for miles to get to a supermarket.
5 Tony *should / ought / had better* to be taking care of that, but he's so lazy.
6 The match *had to / was supposed to / was required to* begin at 7:00, but heavy rain delayed the start.

b Rewrite the sentences with the words in brackets.
1 You should use chains on your tyres if you drive in the snow. (advisable)
   It is advisable to use chains on your tyres if you drive in the snow.
2 Applicants should arrive at least ten minutes before their interview. (expected)
3 I'm afraid the only option I have is to cancel the trip. (no choice)
4 Members of the public cannot go beyond this point. (forbidden)
5 You can decide when to leave. (up to)
6 Gerald will have to attend the meeting. (got)

c Complete the text with the correct form of the phrases in the box. More than one answer may be possible.

> be expected to   be obliged to   be permitted to
> be under no obligation to   ought to   be up to you   ~~have to~~

If you earn money, you normally [1] *have to* pay income tax to the government, usually at least 20%. But if you inherit money from your parents, should you [2] _____ pay tax on it? In most countries, there's a law which states that people [3] _____ declare any money they receive from their family, whether it's a gift or an inheritance, although usually people [4] _____ pay tax on smaller sums of money of up to a few thousand that they might inherit. But is it fair to ask people to pay inheritance tax at all? Some people argue that this is money that your parents earned and so it should [5] _____ what you do with it, and you should [6] _____ inherit it tax free. But other people feel that this is money you haven't earned yourself and so you [7] _____ pay more tax on it than you do on income you have earned from working.

d ≫ Now go back to p. 61.

147

6A Simple and continuous verbs

▶ 06.05 **Simple verbs**
We use simple verbs to talk about routine habits and repeated actions:
*I **usually catch** the bus just after 8 o'clock.*
*They**'ve always gone** on holiday to Greece in the summer.*
We also use simple verbs to talk about facts, general truths or attitudes and unchanging states:
*The camera **takes** up to ten photos per second in this mode.*
*I **don't like** the smell of liquorice and I**'ve never wanted** to eat it.*
We use simple verbs to talk about completed actions, events or activities:
*I**'ve just taken** an amazing photo of two foxes.*
*We **trained** really hard for the marathon we **ran** in April.*
We use a simple verb when we say how many times something happens or how much is complete:
*I **went** to the Museum of Modern Art three times last year.*
*We**'ve carried out** about half of the interviews.*

▶ 06.06 **Continuous verbs**
We use continuous verbs to talk about temporary or incomplete activities:
*I**'m doing** a lot of extra overtime, but only this month.*
*They**'ve been redecorating** their bedroom, but still have to put down new carpet.*
We usually use continuous verbs to emphasise activity as opposed to result:
*I**'ve been knitting** a scarf – it's taking ages to finish.* (emphasis on activity)
Compare: *Here's a new scarf I**'ve knitted** for you.* (emphasis on result)
Continuous forms also emphasise duration:
*In March, we **will have been living** here for four years.* (emphasis on duration)
Compare: *In March, we **will have lived** here for four years.* (emphasis on completion)
We can use continuous verbs with the adverbs *always*, *continually*, *constantly* and *forever* to talk about bad or annoying habits or express surprise about how frequently something happens:
*James **was constantly taking** photos of every little thing he saw.*
*It**'s always raining** in this part of the world.*

Verbs not usually used in the continuous
Some verbs are almost never used in the continuous, e.g., *know* and *suppose*:

*I **have known** Nina for ages.* NOT ~~have been knowing~~
*I **don't suppose** you know where the paints are?* NOT ~~'m not supposing~~.
Below are some verbs that are not usually used in the continuous:

Thinking
believe, despise, know, recognise, regard, suppose, realise
*I'm sure Trevor **despises** everything we are trying to do.* NOT ~~is despising~~

The senses*
hear, see, smell, sound, taste, look (= appear)
*What's that noise? It **sounds** like a car.* NOT ~~is sounding~~

Communicating
astonish, deny, impress, mean, satisfy, take (= understand)
*Nothing about his behaviour that day **impressed** me.* NOT ~~was impressing~~

Other
belong, consist, depend, fit, possess
*The corner office now **belongs** to you.*

*We often use *can* with sense verbs rather than the simple form:
*I **can hear** someone coming.* (rather than 'I hear someone coming.')
*I **can't** see anything.*

Some verbs have different meanings in the simple and continuous, e.g.:

This cake **weighs** just under one and a half kilos. (a fact)	Rachel **is weighing** the flour for the cake. (an activity)
What **do** you **think** of digital cameras? (an opinion)	I**'m thinking** of going to art school. (an activity)
Ella **is** a difficult child. (a characteristic)	Ella**'s being** difficult. (behaviour)
What can you **see** in this picture? (see = look at) Do you **see** what I mean? (see = understand)	The doctor **is seeing** a patient. (see = meet)

---

a Match 1–8 with the correct endings a or b.
1 Chiara ate the chocolate
2 Chiara was eating the chocolate
3 Simon had a bath
4 Simon was having a bath
5 My boss is unreasonable
6 My boss is being unreasonable
7 Nina comes from Russia
8 Nina is coming from Russia

a when she noticed something hard in it.
b and then started on the peanuts.
a and went straight to bed.
b when someone knocked at the door.
a at the moment: we have to do a lot of overtime.
b and always expects us to work late.
a to attend a conference in Bristol.
b but now lives in the UK.

b Choose the correct options. In some examples, both options are possible.
1 I *think* / *'m thinking* photography is more about technology than art.
2 I'll *be learning* / *learn* English for the rest of my life.
3 *Are you* / *Are you being* obstinate just to annoy me?
4 Everyone had *left* / *been leaving*, and there was complete silence.
5 Jon *thinks* / *'s thinking* of joining the army next year.
6 *Do you realise* / *Are you realising* how this makes me look?
7 Someone has *been gossiping* / *gossiped* and I'm really upset.
8 Unemployment *increases* / *is increasing*, but the government doesn't care.
9 We *opened* / *were opening* our first office in summer 2012.
10 I *suppose* / *'m supposing* we'll have to wait for the bus.

c Complete the text with the verbs in brackets. Change the verbs into the correct form, using simple or continuous forms. More than one answer may be possible.

Roma So ¹<u>do you think</u> (you / think) graffiti could be called art?
Judy Why not? Graffiti has a long tradition, and we know the Romans ² _____ (have) it.
R Yes, but people ³ _____ (complain) about graffiti for a long time, too. I must admit that every time I ⁴ _____ (see) a wall covered in the stuff, it annoys me.
J Well, obviously you ⁵ _____ (decide) that real art ⁶ _____ (belong) in museums and nowhere else. Graffiti is the most natural form of street art there is. ⁷ _____ (you / watch) that series about popular art that's on TV? It ⁸ _____ (change) my idea of art for good. Actually, I ⁹ _____ (always / want) to have a go at some kind of painting.
R What ¹⁰ _____ (say)? Are you going to go out and paint some graffiti on a train station wall?
J No, I ¹¹ _____ (think) train passengers would think much of that.

d ⟫ Now go back to p. 70.

148

Grammar Focus

6B Participle clauses

We use participle clauses to add more information to a sentence.
We can use either present or past participle clauses:
Hiding behind the bushes, I held my breath.
The stranger staggered into the room, **covered in snow**.

▶ 06.09 Participle clauses as adverbials

Adverbial participle clauses are mainly used in more formal spoken language and in writing. They say why, when, where and how:
Frightened by what he saw, he never returned.
= Because he was frightened …
Having thought it over, I've decided to refuse their offer.
= Because I've thought about it …
Stopping for a break, we discussed what to do next.
= After we stopped …
Standing by the fire, Mary thought about her next step.
= While she stood …
Climbing out of the window, he managed to escape. = By climbing …
Using my knife, I forced the box open. = With my knife …

Participle clauses always start before or at the same time as the main verb in the sentence:
The man **running alongside me** tripped and fell.
Sensing I was being watched, I looked into the shadows.
To talk about events that happened earlier, we use a clause with the perfect participle: *Having* + past participle:
Having finally **found** a job, I called my parents with the happy news. NOT *Finally finding* …
Not having seen the incident, I'm not the best person to tell you what happened.

> **Tip**
> We can use *-ed* adverbial participle clauses after time conjunctions in formal language:
> **When faced with danger**, most people would just panic.
> The holiday of a lifetime! **Once experienced**, it will never be forgotten.

▶ 06.10 Participle clauses after nouns

We can sometimes use participle clauses after nouns and pronouns. They are similar to defining relative clauses that have continuous and passive verbs. Look at the following examples:
We found the wallet (*that was*) **lying by the side of the road**.
Everybody (*who had been*) **affected by the fire** was told to leave their homes.
The streets were full of people (*who were*) **dancing for joy**.
Alice in Wonderland was the **book** (*which was*) **chosen by the majority** of students.
But:
Joanna is a **woman who says** what she thinks. NOT ~~woman saying~~
(*says* is not a continuous verb)
The **building that collapsed** was to be rebuilt. NOT ~~building collapsed~~
(*collapsed* is not a passive)
The subject of a participle clause must be the same as the main clause:
Opening the door slowly, she hesitated before entering the room.
NOT ~~Opening the door slowly~~, it was heavy for her to push.
We can't form a participle clause when a modal verb is necessary for the full sense of the clause:
Animal Farm is a book which **should be read** by everyone. NOT ~~book read~~

> **Tip**
> We can use participle clauses with verbs not usually used in continuous tenses:
> You will come to a large rock **resembling** a castle. = rock which resembles a castle NOT ~~rock which is resembling~~
> I wasn't sure where to go, **not being a local**.

Standing as still as he could, he waited for the next throw.

a Tick (✓) the correct sentences. Correct the mistakes you found in the remaining sentences.

1. ☐ ~~Tony~~ running at full speed, he managed to jump on the train. [R]
2. ☐ Remembering my appointment, I jumped up and left.
3. ☐ I will find the person committed this crime.
4. ☐ There was a terrible smell coming from the room.
5. ☐ Causing the damage, he offered to pay for it.
6. ☐ Reading the letter, my hands were shaking in excitement.
7. ☐ Not belonging to the group, I felt very out of place.
8. ☐ Johnny is the kind of man never arriving anywhere on time.

b Complete the beginning of the story with the participle clauses in the box.

> being realistic   coming outside   ~~following me~~
> being overworked and underpaid   getting stressed out
> waiting to strike   wearing orange

I knew that there was a man [1] *following me*. That morning, [2] _____, I saw him again. The strange thing was that he made no effort to hide; [3] _____, he seemed to want to be seen. Anyway, [4] _____, what could I do? [5] _____, the local police would hardly have time to listen to my suspicions. It wasn't exactly the crime of the century, either. Maybe it was just me [6] _____ as a result of too much work. As things turned out, my stalker, [7] _____, was a very serious threat indeed.

c Rewrite the next part of the story using participle clauses where possible.

I went to the café on the street corner. ~~I sat down and~~ *Sitting down,* I ordered a piece of cake. A piece of cake which was covered in chocolate was quickly brought over to my table. I noticed something which was sticking out from under the cake, so I lifted it up. Underneath I found a note which was written in red that said, 'Get into the car which is waiting across the road.' I was frightened by the tone and I feared the worst, so I did what the note said. A thousand negative thoughts were crowding my head when I got to the car. The familiar figure who was dressed in orange was in the front seat, with a sinister smile on his face. 'We meet at last,' he said.

d ▶▶ Now go back to p. 73.

149

7A Speculation and deduction

We can use modal verbs and other expressions to say how certain, probable or possible something is, in the future, present or past. We do this for two main purposes:
1. to make **deductions** (say what we think is true or possible from what we see, hear, etc.)
2. to **speculate** (make guesses about things we don't know).

▶ 07.05 **Deductions: modal verbs**

To make deductions, we can use the modal verbs *must*, *should*, *may/might/could*, *can't/couldn't*, followed by an infinitive form without *to*. Possible infinitive forms are:

(Present states or future events) **Modal verb + infinitive** They **should be** here soon. (= They'll probably be here soon.)	(Present activities – things going on now) **Modal verb + *be* + verb + *-ing*** He **could be working**. (= Perhaps he's working.)
(Past actions and states) **Modal verb + *have* + past participle** They **might have gone** away for the weekend. (= Perhaps they went away.)	(Past activities – things going on in the past) **Modal verb + *have been* + verb + *-ing*** She **must have been trying** to call us. (= I'm sure she was trying to call us.)

Different modal verbs express different degrees of certainty.

It's certain: *must*
We use *must* to say something is logically true or that we believe it from the evidence:
Lisa is all dressed up. She **must be going** somewhere nice.
We can also use *must* to imagine how things are/were:
I hear you went to Antarctica last year. That **must have been** a wonderful experience.

It's probable: *should*
We use *should* to say that something is probable because it is expected:
It's 6:00, so they **should have arrived** by now.

It's possible: *may (not), might (not), could*
When used to express possibility, *may*, *might* and *could* mean the same:
Fuel **could/may** run out in the near future.

It's impossible: *can't, couldn't*
We use *can't* or *couldn't* to say that something is logically impossible or very unlikely:
The exam **can't/couldn't have been** very difficult if you finished in 20 minutes.
We can also use *can't* and *couldn't* to imagine how things are/were:
She had to bring up three children on her own. That **can't have been** easy. (= I'm sure it wasn't easy)

> **Tip**
> We also use *could(n't) + have* + past participle with a different meaning, to imagine possibilities in the past:
> I didn't know you were in town. We **could have met** up. (= We didn't meet, but it would have been possible)

▶ 07.06 **Speculating**

We can use the modal verbs *might*, *may* and *could* to speculate (i.e., what we are saying is just a guess, not a deduction from evidence).
I wish I could call her. She **might be wondering** where we are.
To express slightly stronger probability, we can use *may/might well* (= I don't know but I think it's probable):
Solar power **may well be** the answer to our energy problems.
To speculate about the future, we can use *will/won't* + an adverb:
Fuel **will almost certainly** run out in the near future.
We **probably won't** have time to visit the museum.

▶ 07.07 **Other expressions**

Other expressions used for speculating and expressing varying degrees of certainty are:
It's + adjective + that: It's possible/probable/likely/unlikely/certain that ...
It's quite possible that we'll invent a new way to reduce CO_2 levels.
I think **it's unlikely that** people will ever live on Mars.
is + adjective + to: is certain/sure/bound/likely/unlikely to ...
We **are bound to** find a cure for cancer one day.
He's **unlikely to** get a place at university. His marks aren't good enough.
Expressions with 'I ...': I'm sure, I'm certain, I bet, I reckon, I imagine:
We don't know exactly why the plane crashed, but **I imagine** there was a technical fault of some kind.
There's a (good/slight/reasonable) chance that ...
There's a reasonable chance that he'll be the only applicant for the job.

a Rewrite these sentences using the words in brackets.
1. It was impossible for Adam to do any more. (couldn't)
   Adam couldn't have done any more.
2. I'm sure that customers will complain. (bound)
3. It is very possible that I'll see Ian tomorrow. (well)
4. I'm sure Barbara broke the window; she was playing round here. (must)
5. There's no way the referee saw the incident. (can't)
6. Damien probably knows the answer. (should)
7. It's obvious to me that Greta is dissatisfied. (tell)
8. Karen isn't at her desk, so I'm sure she's having a coffee break. (must)

b Add words or phrases from the box in the gaps. More than one answer may be possible.

---
a good chance that   could   must have   probably
almost certainly   may well   possible that   unlikely to

Only 50 years ago, the idea of asking your mobile phone for advice [1]_____ seemed like science fiction, but now the use of 'intelligent assistants' like Alexa or Siri seems to us quite normal. And in the near future, robots will [2]_____ be able to replace human beings in jobs which require interaction with people. Soon, humanoid robots [3]_____ be taking care of patients in hospitals, though it will [4]_____ be a long time before they can do skilled jobs like surgery. And robots that can express and respond to feelings [5]_____ be developed in the next 50 years, so it's [6]_____ they could take over caring roles, for example, keeping people company in care homes or treating people with psychological problems. Although humanoid robots are [7]_____ take over completely from humans any time soon, there's [8]_____ they will become a normal part of our children's everyday lives, or even of our own.

c ▶▶▶ Now go back to p. 81.

Grammar Focus

7B Cleft sentences

We use cleft sentences to correct, emphasise or point out information.
We form **a focusing clause ending in *be*** at the beginning of the sentence.

▶ 07.13 **Wh- cleft sentences**
Note how the following examples become cleft sentences:
It's amazing that nobody found out.
He wanted a fresh start.
I really like watching crime series.

What	noun	verb phrase	be	information focused on
What		is amazing	is	that nobody found out. ('that' clause)
What	he	wanted	was	a fresh start. (noun)
What	I	really like	is	watching crime series. (-*ing* form)

> **Tip**
> - *be* can be plural if what follows it is plural:
>   *What patients demand **is/are** better hospitals.*
> - In informal speech we can also use *where/when/why/how* in the *Wh-* cleft structure:
>   *Where I was born is London.*
>   *How I feel is angry.*
>   *Why I left was to get a job.*

We frequently emphasise an action or activity with *What + happen + be + (that) + clause*:
What happened was that we had to throw all the food away.
What happens is that you get a quick orientation on your first day.
We can emphasise actions with *What + noun phrase + do + be + (to) + base form*:
What she did was (to) phone the police.
What Sheila had done was to get married.

- **The point**
  We can begin cleft sentences with *The point*:
  The point is that you should have asked before borrowing the car.
  The point I'm making is, everyone has their reasons.

- **All**
  We can begin cleft sentences with *All*:
  All (that) she wants is a new phone.
  All I did was ask her how she was feeling.

- **The thing / The main thing, etc.**
  We can begin cleft sentences with *The thing, The main thing,* etc.:
  The main thing is that you two stop quarrelling.
  One thing you can do is to promise it won't happen again.

- **The place where / time when / reason why**
  We use *place where, time when* and *reason why* to emphasise a place, time or reason. We can use *that* instead of *where, when* and *why*:
  The place (where) I was born is London.
  The time (when) you find out who your real friends are is when you have no money.
  The only reason (why) I stay in this job is Mike.
  The main reason (why) I do it is to make a little money.

▶ 07.14 ***It* cleft sentences**
Cathy had the idea.
***It was** Cathy who had the idea.*

It	be	information focused on (noun/place/time phrase)	that / which / when clause
It	is	technology	that is causing increased shyness.
It	was	a month later	when she finally got back to me.
It	is	working all day for nothing	which gets me down.
It	is	only in big cities	that smog is a problem.

We can also emphasise time with *It is/was not until ... that* and *It is/was only when ... that*:
It was not until Lesley went away that I realised how much I missed her.
It's only when I'm alone that I feel insecure.

What technology does is to bring people together.

a Match the sentence halves.

1. [g] What he wanted was
2. [ ] What I did was
3. [ ] It was my teacher
4. [ ] The main thing is
5. [ ] All you can do is
6. [ ] It's only when we're busy
7. [ ] What happened was
8. [ ] How she earns a living is

a write an angry letter back.
b that the problems start.
c that the boat started to sink.
d who encouraged me to write.
e hard to say.
f that nobody got hurt.
g to change the world.
h try harder next time.

b Correct the mistakes in the sentences.
1 ~~There~~ It is Paris that I've always wanted to visit.
2 The captain of the ship was who sensed the storm coming.
3 All what students want is an affordable educational system.
4 All she did was taking out the cable.
5 What happens next is to fill out an application form.
6 The most important thing is which he is innocent.
7 What was the weather that was beginning to worry me.
8 Is a unique situation that we find ourselves in.

c Rewrite the sentences as cleft sentences using the words in brackets.
1 I want coffee. (what) *What I want is coffee.*
2 I only need ten euros. (all)
3 Nobody wants to do this job. (it)
4 You are asking for something unreasonable. (what)
5 We chose Portugal because of the friendly people. (reason)
6 Our car ran into a tree. (happened)
7 Her cousin was causing all the trouble. (it)
8 I don't know Jason so well and this bothers me. (the thing)

d ≫ Now go back to p. 83.

151

8A Gerunds and infinitives

▶ 08.02 **Gerunds**
Gerunds are *-ing* forms that function as nouns in a sentence:
Most people agree that **smoking** is bad for your health.
We can form compound nouns with gerunds:
sleeping pills, **training session**
Gerunds are more commonly used than infinitives as subjects of a clause:
Staying in bed all day is not a great use of your time.
To stay in bed all day … is possible, but less common and more formal.
We use gerunds after prepositions:
I'm not interested **in becoming** a member of your club. NOT *in to become*
Do you ever get tired **of doing** the same thing every day? NOT *of to do*
Gerunds are also used after some fixed expressions:
Was it worth spending all that money on a sofa bed?
It's no use leaving before eight o'clock.
There's no point worrying and losing sleep over it.

▶ 08.03 **Infinitives**
We use the infinitive without *to* after modal verbs, expressions like *may well*, *had better*, *would rather* and some verbs like *let* and *make*:
The situation <u>may well</u> **get** worse before it gets better.
I <u>would rather</u> **sleep** in my own bed than in a hotel room.
Drinking hot milk at bedtime <u>makes</u> me **fall** asleep easily.
We use *to* + infinitive after …
- many adjectives, comparatives, superlatives and ordinal numbers:
  I was **delighted to hear** that you had won first prize. NOT *hearing*
  Who is the **greatest** athlete ever **to represent** Great Britain? NOT *representing*
  She was the **first** woman **to climb** Everest. NOT *climbing*
- certain verbs, e.g., *decide, plan, agree* and also the nouns which are formed from these verbs:
  Sally **decided to resign**. → Sally made a **decision to resign**.
  He **agreed to repair** the damage. → He signed an **agreement to repair** the damage.
- time:
  It's **time to go** to bed.
- quantifiers like *enough*, *little* and *many* + nouns:
  Do you have **enough** money **to start** your own business?
  I've seen **too many** films like that **to be** very impressed.

💡 **Tip**
Negative forms of gerunds and infinitives are made by placing *not* before the gerund and infinitive:
Not eating just before bedtime is better for your health. NOT ~~Eating not just before~~ …
I'd rather **not go** out tonight. NOT ~~I'd rather go not out tonight.~~
It's nice **not to go** to work today. NOT ~~It's nice to not go work today.~~

Gerunds can occur in present and perfect forms and also in the passive:
- Present gerund: verb + *-ing*
  Shouting a lot isn't very good for your voice.
- Perfect gerund: *having* + past participle
  I'm sorry for ever **having mentioned** the subject.
- Passive gerund: *being* + past participle
  Winning is better than **being beaten**.

Infinitives occur most frequently in simple, continuous and perfect forms:
- Simple: I'll **come** later. / Try **to help** if you can.
- Continuous: I'd rather **be going** with you. / She seems **to be feeling** better.
- Perfect: You should **have phoned** last night. / It's important **to have tried**.

Passive infinitives are most commonly used in the simple form:
It can **be thrown** away. / This offer is **not to be missed**.

💡 **Tip**
In many cases the present and the perfect forms of gerunds and infinitives have the same meaning:
Her proudest moment to date is **having won** / **winning** Olympic gold.
You were supposed **to have finished** / **to finish** it yesterday.
However, this is not the case after modal verbs where there is a difference in meaning between the simple and perfect forms:
You **should tell** me. (= I want to know now.)
You **should have told** me. (= I needed to know in the past.)

Certain verbs can be followed by either a gerund or an infinitive, e.g., *remember, forget, try, prefer, stop, regret, mean*. However, there is usually a change in meaning between the two forms. Compare:
I **remember reading** that book at university. (= This is a past memory.)
I **remembered to pick up** your book from the library. (= I didn't forget to do this.)

---

a Choose the correct options.
1 *Choosing* / *Having chosen* / *To be chosen* a pillow that is right for your back is not easy.
2 *Picking* / *Being picked* / *Having been picked* for my university team would be a great achievement.
3 There was no point *waiting* / *having been waited* / *to wait* for him.
4 Jane is furious with me for *mislead* / *having misled* / *having been misled* her.
5 The suspect claims *to have been visiting* / *to be visiting* / *to have been visited* her sister at that time.
6 I would prefer *not to have known* / *to have known not*.
7 Sorry, but there are too few players *to have* / *having* a real game.
8 There's no use *having complained* / *complaining* / *to complain* about it all the time.
9 Look, it's time *to forget* / *forgetting* everything that happened.
10 The views from the top are worth *describing* / *to be described* in detail.

b Correct the mistakes in the gerunds and infinitives in *italics*.
Is it possible for someone never ¹*to be sleeping* (to sleep)? The answer is (almost) yes if you have Fatal Familial Insomnia, in which ²*to have fallen* asleep is almost impossible. For sufferers, it's not even worth them ³*to go* to bed because sleep won't come. As the name suggests, ⁴*affecting* by this rare but dreadful condition can cause death, depending on its severity. If we don't get enough sleep ⁵*carry out* our day-to-day life, the damage to our physical and mental health can be very serious. ⁶*To not sleep* for days often makes people ⁷*to feel* weak and disoriented. There can be some benefit in ⁸*being taken* sleeping pills, but this puts a different kind of stress on the body, and the drugs can become addictive. There is a need for more research ⁹*doing* in this area, and it is sure ¹⁰*being* a very deserving way for government money ¹¹*to be spending*.

c ⏵⏵ Now go back to p. 92.

8B Conditionals

▶ 08.09 Real and unreal conditionals

Real conditionals are used to talk about things that are possible or likely. In the *if* clause, we use the present tense to refer to either the present or the future:

Present real (Zero conditional)
If I **want** a snack, I **have** one.
Future real (First conditional)
She**'ll recover** quickly if her temperature **goes** down. (NOT *will go down*)
In unreal conditionals we show that a situation is hypothetical or unlikely by changing the verb forms 'one tense back' (present → past, past → past perfect, *will* → *would*, etc.).
Present and future unreal (Second conditional)
If it **weren't raining**, I **would go** out somewhere. (= It is raining now, so I won't go out.)
If I **studied** abroad next year, I'**d have to** delay my graduation. (= … but I probably won't study abroad.)
Past unreal (Third conditional)
Megan **wouldn't have missed** her plane if she **hadn't lost** her passport. (= She lost her passport so she missed the plane.)
The car **could have gone** off the road if he **had been driving** any faster. (= He wasn't driving too fast, so the car didn't go off the road.)
Mixed conditionals
Conditional sentences can also refer to both present and past time within the same sentence:
I **would speak** French more fluently (= now) **if I had done** my degree in France. (= in the past.)
If I **weren't** so lazy (= now), I'**d have done** it a long time ago. (= in the past).

💡 Tip

In more formal style, we can begin conditional clauses with:
- inverted past perfect (for unreal past):
  Had I known about your plans earlier, I would have acted differently. (= If I had known …)
- Should … (for real present or future):
  Should her condition get worse, we will contact you immediately. (= If her condition gets …)
- Were … to + infinitive … (for unreal present or future):
  Were humans to live to 150, there would be many health complications. (= If humans lived …)

▶ 08.10 Other conjunctions and phrases

as/so long as, on (the) condition that = only if (real conditions)	You can borrow my shirt **as long as** you don't get it dirty. Goods can be returned **on condition that** you have the original receipt.
providing, provided (that) = if (real conditions)	**Provided that** you repay it within three months, the bank will issue the loan.
if it weren't / hadn't been for + noun phrase **but for** + noun phrase (unreal conditions – formal)	**If it weren't for** Simon, I would never have known about the cucumber diet. The negotiations would have failed **but for** my efforts.
suppose, imagine (that) (unreal conditions – often introducing a question)	**Suppose** we could live to 100, what would we look like? **Imagine** there were no school today. Wouldn't that be great?
assuming (that), supposing = this might be the case (real or unreal conditions)	Let's meet on Sunday, **assuming** that is everyone's day off. **Supposing** you could find the treasure, what would you do with it?
(just) in case = because this might happen (real conditions)	Write down the phone number **just in case** you forget it.
otherwise = if not that, then this (real or unreal conditions)	I need to get to bed, **otherwise** I won't be able to get up on time.

💡 Tip

We usually use *as long as*, *provided (that)* and *providing* about good things or things we want to happen:
We'll be able to have a picnic **provided** the weather clears up.
NOT *We'll have to stay at home provided it rains.*
We often use *in case* about risks or things we don't want to happen:
I'll take a book **in case** I have to wait a long time.

---

a Match the sentence halves and complete them using the correct form of the verbs in brackets.

1. [h] If Sandra _gets_ (get) here early,
2. [ ] If I _____ (still / work) in an hour,
3. [ ] If you _____ (bother) to ask,
4. [ ] If the story _____ (be) to get out,
5. [ ] I don't mind going to the party
6. [ ] You're welcome to stay the night,
7. [ ] If it _____ (be) for evening classes,
8. [ ] You'd better leave now,

a I could have explained everything to you.
b provided that you _____ (bring) your own sleeping bag.
c otherwise you _____ (miss) the last bus home.
d stop me and tell me to go to bed.
e I would never have met my wife.
f it wouldn't look very good for the firm.
g as long as it _____ (not/finish) too late.
h let her in for me, please.

b Write conditional sentences using the words in brackets, so that they mean the same as the original sentence.

1. I'll give you my phone number because you may need to call me. (case)
   I'*ll give you my phone number in case you need to call me.*
2. I'll give you a key so that you'll be able to get into the flat. (otherwise)
3. You can stay here but you have to keep quiet. (as long)
4. I don't live in the country, so I won't get a dog. (if)
5. I wasn't disappointed because a lot of people came to my party. (if)
6. I'll show you the letter, but you must agree to keep it confidential. (condition)
7. You will be the first to know if I decide to get married. (should I)
8. I think we have everything we need, so the job shouldn't take long (assuming)

c ▶▶ Now go back to p. 96.

9A Reflexive and reciprocal pronouns

▶ 09.04 **Reflexive pronouns**
We use reflexive pronouns when the object is the same as the subject. They are placed after a verb or a preposition:
*They blamed **themselves** for the accident.*
*She was always looking at **herself** in the mirror.*
We use *by* + reflexive pronoun to mean without anybody else:
*My friends were busy, so I went into town **by myself**.*
We use *beside* + reflexive pronoun to mean worried/upset:
*After the last heavy defeat, the manager is **beside himself**.*
Some verbs have a different meaning when the object is a reflexive pronoun:
*He didn't **behave himself**.* = behave well
*Just **be yourself** in the interview.* = act naturally
*You don't want to **find yourself** alone.* = get into a situation
***Enjoy yourself** at the party.* = have a good time
*I **helped myself** to the sandwiches.* = take without invitation
*I did**n't feel myself**.* = feel different from usual
Verbs which are usually done by an individual, for example *shave*, *wash*, etc., don't need a reflexive pronoun, unless we want to make a point of the ability:
I washed and dressed in five minutes.
*The twins are old enough to dress **themselves**.*

*Cars that park **themselves** do save a lot of space.*

Reflexive pronouns are also used:
- after nouns and pronouns to emphasise importance, and for contrast with other people/things in general:
  *The president **himself** has shares in the company.*
  *The boss **herself** does not believe any of these rumours.*
- after the verb phrase to emphasise independence/achievement:
  *We designed the house **ourselves**.*
  *They cleaned up the city **themselves**.*
- after the verb phrase to show similarity to another person/thing = as well
  *He went to have a shower. I needed one **myself**.*

> 💡 **Tip**
> In English we do not generally use the verbs *concentrate*, *feel*, *hurry*, *lie* (*down*), *relax*, *sit* (*down*) with reflexive pronouns:
> *Rebecca didn't feel comfortable living in such a huge city.*
> NOT ~~feel herself~~
> *I spent some time relaxing before the busy day ahead.*
> NOT ~~relaxing myself~~
> *I concentrated on my work.* NOT ~~concentrated myself~~

▶ 09.05 **Reciprocal pronouns**
We use *each other* and *one another* with plural subjects when two or more people are involved in the activity:
*We always speak to **each other** with the utmost respect.*
*We chatted with **each other**.*
One another is more formal than *each other*:
*They greeted **one another** before addressing the room.*
Compare reflexive and reciprocal pronouns:
*Mr and Mrs Smith bought **themselves** a car.* (= one car for them both)
*Mr and Mrs Smith bought **each other** a present.* (= two presents, one each)
*We smiled at **each other** and said hello.*
*We smiled to **ourselves** but gave no sign of any emotion.*
We use the possessives *each other's* and *one another's*:
*They were friends and regular visitors at **each other's** houses.*
*The purpose of this session is to listen to **one another's** problems sympathetically.*

a Match a and b in each pair with the best endings.

1 a ☐ We looked at ourselves   1 and smiled.
   b ☐ We looked at each other   2 in the mirror.

2 a ☐ They usually behave themselves   1 when the teacher's around.
   b ☐ They usually behave   2 better when the teacher's around.

3 a ☐ Mike helped him   1 clean up the room.
   b ☐ Mike helped himself   2 to a slice of cake.

4 a ☐ He looked really upset, so I sat down   1 beside himself.
   b ☐ He looked really upset. He was   2 beside him.

5 a ☐ They found themselves   1 after searching for hours.
   b ☐ They finally found each other   2 in a very awkward situation.

6 a ☐ The three medalists shook hands to   1 congratulate themselves on their success.
   b ☐ Atlético Madrid can   2 congratulate each other on their success.

b Choose the correct options.

1 I think we'll treat *us / ourselves* to a nice box of chocolates.
2 John would never have thought of that *himself / beside himself*.
3 Laura only thinks *by herself / of herself*. She's so selfish.
4 'Can I borrow a pen?' 'Sorry, I haven't got one *myself / itself*.'
5 You don't need to help. I can do the puzzle *itself / myself*.
6 Dom can't imagine *by himself / himself* in a different job.
7 They kissed *one another / themselves* and said goodbye.
8 The students checked *each other's / each others'* answers.

c Add the missing reflexive and reciprocal pronouns. More than one answer may be possible.

Have you ever thought to ask^yourself whether you would like to live in space? As the world population grows, towns and cities find under tremendous pressure, and it is becoming more difficult and expensive for us just to live in urban areas, let alone enjoy there. So maybe we would feel more comfortable in space. But, let's just remind of the challenges of doing such a thing. The technology may be there, but we would be opening up to lots of problems we can't even imagine. Unfortunately, there are no easy solutions. The world needs to sort out, and we need to learn to live with. I hope I've made clear.

d ▶▶ Now go to p. 106.

154

9B Ellipsis and substitution

We can avoid repeating our own or other people's ideas by using ellipsis (leaving out words and phrases) and substitution (replacing words and phrases).

▶ 09.12 Leaving out verb phrases
One of the most common forms of ellipsis is in short answer forms where the main verb is not repeated:
Have you been to Venice? Yes, I **have**. (been to Venice)
We can leave out repeated verb phrases and use an auxiliary or modal instead. The auxiliary or modal may change in the second verb.
The city council promised to **build a new playground**, *but it never* **did**.
(*did* auxiliary replaces 'build a new playground')
We can leave out the infinitive but not *to*:
I needed to go shopping, but the kids didn't want to. (go shopping)
NOT ~~the kids didn't want~~

▶ 09.13 Leaving out subjects, main verbs and auxiliaries
We can leave out repeated subjects, main verbs and auxiliaries after *and/or/but/then* when the subject is the same:
The council has spent a lot of money but (it has) changed nothing.
The architect designed an iconic office tower, then (the architect designed) a bridge.
We usually can't leave out subjects and auxiliaries in clauses connected with words like *although, because, before, if, when*, etc.:
I changed my mind when I saw the building. NOT ~~when saw~~ …

▶ 09.14 Other examples of ellipsis
We can leave out adjectives and repeat *be*:
The first room **was beautiful**, *but the second* **wasn't** (beautiful).
We can leave out noun phrases after determiners and superlatives:
This is **my** *favourite picture, and that's* **my husband's** (favourite picture).
There were **a few** *flats in my price range, and I chose the* **cheapest** (flat in my price range).
We can leave out repeated verbs and nouns in comparative structures:
They built the **first floor more quickly** *than (they built) the* **second** (floor).

▶ 09.15 Pronouns
We can use pronouns like *one* and *ones* to substitute noun phrases:
I like the blue scarves much better than the green **ones**.
We can use *that* instead of a phrase or clause.
Don't interrupt me! I hate **that**.
We can use possessive pronouns, *yours*, *mine*, etc., to substitute noun phrases:
You've got a decent view. **Mine** *is terrible.*
You know my views on private education, so tell me **yours**.

▶ 09.16 so and not
To substitute clauses after verbs, we usually use:
* *so* (positive) and *not* (negative) after the verbs *hope, guess, be afraid*:
  '*Are we getting paid today?*' '*I hope* **so**.' (= we are getting paid today)
  '*Is Danny coming to dinner?*' '*I'm afraid* **not**.' (= he isn't coming to dinner)
* *so* for both positive and negative forms of the verbs *think, expect, imagine, believe, say*:
  '*Will you be home for dinner?*' '*I expect* **so**.' (= I'll be home for dinner)
  '*Do you think it'll rain today?*' '*No, I don't think* **so**.' (= it won't rain today)

We can use *if not* and *if so* to substitute clauses:
I hope the jumper is the right size. **If not**, *you can exchange it.* (= if it's not the right size)
It looks like some of you have finished. **If so**, *you can check your answers together.* (= if you have finished)

▶ 09.17 so / neither / nor
We use *so* and *neither/nor* + auxiliary to substitute exactly the same idea for a new subject and avoid repetition:
The old town is amazing, and **so** *are the views* (= both clauses positive – the views are also amazing.)
If Gerald doesn't like it, **neither/nor** *will his wife* (= both clauses negative – his wife also won't like it.)
nor can also mean *and not*:
She doesn't want to live in the country **nor** *in the town.* (= and she doesn't want to live in the town.)

---

a Cross out the words that can be left out of each sentence with no change of meaning.
1. The president arrived and he made a speech.
2. You don't know and you never will know.
3. I will tell you because I value and I respect your opinion.
4. We have been thinking about our reputation, we have not been thinking about money.
5. I said I would be volunteering, so I will be volunteering.
6. If they are hungry, bears can be dangerous and they can be unpredictable.
7. My first impression was very positive, but my second impression wasn't very positive.
8. We can meet up at seven if you'd like to meet up at seven tonight.
9. 'Are we in room six?' 'I guess we are not in room six.'
10. The Nile is the longest river in the world, and the Amazon is the second longest river in the world.

b Shorten the sentences using substitution.
1. My exam was a lot tougher than ~~your exam~~. *yours*
2. 'Is this the right page?' 'I think it is the right page.'
3. 'I don't know where we are.' 'I don't know where we are, either.'
4. I love holidays abroad, especially long holidays abroad.
5. 'Who's got a dress with short sleeves?' 'Borrow my dress with short sleeves.'
6. 'Did you get my message?' 'I'm afraid we didn't get it.'
7. 'George has got married.' 'I didn't know George had got married.'
8. Klaus is very enthusiastic and his sister is very enthusiastic, too.
9. Tina had always wanted to go parachuting, and one day she went ~~parachuting~~.

c Use ellipsis and substitution to shorten the conversation and make it more natural.

Damien I've been thinking about the office of the future.
Rachel What do you mean by ~~the office of the future~~? *that*
D The place where we are going to work and where we are going to do business, say, 50 years from now. Those offices will look completely different compared to the offices today.
R I expect they will look completely different.
D For example, imagine there are no walls and there are no doors. All barriers to communication will be broken down and all barriers to communication will be a thing of the past. This is hard to imagine, but you don't need to imagine it. Just go to any successful company today.
R I think successful companies today have walls and have doors.
D You are being sarcastic and you are trying to make fun of me.
R Sorry, I didn't mean to make fun of you. I'd like to travel in time and I'd like to visit an office of the future. Tell me when you have built an office of the future.

d ▶▶ **Communication 9B** Work in pairs. Student A: Go to p. 135. Student B: Go to p. 136.

10A Regret and criticism structures

Regrets are things we feel sorry or annoyed about because we think the action or situation could be or have been better. Criticism involves complaining about a problem and is directed at another person or a situation. Some regrets can be a way of criticising yourself.

▶ 10.06 Present and future regrets
We use the verb *wish* and the phrase *if only* followed by the past simple to talk about present and future regrets, but *if only* has a stronger meaning. The past simple is used to indicate the fact that the situation is imagined and not real:
He **wishes** (that) he **was/were** better at maths. (present regret – he's not good at maths)
They **wish** they **had** a larger house.
If only I **could** go to Rome with you next month. (future regret – I can't go to Rome)
Note: where *was* is an option (in first and third person), *were* can also be used.

▶ 10.07 Past regrets
We use a wider range of structures to express regrets about the past.
- *I wish / if only* + past perfect:
  She **wishes** (that) she **had studied** Mandarin at university. (present wish about past event)
  They **wished** they **had sold** their house before the stock market crash. (past wish about a past event)
  If only I'**d booked** online last night.
- Past unreal conditionals (see 8B):
  If I **hadn't gone** to the party, I **would never have met** that awful man.
  If he'**d applied** for that job, he **wouldn't be** unemployed now.
- The past modals *could* and *should* can also express past regrets:
  I **could have timed** my talk better.
  We **should have checked** our equipment before leaving.
- The verb *regret* followed by a gerund can be used:
  She **regrets leaving** her old job.
- *would like / love* + perfect infinitive can also express past regrets:
  I **would like to have spent** more time with you.

▶ 10.08 Present criticism
We use *wish / if only* + *would* to criticise people or situations regarding present events:
I **wish** (that) the council **would** look after the parks better.
If only you would stop checking your phone at mealtimes.
A mixed conditional can be used to criticise someone in the present for something that happened in the past:
If you had been watching properly, you'd be able to do it.
We can use *must*, *need*, *can* and imperatives to express very strong, direct personal criticism:
You really **must** train harder if you want to get to the finals.
You **need** to start saving for your retirement.
Don't put so much garlic in the pasta sauce next time.
To soften the criticism, we use *should* and *ought to*:
You **should** add the milk to the flour more slowly.
They **ought to** turn off the lights when they go out.

▶ 10.09 Past criticism
To criticise people or situations regarding a past event, we use *wish / if only* + past perfect:
I **wish you hadn't brought** home that lost dog.
If only the government hadn't cut spending on health.
Past unreal can be used to express criticism of the past:
If you'**d read** the essay question more carefully, you **would have written** a better answer.
We can also use modals + perfect infinitive to criticise past actions:
You **could have phoned** him sooner.
They **needn't have bothered** getting in touch.
He **should have asked** me first.

> 💡 **Tip**
> We can use *must* to criticise people strongly in the present, but not *must* + perfect infinitive in the past:
> You **must** study the road rules harder to pass the test.
> You **should have studied** the road rules harder to pass the test.
> NOT ~~must have studied~~.

[Cartoon: A speaker at a lectern in front of an audience, saying "Anyway, it's time I came to my conclusion."]

a Match sentence halves 1–10 to a–j.

1 He wishes
2 They could have
3 I regret
4 If she'd gone shopping earlier,
5 You ought to
6 If only we
7 I wish you
8 I would like to
9 If you'd checked
10 They very much regret buying

a clean your car more often.
b smartphones for their children.
c she'd be home by now.
d let us know they were coming.
e he was still living at home.
f your email, you'd have found out about the meeting.
g could afford to buy this car.
h not going to university.
i would try a bit harder.
j have visited my uncle and aunt.

b Choose the correct options.

1 If only I *would / could* find a better job.
2 If we'd left earlier, we *wouldn't be / would have been* late for the meeting now.
3 She wishes her teacher *could / would* stop correcting her all the time.
4 We *must / should* have printed out tickets before leaving.
5 If only I *chose / had chosen* a more suitable colour when we did the painting.
6 If you'd rung and booked yesterday, we would *get / have got* a table.
7 I really regret not *enrolling / enrolled* in the cooking class.
8 Excuse me, sir, you *shouldn't / don't* leave your rubbish behind.
9 I wish I *stayed / had stayed* in touch with more of my friends from school.
10 You needn't *bother / have bothered* telling everyone about last month's profit loss.

c Rewrite the sentences as regrets or criticisms, using the words in brackets.

1 I hate the new chair I've just bought. (only)
2 I want to go on holiday to Australia next year but can't. (wish)
3 We didn't service the washing machine, so it's broken down. (if)
4 You didn't turn off your phone before going into the cinema. (should)
5 I'm unhappy about the fact the council closed the library. (wish)

d ▶▶ Now go back to p. 118.

Grammar Focus

10B Passive reporting verbs

We use passive reporting verbs (*say, think, know, believe, report*, etc.) when we are generalising about what most people say or think. We can use two different passive reporting structures:

1 *It + passive + that*
It is known that the colour white represents purity in many cultures.
In ancient times, *it was believed that* the sun went around the Earth.

2 *Subject + passive + to + infinitive*
The colour white **is known to** represent purity in many cultures.
He **is understood to** be furious about the election result.
We can follow this structure with perfect infinitives to refer to the past, or continuous infinitives for the present and future:
She **'s said to have met** him while making a film. (= It is said that she met him ...)
They **are believed to be living** in the Bahamas. (= People believe that they are living ...)

We often use passive reporting verbs to report information from other sources. They are common in:

- academic writing, in order to appear objective:
It has been shown (Smith, 2012) *that* superstition influences behaviour.
- news, either to avoid mentioning the source or because the source is unimportant:
The suspect **is reported to have escaped** in a car.

It + passive + wh- word
We can use passive reporting verbs + a *wh-* word for unknown facts:
It is not known what was said in the meeting.
It was not made clear whether or not they would be challenging the decision.
The sentence can begin with the *wh-* clause:
What was said in the meeting is not known.

▶ 10.15 **Common passive reporting verbs**

It + passive + *that* only: announce argue note explain suggest

It was **announced** that changes would be made. NOT ~~were announced to be made~~
It is often **argued** that Cleopatra was one of the most influential women in history.
It was **explained** that the mysterious marks were, in fact, animal tracks.
It has not been **suggested** that any jobs will be affected.

Subject + passive (+ infinitive) only: consider

He was **considered** (to be) one of their best players. NOT ~~It is considered that he...~~

Both structures:
agree assume believe claim expect know report reveal say show suspect think understand

The parcel **isn't expected to arrive** before the weekend.
She **is reported to have made** over ten million dollars.
It is said that K2 is harder to climb than Everest.
The story **has been shown to be** a complete lie.
It is thought that Latin was the first international language.

Subject + passive + *as* + adjective/noun phrase: regarded seen

Serena Williams **is regarded as** one of the greatest tennis players ever. NOT ~~It is regarded that Serena...~~
Sending cards on special occasions **may be seen as** old-fashioned by some people.

Walking under a ladder is believed to be unlucky!

a Correct the mistakes in the sentences.
1 It *is* argued that Vancouver is the most diverse city in the world.
2 He is said that he lived in a cave.
3 It is seen that basketball is a very important sport in Asia.
4 It was not reported her reply was.
5 It is suspected to the people responsible have left the country.
6 The winters are thought that they get very cold in this part of the world.
7 She is regarded to be the most exciting writer of her generation.
8 Quinoa is considered as very good for your health.

b Complete the text with the past participle of a verb in the box.

consider expect suggest know not understand
see think

There is significant cultural variation today, but it is
[1] *thought* that one of the most common, yet oldest, customs is shaking hands. From vases and other archaeological evidence, the ancient Greeks are [2] _____ to have shaken hands, and the custom was [3] _____ as a sign of respect and affection. In fact, the handshake is [4] _____ to be a form of ritual because it is done in so many contexts with great attention to detail. For example, in Eastern Europe it is [5] _____ that a man's, but not a woman's, hand will be shaken every time people meet. It is [6] _____ how the custom originated, but in some books it is [7] _____ that by offering your hand without a weapon you show that you come in peace.

c Rewrite these sentences using (1) *It + passive + that* (2) *Subject + passive + to + infinitive*. Keep the meaning of the sentences the same.

1 People think that sports rituals give you a feeling of control.
2 Many people believe that superstitions reduce anxiety.
3 People have reported that the president has left the country.
4 They say that the inventor Thomas Edison slept only four hours a night.
5 We know that obesity is a factor in developing diabetes.

d ≫ Now go to p. 121.

157

VOCABULARY FOCUS

1A Language learning

Verb phrases

a ▶ 01.05 Complete the expressions in **bold** with the words in the box. Listen and check.

ear	acquire /əˈkwaɪə/	rusty	brushed
pick	struggle /ˈstrʌgəl/	keep	
get	accustomed /əˈkʌstəmd/	hold	
practice	immersed /ɪˈmɜːst/	attain /əˈteɪn/	

1 Some learners appear to be able to _____ **language** without much formal study.
2 I really _____ **with** English idioms. I can never remember them.
3 I'm not sure if I'll ever _____ **a** native speaker **level** of competence, but I'm not sure I really need to.
4 When he went to live in Korea, he quickly **got** _____ **to** the sound of the language.
5 I've _____ **up on** my Arabic because I'm going to Riyadh next week.
6 Penny's lucky – she **has an** _____ **for** languages. She learns them much more easily than me.
7 After about a year, he found he could _____ **a conversation** in Italian without too much effort.
8 Unless I **put** a new piece of language **into** _____ immediately, I find I forget it.
9 People tend to give up on learning a second language too easily. You need to _____ **at it** if you want to succeed.
10 She spent six weeks in Poland and really _____ herself **in** the language and culture.
11 It's easy to _____ **up** phrases like 'hello' and 'excuse me' wherever you are in the world.
12 The sounds of Finnish are unique, so I found it difficult to _____ **to grips with** the pronunciation.
13 I need to practise my speaking now I'm back. I'm sure I'm really _____.

b Match the verbs 1–6 with the phrases a–f.

1 ☐ hold   a new ideas
2 ☐ grasp   b a level/degree of competence /ˈkɒmpɪtəns/
3 ☐ get   c a conversation
4 ☐ put   d accustomed to
5 ☐ acquire   e into practice
6 ☐ attain   f a new/second language

c ⟫ Now go back to p. 9.

Noun forms

d Complete the table with the missing noun forms. Use a dictionary to help you if necessary.

Adjective	Noun	Verb
1 interactive /ɪntəˈraktɪv/		interact
2 distracted /dɪˈstraktɪd/ distracting /dɪˈstraktɪŋ/		distract
3 dedicated /ˈdedɪkeɪtɪd/		dedicate
4 limited /ˈlɪmɪtɪd/		limit
5 motivated /ˈməʊtɪveɪtɪd/ motivating /ˈməʊtɪveɪtɪŋ/		motivate
6 necessary /ˈnesəseri/		necessitate
7 capable /ˈkeɪpəbl/		–
8 mental /ˈmentəl/		–
9 reluctant /rɪˈlʌktənt/		–
10 interfering /ɪntəˈfɪərɪŋ/		interfere
11 competent /ˈkɒmpɪtənt/		–
12 literate /ˈlɪtərət/		–
13 exposed /ɪkˈspəʊzd/		expose
14 –		acquire
15 insightful /ˈɪnsaɪtfəl/		–
16 prestigious /presˈtɪdʒəs/		–
17 disciplined /ˈdɪsəplɪnd/		discipline

e ▶ 01.08 **Pronunciation** Listen to some of the adjectives and nouns in the table.

1 Which nouns have more syllables than their adjectives?
2 Notice the stressed syllables in the adjectives. Practise saying the words and underline the stressed syllables in the nouns. Listen again and check.
3 Notice that the stress sometimes changes in the noun. Choose the correct option to complete the rule.

In nouns with the suffixes *-tion* and *-ity*, the stressed syllable is always *the first syllable* / *the syllable before the suffix*.

💡 **Learning Tip** Organising your records of word families by suffix can make features such as sound and spelling relationships easier to remember.

f What other nouns do you know with the suffixes *-tion* and *-ity*? Make a list and practise saying the words.

g ⟫ Now go back to p. 10.

Vocabulary Focus

2B Verbs of movement

a. They **soared** into the air. /sɔːd/ 
b. She **hurtled** down the slope. /ˈhɜːtəld/ 
c. They **zoomed** /zuːmd/ / **whizzed** /wɪzd/ along the road. 
d. It **rolled** across the floor. /rəʊld/ 
e. He **plunged** into the water. /plʌndʒd/ 
f. They **whirled** around the room. /wɜːld/ 
g. It **whooshed** through the station. /wuːʃt/

a ▶ 02.10 Match the sentences 1–10 with the pictures h–q. Listen and check.

1. ☐ He **crawled** up the stairs. /krɔːld/
2. ☐ They **marched** through the square. /mɑːtʃt/
3. ☐ She **leaped** over the rocks. /liːpt/
4. ☐ It **drifted** out to sea. /ˈdrɪftɪd/
5. ☐ He **crept** into the house. /krept/
6. ☐ He **limped** off the pitch. /lɪmpt/
7. ☐ He **staggered** across the desert. /ˈstagəd/
8. ☐ We **slid** down the slope. /slɪd/
9. ☐ They **rushed** to catch the train. /rʌʃt/
10. ☐ They **strolled** through the park. /strəʊld/

b Which verbs of movement in pictures a–q mean … ?

1. to move slowly
2. to move quickly
3. to move quietly
4. to move with difficulty

c Which verbs in **bold** in a are irregular past forms? What's the infinitive form of each?

d In pairs, take turns testing each other on prepositions of movement, using the sentences for pictures a–q. (Don't use picture h.)

> He crawled _____ the stairs.

> He crept _____ the house.

e Change the sentence He/She/It + (past simple verb of movement) *down the road* so that it matches the situations below. More than one verb may be possible.

1. He was a soldier. *He marched down the road.*
2. She was exhausted.
3. He didn't want anyone to hear him.
4. She was late for an appointment.
5. His right leg was injured.
6. She wasn't in a hurry.
7. He was on a sledge.
8. It was a bird.
9. He was on a motorbike.
10. I let go of my balloon.
11. It was a spider.

f Write a few sentences about an experience you've had that involved moving fast. Compare what you have written with other students.

I went on an incredibly fast ride at a theme park. The Nemesis hurtles along a track with lots of twists and turns. You whirl through the air at such high speed that you hit zero gravity. I lost both my earrings!

g ≫ Now go back to p. 25.

159

3B Landscape features

a Read the extracts from the travel stories and match them with the photographs.

1. ☐ We made slow progress through the **mosquito-infested swamp**, knee-deep in mud. We avoided the **dark** [1]_____ **of stagnant water** and eventually reached the firmer ground beyond.
2. ☐ We visited **a remote village in the foothills**. In front of the cottage was a **rich green** [2]_____ where cows grazed. In the distance, beyond **wooded** [3]_____, the mountains rose up into the sky.
3. ☐ To the north lies **an untouched wilderness**. The **rocky** [4]_____ is unsuitable for farming. **Empty** [5]_____ stretches towards the distant mountains.
4. ☐ The **rugged coastline** is famous for its beauty. From where I stood, **sheer** [6]_____ dropped to the sea and, looking down, I saw **the mouth of a** [7]_____ in the **cliff** [8]_____.
5. ☐ Never before had I been to such an **arid desert**. On our third day, we came to some **huge sand** [9]_____. We knew there was no way our 4X4 would be able to cross them.
6. ☐ We were deep in **the heart of the jungle** now. Quietly, we moved through the **dense** [10]_____. Looking up, I saw the **forest** [11]_____ far above my head and heard the cries of monkeys and birds.
7. ☐ The island can only be described as **a tropical paradise**. The sight of **pristine** [12]_____ and **calm turquoise** [13]_____ made us forget our long journey in an instant.

> **Tip**
>
> *Swamp*, *bog* and *marsh* all describe types of muddy wetlands.
> - In a marsh, the main plant life is types of grasses.
> - In a swamp, woody plants and trees can grow.
> - In a bog, the soil is poor so there is less plant life.

b ▶ 03.05 Complete the collocations in **bold** in **a** with the nouns in the box. Listen and check.

dunes /dʒuːnz/   moorland /ˈmɔːlənd/
meadow /ˈmedəʊ/   undergrowth /ˈʌndəɡrəʊθ/
slopes /sləʊps/   canopy /ˈkænəpi/
pools   cliffs   waters   cave
face   ground   beaches

c 💬 Ask and answer the questions.
1. Which of the words and phrases in **a** and **b** could describe places in your country?
2. Which other types of environment have you visited in other countries?
3. What's your favourite and least favourite type of environment to be in? Why?

d ▶▶ Now go to p. 36.

160

Vocabulary Focus

4A Instinct and reason

a ▶ 04.01 Listen to sentences 1–10. Match the words and phrases in **bold** with their meanings a–f.

1. ☐ I'm a very **rational** thinker.
2. ☐ **On impulse**, I married someone I'd only just met.
3. ☐ I know **subconsciously** when people are lying to me.
4. ☐ If I need to decide quickly, I always go with my **gut instinct**.
5. ☐ It's important to **weigh up** the pros and cons before taking action.
6. ☐ I **had a hunch** that I should resign, and I was right.
7. ☐ I'm successful in business because I think **logically**.
8. ☐ I'd always **think twice** before trusting a stranger.
9. ☐ I'll need time to **think it over** before I decide.
10. ☐ I love taking **spontaneous** decisions. They're more fun!

a an intuitive feeling (x2)
b step by step, using reasons
c think carefully (x3)
d without planning (x2)
e without being aware
f based on facts, not emotions

b ▶ 04.02 **Pronunciation**

1 Listen to the pronunciation of the letters in **bold** in these words. Which sound has more than one syllable?

1 /ʃəs/	2 /iəs/	3 /dʒəs/
cau**tious**	spontan**eous**	gor**geous**

2 ▶ 04.03 Copy the table in **b1** into your notebook. Then add these words to the correct columns. Listen and check. Practise saying the words.

subcon**scious**   presti**gious**   hila**rious**   coura**geous**   ambi**tious**
simultan**eous**   pre**cious**   cu**rious**   outra**geous**   conscien**tious**

c The words in **bold** below are about the mind and feelings. What is the difference between them? Use a dictionary to help you.

1 He's a very **reasonable** / **rational** person.
2 She's a very **sensitive** / **sensible** person.
3 He's very money-**conscious** / **conscientious**.
4 She's very **self-conscious** / **self-confident**.

d 💬 Which adjective in each pair in **c** do you think describes you better?

e ≫ Now go back to p. 45.

4B Memory

a ▶ 04.11 Complete the sentences with the correct adjectives. Listen and check.

1 I only ever **have a v_____ memory of** my journey to work. I do it on auto-pilot.
2 I **have a p_____ memory of** my cat getting run over when I was a child. 
3 Once the city was rebuilt, the storm **became a d_____ memory** for most people. 
4 Their trip to Venice **was a l_____ memory**, full of magic. 
5 I **have a v_____ memory** of our team winning the World Cup when I was a kid. 
6 He **has a p_____ memory** and can paint places he hasn't seen since childhood. 

b ▶ 04.12 Match 1–7 with a–g to make complete sentences. Check the meaning of any expressions in **bold** that you don't know. Listen and check.

1 ☐ I **vaguely remember** seeing that film years ago,
2 ☐ If I think of my time in New York,
3 ☐ I told him you were coming today,
4 ☐ The smell of freshly baked bread always **triggers a memory** of
5 ☐ Before going into class, she reads the register
6 ☐ If you **cast your mind back** to the last meeting,
7 ☐ I'll always **treasure the memory** of

a but it must have **slipped his mind**. Sorry, he's not here.
b the warm welcome they gave us. It was a very special occasion.
c but I've got no idea what the story of it is.
d staying with my grandmother in the school holidays.
e the first thing that **comes to mind** is a yellow taxi.
f you'll remember we agreed to increase the fee by £10.
g to **refresh her memory** of her students' names.

c ≫ Now go back to p. 49.

161

5A Crime and justice

a ▶05.06 Listen to the sentences. What is the difference between the legal terms in **bold**? Discuss the meanings with a partner.

1. a Thousands of pounds in cash were found on the premises, and a 35-year-old woman was **arrested on suspicion of** money laundering.
   b When the missing money was noticed, they **made an allegation of** fraud against him.

2. a She is **being held in custody** while waiting for her trial.
   b He's **been convicted of** murder and sent to prison.

3. a The defence **showed evidence in court** which supported the accused's alibi.
   b She **gave testimony in court** that she had seen the accused running from the scene of the crime.

4. a He was given a lighter prison sentence because he **pleaded guilty to** the crime.
   b Despite a strong defence case, he **was found guilty of** the crime.

> **Learning Tip**
> When you record new words and expressions in your vocabulary notebook, it is useful to make a note of others that have a similar but slightly different meaning. This can help avoid confusion when you want to use the new language.

b 💬 Look at the phrases in **bold** in **a**. In your country, who does each thing? Who do they do it to? Use the words in the box to help you.

judge /dʒʌdʒ/
jury /ˈdʒʊəri/
police officer /pəˈliːs ˌɒfɪsər/
criminal /ˈkrɪmɪnəl/
witness /ˈwɪtnəs/
victim /ˈvɪktɪm/
defence lawyer /dɪˈfens lɔɪə/
prosecution /ˌprɒsɪˈkjuːʃən/
someone else

c ▶05.07 Listen to the sentences. Which of these forms of punishment and rehabilitation are possible in your country's legal system?

a He was **sentenced to life imprisonment**.
b He had to **do community service**.
c She **served a reduced sentence for good behaviour**.
d The judge insisted that she **serve the full ten years**.
e The company was **fined** a six-figure sum.
f He was **banned from driving**.
g They suggested he be **brought face-to-face with his victim**.
h All prisoners receive either **one-to-one** or **group counselling**.
i Prisoners with mental health issues **receive psychiatric help**.
j It is necessary to hold some prisoners **in solitary confinement**.

d 💬 Order the forms of punishment and rehabilitation in **c** from 1 (= least harsh) to 10 (= most harsh), in your opinion. Compare your order with a partner.

e 💬 Discuss which crimes or types of criminals might receive each form of punishment or rehabilitation in **c**.

> Prisoners who are a danger to other inmates might be held in solitary confinement.

f ≫ Now go back to p. 58.

Vocabulary Focus

6A Adjectives: Describing images

a ▶ 06.01 Complete the sentences below with the adjectives in the box. Listen and check. Sometimes more than one answer is possible.

playful /ˈpleɪfəl/
powerful /ˈpaʊəfəl/
humorous /ˈhjuːmərəs/
raw /rɔː/
meaningful /ˈmiːnɪŋfəl/
well-composed /welkəmˈpəʊzd/
exotic /ɪɡˈzɒtɪk/
iconic /aɪˈkɒnɪk/
gritty /ˈɡrɪti/
evocative /ɪˈvɒkətɪv/
ironic /aɪˈrɒnɪk/
nonsensical /nɒnˈsensɪkəl/

1 The strength of emotion in this close-up of her face seemed to almost hit me. It's a truly _____ image.
2 He appears to be lifting a car with one hand. It's just not possible – it's completely _____.
3 The kittens are loving that ball of wool! It's an extremely _____ photo.
4 The photographer has captured _____ scenes of inner-city poverty. It isn't pretty.
5 It's a very _____ photo. There's a perfect balance between the foreground and the sky and the land.
6 These photos make a more _____ statement about man's impact on the environment than words could.
7 This is the most gently _____ photo in his portfolio. The expression on the man's face really makes me smile.
8 For me, the most wonderfully _____ photo in the exhibition is the frozen desert. It's another world for me.
9 It's a very _____ image. You can't look at it without feeling something.
10 This photo was taken just after he lost the match. The _____ emotion is painful to look at.
11 The picture of Neil Armstrong stepping on to the moon in 1969 is truly _____.
12 The rather _____ expression on the woman's face seems to be saying, 'Oh well, life's like that'.

b Notice the suffix in these adjectives:
- play**ful**
- power**ful**
- meaning**ful**

Underline more adjective suffixes in **a**. Which adjective doesn't have a suffix? Think of two more adjectives which have each suffix you underlined.

c ▶ 06.02 Match sentences 1–6 with a–f. Listen and check.

1 ☐ The angle of this photo shows off the iconic architecture of the new art gallery. 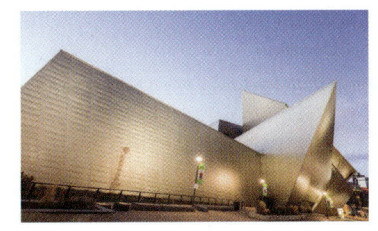
2 ☐ In this powerful photo, the house stands alone against its environment. 
3 ☐ I like this photo of the room with very little furniture in it. 
4 ☐ In this photo, he's wearing an exotic costume with feathers and gold ribbons. 
5 ☐ All the pictures in the exhibition are virtually the same. 
6 ☐ You need the perfect flower and the perfect light.

a It's not too **cluttered**. /ˈklʌtəd/
b It looks **sensational**. /senˈseɪʃənəl/
c It's quite a **bleak** image. /bliːk/
d It gets a bit **repetitive**. /rɪˈpetətɪv/
e If these elements are right, you can create an absolutely **flawless** image. /ˈflɔːləs/
f It all looks very **elaborate**. /ɪˈlabərət/

💡 Tip
Many adverbs of degree and adjectives form very strong collocations. For example, we say *utterly miserable* and *incredibly elaborate*, but ~~utterly elaborate~~ isn't a natural collocation. It's a good idea to note adverb + adjective collocations in your vocabulary notebook.

d Underline the adverb of degree + adjective collocations in the sentences in **a**.

e Which of the adverbs of degree in the box can be used with which adjectives in **bold** in **c**?

| incredibly | pretty | a bit | wonderfully |
| extremely | utterly | rather | truly |

f ≫ **Communication 6A** Now go to p. 134.

163

7A Compound adjectives: Parts of the body

> **Tip**
> Compound adjectives are formed in many ways:
> - noun + adjective: **world-famous**, **self-confident**
> - adjective + noun + -ed: **short-sleeved**, **cold-blooded**
> - adjective + participle: **good-looking**, **long-running**
> - adverb + participle: **hard-working**, **well-written**
> - noun + participle: **heartbreaking**, **self-made**
>
> Unless they have become one word, e.g., *heartbreaking*, the forms listed here always require a hyphen (-) between the two parts.

> **Tip**
> Compound adjectives are usually well-established collocations.
> *The novel is **heartbreaking** / **mind-blowing**.* NOT ~~*The novel is **heart-opening** / **mind-breaking***~~ etc.
>
> Many have idiomatic meanings. For example, if a person is **tongue-tied**, it does not literally mean that their tongue is tied. It means they find it difficult to speak because they are shy, nervous or embarrassed.

a ▶07.01 Look at examples 1–4 and then complete 5–9. Listen and check.

- **adjective + noun + -ed**
  1. He considers other points of view – he has an open mind. → He's **open-minded**.
  2. She will always help her friends – she has a warm heart. → She's **warm-hearted**.

- **noun + present participle**
  3. Carrying boxes upstairs nearly broke my back.
     → It was **backbreaking** work.
  4. The sight of elderly people in love always warms my heart. → It's a **heartwarming** sight.
  5. She always uses her left hand.
     → She's … 
  6. Don't expect any sympathy – he has a very hard heart. → He's … 
  7. She made the decision with a clear head.
     → She's … 
  8. Thai food makes my mouth water.
     → It's … 
  9. The sight made my jaw drop.
     → The sight was …

b ▶07.02 Match the words in the boxes to make compound adjectives that can replace the definitions in *italics*. Use some words more than once. Listen and check.

half short hair	sighted /saɪtɪd/ headed /hedɪd/
absent narrow	raising /reɪzɪŋ/ hearted /hɑːtɪd/
light mind	boggling /bɒglɪŋ/ minded /maɪndɪd/

1. Everyone in the village disapproves of my lifestyle. They're all so *unwilling to accept different ideas*.
2. He agreed to help us move the furniture, but it was very *lacking in enthusiasm*.
3. He may forget to phone you. He's rather *likely to forget things because he's thinking about something else*.
4. Can you tell me what that sign says? I'm afraid I'm *unable to see distant things clearly*.
5. After eating nothing for ten hours, I began to feel a bit *as if I might lose my balance*.
6. I'm fed up with serious films. I'd like to see something more *happy and not too serious*.
7. The brakes on the bus weren't working properly, so it was a *terrifying* journey.
8. Did you know there are 100 billion stars just in our own galaxy? It's *almost impossible to imagine*.

c ▶07.03 **Pronunciation**

1. Listen to the two pairs of compound adjectives. <u>Underline</u> the main stress. Is it on the first or the second word?

   mind-boggling   open-minded
   heartwarming   short-sighted

2. <u>Underline</u> the main stress in these patterns. Practise saying the compound adjectives in **a**.
   - adjective + body part + -ed
   - body part + present participle

d 💬 Find someone in the class who:
1. is left-handed
2. ate something mouthwatering yesterday
3. has done a backbreaking job at some time in their life
4. thinks they're open-minded
5. thinks they're absent-minded
6. has been on a hair-raising journey
7. knows a mind-boggling fact
8. has never felt tongue-tied

e ≫ Now go back to p. 81.

8B Ageing and health

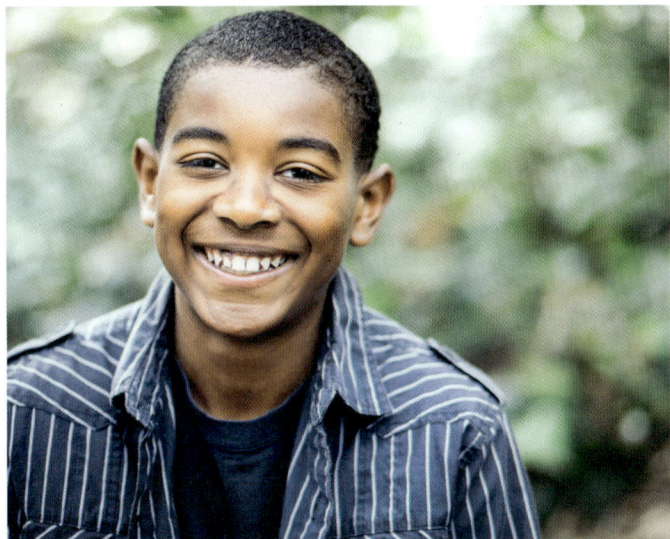

a ▶ 08.07 Listen to the words and phrases in the box.

> a glowing complexion   smooth skin   saggy skin
> oily skin   dry skin   wrinkles / fine lines   freckles
> a rash   blotches   spots/acne   firm skin   clear skin

Which words in the box are usually associated with … ?

- youthful skin
- mature skin
- all ages

b Complete the collocations in **bold** with as many words and phrases as possible from the box in **a**. Compare your ideas with a partner. Are they the same?
1 Sunbathing can **cause** …
2 If you have an allergic reaction, your skin might **come out in** …
3 **Anti-ageing creams** are designed to **prevent** …
4 Young people are often **prone to** …
5 Most people hate it when they start **getting** …
6 A **facial** can be helpful if you **have** …
7 If you want to be a model, it helps to **have** …

Vocabulary Focus

c ▶ 08.08 Match 1–9 with a–i. Listen and check.
1 ☐ He was **showing his age**. His
2 ☐ Her **eyesight is deteriorating** and
3 ☐ **Yellowing teeth**? Try our new
4 ☐ **Moisturising** daily combined with **weekly facials**
5 ☐ **Tooth loss** and **heart trouble** are
6 ☐ **Strengthening** and **toning** exercises
7 ☐ **Poor circulation** can be improved by
8 ☐ **Weight loss** can be aided by
9 ☐ There's no need to resort to painful **injections**

a **whitening** toothpaste. You'll be amazed.
b **regular cardiovascular exercise**.
c **eating a varied and balanced diet**.
d helps to **tighten** and **plump** the skin.
e hair was **thinning** and **greying** around the temples.
f like yoga and Pilates help to give you energy.
g or **plastic surgery**.
h not inevitable parts of ageing.
i she**'s got arthritis** in her knees.

d Look at the words and phrases in **bold** in **c**. Complete the table.

Anti-ageing treatments/effects	
Superficial effects of ageing	
Health problems caused by ageing	
Healthy living	

e 💬 Answer the questions about the things in **d**.
1 What anti-ageing techniques do you think are reasonable steps to take to stop the ageing process?
2 Do you think that any of the superficial effects of ageing can be prevented/cured?
3 Which health problems caused by ageing have affected people you know? What happened?
4 Which healthy living technique is the most important? Can you add any more to the table?

f ≫ Now go to p. 96.

165

9B Describing buildings

a ▶ 09.10 Complete the sentences with the adjectives in the box. Listen and check.

imposing /ɪmˈpəʊzɪŋ/	nondescript /ˈnɒndɪskrɪpt/	graceful /ˈɡreɪsfəl/
innovative /ˈɪnəvətɪv/	tasteless /ˈteɪstləs/	over the top /ˌəʊvə ðə ˈtɒp/
out of place /aʊt əv ˈpleɪs/	stunning /ˈstʌnɪŋ/	dated /ˈdeɪtɪd/

1 The council favoured an original design by a young architect because they wanted a striking and _____ town hall to bring a modern edge to their city.
2 As the town is fairly small, the large castle on the hill is really too _____ and seems _____.
3 I'm sorry, but there's nothing remarkable or new about the design of those houses – they're totally _____ and pretty _____.
4 I really like the gold leaf in the ceiling decorations, but for some people it's _____ and _____.
5 The _____, elegant lines of the building are very pleasing to the eye. It's _____!

b ▶ 09.11 Match words 1–12 with the pictures below. Listen and check.

1 ☐ cabin /ˈkabɪn/
2 ☐ skyscraper /ˈskaɪskreɪpə/
3 ☐ power station /ˈpaʊə steɪʃən/
4 ☐ housing estate /ˈhaʊzɪŋ ɪsteɪt/
5 ☐ warehouse /ˈweəhaʊs/
6 ☐ tower block /ˈtaʊə blɒk/
7 ☐ penthouse /ˈpenthaʊs/
8 ☐ studio /ˈstjuːdiəʊ/
9 ☐ bungalow /ˈbʌŋɡələʊ/
10 ☐ semi-detached /semidɪˈtatʃt/
11 ☐ mansion /ˈmanʃən/
12 ☐ retail park /ˈriːteɪl pɑːk/

c Put the words in **b** in these groups.
1 places that can be homes
2 places that are businesses
3 places that can be both

d 💬 Discuss the questions.
1 Which residential buildings are common in your country? Which are less common?
2 If you had a lot of money, would you live in a mansion, a penthouse or neither? Why?
3 If you had to live in a small space, would you prefer a cabin or a studio? Why?

e ⟫ Now go back to p. 107.

Vocabulary Focus

10A Communication verbs

a ▶10.02 Complete the sentences with the verbs in the box. Listen and check.

> address /əˈdres/   presented /prɪˈzentɪd/   go into
> demonstrated /ˈdemənstreɪtɪd/   made
> move on to   illustrate /ˈɪləstreɪt/

1 She _____ **her understanding** of complex social issues by explaining them in everyday language.
2 I've been invited to _____ **an audience** of business experts at a conference in London.
3 If you sense the audience is getting bored, you should _____ **a new subject** to keep their interest up.
4 Every time she got the wrong slide, she _____ **comments under her breath** that I couldn't hear.
5 She _____ **key information** in easy-to-read tables.
6 It really helps if you can _____ **the points** you want to make with specific examples.
7 Don't _____ **too much detail** during your presentation – people can only process so much new information.

b Match the phrases in **bold** in 1–8 with the definitions a–h.

1 ☐ She began by **paying tribute to** all the teachers who had inspired her throughout her school years.
2 ☐ During the speech, he **asserted** his right to express his opinion even if it wasn't a popular one.
3 ☐ He **backed up** the arguments he made by providing examples from recent research.
4 ☐ She **summarised** the key ideas in her presentation with a list of bullet points.
5 ☐ He saw his speech as an opportunity to **voice concerns about** the rise in crime in his neighbourhood.
6 ☐ The leader of the opposition **attacked** government policies in a speech that focused on the rise in unemployment.
7 ☐ In her presentation, she **sold the idea** of more flexible working hours to her managers.
8 ☐ She **concluded** by encouraging more people to try one of their free community education courses.

a   to criticise a person or people strongly
b   to say the most important facts in a short and clear way
c   to publicly praise somebody in front of an audience
d   to end a speech or presentation
e   to persuade a person or people that something is a good plan
f   to publicly say what you think about worrying issues
g   to prove that something is true
h   to make a statement strongly

c 💬 Think of people you know or in the media who do / have done the things below. Tell a partner about what happened.

1 attack government policy
2 have paid tribute to another person
3 often go into too much detail
4 sometimes make comments under their breath
5 often voice concerns about something
6 sell their ideas well

d 💬 Discuss the questions.

1 Have you ever addressed an audience of more than 100 people? If so, how did it feel? If not, how would you feel doing this?
2 If you were giving a presentation, what could you use to illustrate the finer points of a topic to other people?
3 Do you ever make throwaway remarks? If so, do other people take them seriously? If not, why don't you do this?
4 Who's an influential person from your past that you would feel comfortable paying tribute to? What would you say about them?
5 What do you think is a good way to back up your opinion on something?

e ⟫ Now go back to p. 116.

10B Superstitions, customs and beliefs

a ▶10.11 Complete the sentences with the words and phrases in the box. Listen and check.

> make a wish   traditionally   customary   good fortune
> good luck charm   ward off evil

1. She wore a _____ around her neck until the day she died at the ripe old age of 104.
2. I had the _____ to invest at exactly the right time and made millions.
3. The cautionary tales are _____ told by each generation of parents to teach their children morality.
4. It is _____ to decorate the house with branches from pine trees at this time of year.
5. They sprinkle the beans and then sweep every room to banish demons and _____ .
6. Children _____ and try to blow out the candles. It will come true if they manage to blow them all out.

b ▶10.12 The words in the box are all used for talking about beliefs. Tick (✓) the ones you think you know. Try saying the words. Then listen and check.

gullible /ˈgʌləbəl/	convinced /kənˈvɪnst/
plausible /ˈplɔːzəbəl/	convincing /kənˈvɪnsɪŋ/
persuasive /pəˈsweɪsɪv/	far-fetched /fɑːˈfetʃt/
dubious /ˈdjuːbiəs/	

c Use the words in **b** to replace the definitions below in *italics*. Use a dictionary to help you. There may be more than one possible answer. Which words are very similar in meaning?

1. My friend says a fortune teller's advice led him to success, but I don't find this very *easy to believe*.
2. People who believe in good luck charms must be very *ready to believe anything people tell them*.
3. When she talks about magic, I'm sure what she says is true. She's very *able to make other people believe her*.
4. The idea that horseshoes bring you luck doesn't seem very *likely to be true* to me.
5. I think most things that fortune tellers say are *unlikely to be true*, to say the least.
6. My grandmother was absolutely *certain in her belief* that black cats were unlucky.
7. People's stories about seeing ghosts usually sound rather *difficult to believe* to me.

d Discuss the questions.

1. Which of the beliefs in the pictures 1–3 do you find … ?
   • convincing   • plausible   • dubious   • far-fetched
2. As a child, how gullible were you? Can you think of an example?
3. Who do you know (personally or someone well known) who you'd describe as a persuasive person?
4. 'People who are convinced they're right are usually wrong.' How true do you think this is?

e ▶▶ Now go back to p. 119.

---

1 If you blow out all your birthday candles with one breath, your wish will come true.

2 They say that black cats are unlucky.

3 Some people believe that four-leaf clovers bring good luck.

WRITING FOCUS

1D Expressing opinions

Disagreement	Agreement
That's nonsense.	You're spot on …
That simply isn't true.	That makes a lot of sense.
There's no way …	You've hit the nail on the head.
You're missing the point.	I would go along with that.
That's easy to say, but …	
How can you possibly think that?	
That's a load of rubbish.	
That doesn't make sense.	

Uncertainty	Partial agreement/disagreement
I'm in two minds about this/that.	You've got a point, but …
I've got mixed feelings about this/that.	On the other hand, I do feel …
	It's true that … but …
	I agree up to a point …

a Read Eva's post and then complete the replies (1–6). Check your answers in the table.

b Which of the replies include words or phrases that soften the opinion? What words or phrases could you add to soften the other opinions?

c 💬 Which opinion do you agree with the most? Which opinion do you agree with the least? Why?

d ≫ Now go to p. 17.

EVA

The trouble with English is it's such a complicated, difficult language and it doesn't have any rules. I think they should create a simpler form of English that could be used internationally and would be easier to learn. It should definitely have simpler grammar, maybe just three tenses. And a more sensible spelling system!

Or they should choose an easier language to be the international language, like Spanish, say. Half the world speaks Spanish already. Or how about Swahili or Malaysian? They've both got nice, simple grammar.

1 How **can you** _____ that? You're completely **missing** _____. English is a beautiful, rich language, and that's exactly why people want to learn it.

2 Well, **that's easy** _____, but you can't just 'create' a language. People speak the languages they choose to. And you say 'half the world speaks Spanish'. Well, **that simply** _____ – 450 million people isn't half the world!

3 I must say I think **you're** _____ about the difficult spelling. I had to learn English in school, so **I'd definitely** _____ **with that**! But **I've got** _____ **about** simplifying the grammar – it would make it easier to learn, but I don't think you can express complex ideas using just three tenses.

4 I'm sorry, but **that's** _____. Of course English has rules – all languages do.

5 What you're saying **doesn't really** _____. Why would you need to 'create' a global language? No one <u>has to</u> speak English, so if people speak it, obviously it means they want to and they find it useful.

6 Good comment – I think **you've hit the nail** _____. Spanish would make a much better world language. It's a beautiful language and easy to learn. I say go for it! (My mother tongue is Spanish, by the way! 😊)

169

2D Linking: contrast and concession

Offering alternatives	Comparing	Conceding
however	however	however
on the other hand	on the other hand	nevertheless
alternatively	by comparison	regardless (of)
Opposing	although	although
on the contrary	unlike	even though
	in contrast to	for all that
	when compared to	in spite of
		despite

a Complete the sentences below with the linkers in the box.

however   when compared to   on the contrary
regardless of   by comparison   even though

1 _____ the effort that has been put into planning the programme, attendance at activities has been disappointingly low.
2 I would recommend reserving a table at a local restaurant. _____, if we are concerned about the budget, we could organise a pot-luck dinner where everyone brings something to eat.
3 The social evening at the theatre was incredibly popular. _____, the turnout for the student party was extremely low.
4 _____ we used high-end caterers for the student dinner, the food was bland and overcooked.
5 Most students clearly indicated that the picnic in the park was not boring at all. _____, they said it was the activity where they had had the most fun.
6 Our social programme includes at least one activity per week. _____ programmes at other institutions, it is very full and extremely varied.

b Which other linkers from the table are possible in each gap?

c Rewrite these sentences using the linkers in brackets.
1 Even though the class was large, it was still possible to get individual attention. (despite)
2 The teacher we had was very strict. By comparison, my old teacher was very easygoing. (unlike)
3 I was very disappointed with the lunches. However, the evening meals were great. (although)
4 In spite of it raining every single day, I enjoyed everything that we did. (for all that)
5 In spite of several injuries, spirits were high among the groups. (nevertheless)

d Complete the examples with your own ideas.
1 Most students say that the social programme is an important part of their time at the university. On the other hand, …
2 Regardless of their heavy study commitments, students …
3 Feedback has generally been positive. Nevertheless, …

e ⟫ Now go back to p. 29.

Sacsayhuamán, Peru

3D Writing briefly

a Read the description of a visit to the citadel of Sacsayhuamán near Cusco. Where might you find this style of writing? Why? Choose more than one answer.
1 an informal tourist review written for a website
2 an official review written in a travel guide
3 a travel blog written for yourself or your friends
4 a message to friends on social media
5 a newspaper article about a visit to Cusco

> Walked up to the citadel in the afternoon. Lots of narrow windy streets, great view from the top. Took hundreds of photos! Fabulous place. Definitely planning to come back here next year.

b In the first sentence, the word *We* or *I* has been left out:

~~We~~ walked up to the citadel in the afternoon.

What words have been left out in the other sentences?

Writing Focus

c What words have been left out to make these reviews shorter?
  1 Not much to do here in the evenings, and food in most places overpriced. Quite a disappointing place to visit.
  2 Been to most resorts in Mexico but nowhere as impressive as Tulum.
  3 Best time to visit: late autumn, no tourists, great weather.
  4 Went to Budapest last year. Much more interesting and more reasonable prices.

d How could you reduce these sentences for an online review?
  1 It would be a great place for a honeymoon because it's so romantic.
  2 There was so much to take photos of. It was a good thing I had my camera with me.
  3 We arrived late and we couldn't find anywhere to eat. I wasn't very impressed!
  4 You should go early to beat the heat. There's a beautiful beach at the foot of the cliff, which is great for cooling off.

e Write a short review (about three sentences) of a tourist attraction you visited recently. Use the same style as in the review of Sacsayhuamán on p. 170.

f Show your review to your partner and answer any questions.

g ≫ Now go back to p. 41.

Tulum, Mexico

4D Showing time relationships

= immediately	The moment …
	The instant …
	No sooner had … than …
= a short time later	Before long, …
	… was closely followed by …
	Shortly after/afterwards …
= a long time later, or longer than expected	It wasn't until … that …
	It was only … that …
	Not until … (did) …
	In time …
	Subsequently, …

a Change these sentences, beginning with the words in brackets.
  1 I saw her paintings. I immediately knew she would be a famous artist. (The moment)
  2 He graduated, and then he got a highly-paid job in the City of London. (Shortly after)
  3 As soon as I started asking questions, she got up and left the room. (No sooner)
  4 We were both made redundant and then we decided to form a business partnership. (It wasn't)
  5 Years later I decided to take up horse riding again. (It was only)

b Join these ideas in any suitable way, using time expressions.
  1 We met – we fell in love.
  2 I got home – I realised that I'd had my wallet stolen.
  3 I arrived in New York – I began to feel at home there.
  4 We went into business together – I discovered that he had a secret life.
  5 She started training for super-marathons – she developed a pain in her knee.

c Compare your sentences in b with other students. Are your sentences similar or different in meaning?

d Write two or three sentences about each of these events, using expressions to show the time relationship.
  1 two events in your life that happened
  2 an event that happened a short time after another earlier one
  3 an event that happened a long time after another earlier one

  No sooner had I turned 17 than my dad bought me an old van to fix up. I didn't know how to do anything mechanical, but before long, I had treated the rust and painted the bodywork.

e Show your sentences to your partner and answer any further questions about the events.

f ≫ Now go back to p. 53.

171

5D Linking: addition and reinforcement

Adding an idea in a new sentence		Adding two ideas in the same sentence
In addition …	Furthermore …	In addition to …
What's more …	Above all …	As well as …
Besides …	… also …	Besides …
Moreover …		Beyond …

a Cover the table. Complete the sentences with one word in each gap. Check your answers in the table.
1 **As well** _____ doing online research on social media, companies usually contact previous employers.
2 Many people are careful about the information they post on social media. _____ **addition**, they often have a private profile under a different name that employers will not recognise.
3 _____ being unethical, using information from social media as a basis for discrimination against a job applicant is illegal in many countries.
4 The private life of employees should remain private. _____ **more**, employers have no right to try and control what employees do in their own time.
5 There should be laws to restrict how much information companies can look for. _____ **all**, they should be banned from trawling for negative information.
6 Companies argue that information that is freely available online can be seen by anyone. _____, they point out that applicants are free to do research on a company.

b Replace the words in *italics* with linkers from the table. Make any other necessary changes.

It is common practice for companies to get useful information about their customers when they sign up for a free offer. Customers accept the free offer, *and* they have to agree to certain terms and conditions that they don't usually read carefully. Companies are then entitled to bombard these customers with spam. *And* they might pass on information to other companies who will send out more spam.
It's always important to read what you sign up for and bear in mind that nothing is completely free. *And most importantly*, make sure you are aware of consumer rights in your country so you can challenge companies who use information about you in an unethical way.

c Add an extra idea to two of these sentences, using an addition linker or a reinforcement linker.
1 I always think carefully about what I write in emails.
2 A lot of companies do not allow their employees to access social media during work hours.
3 I always ask my friends not to post photographs of me on their social media pages.

d ≫ Now go back to p. 65.

6D Application emails; Giving a positive impression

Application emails

Dear (name) / Dear Sir/Madam
I am writing in reply to …
I'd be really/very interested in …, I'd very much like to …
I have / I've got (some/extensive) experience of …
I'm attaching …
(I'm) looking forward to hearing from you.
Kind regards

Giving a positive impression

I am very much in touch with …
This has taught me a lot about …
I played an active role in …
I have taken a keen interest in …
I'm good at …
I think I'd fit in / be good at / be able to …
I feel that, with my …, I would be very well qualified to …

a Look at these extracts from emails. Cross out one word or phrase in each group in *italics* that is less suitable for an application email.
1 I *believe / am certain / guess* that my knowledge of local sporting events will enable me to *do / write / contribute* well-informed reviews.
2 I am writing *in response to / about / in reply to* your advertisement, which *was / appeared / was published* in the March issue of your magazine.
3 I'm looking forward to hearing from you *in due course / in a bit / soon*.
4 I'm *an enthusiastic supporter / a real fan / a keen follower* of the local football team.
5 *Here are / I am attaching / I'm sending* some sample photos which I took recently.
6 I have *some / loads of / extensive* experience of restaurant work.
7 I *can be quite flexible with my working hours / am available at any time / 'm always around*.
8 I spent some time working on a school magazine and I learned some *relevant / great / useful* editorial skills.

b Add additional expressions from **a** to the table.

c Read the job advert and Andy's application email. Rewrite it in a more formal style.

Dear Sir/Madam:
I am writing …

172

STAFF REQUIRED for a bookshop near the university. Flexible working hours, ideal as a part-time job for students.

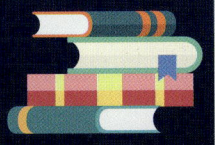

To apply, please call us or send an email.

Job application — Andy_CV

Hi there,

Saw your job ad in the student paper and I'd really like to work for you. I'm doing world literature at university, so I know quite a bit about books written by all kinds of people. I'm really into novels and travel books and that'll be useful, won't it? I've never worked in a bookshop before, but I've done café work and I've spent a bit of time working in a sports shop, so I know all about selling stuff to people. I'm also a nice guy and I've got loads of friends – I can chat to anybody.

So I think I'm just the kind of guy you're looking for. Here's my CV.

I could work whenever you like, mornings or evenings, it's all the same to me.

Hey, get in touch.

Andy

d Now go back to p. 77.

7D Linking: highlighting and giving examples

a Add a linking word or phrase from the table where there is a ^ in 1–7. Often more than one answer is possible.

1. The team is getting on better now. ^ they have decided to have a team dinner once a month.
2. It is already possible to perceive benefits from the training for the company, ^ the increased productivity of the team.
3. The team's productivity has gone up by 10%, ^ the increased number of completed tasks in the past month.
4. Everyone's active listening skills have improved. Masha ^ has become a good listener since doing the programme.
5. Sam and Claudio now work together more effectively. Sam makes a point of consulting Claudio about workflow issues, ^ prioritising tasks on the schedule.
6. The team now deals with tasks in hand. ^ they focus more on getting things done and less on team politics.
7. The programme has also resulted in an improvement in the way all team members deal with people outside the team, ^ their friendlier manner with support staff.

Linkers for highlighting and giving examples	
for instance	specifically
as demonstrated by	namely
as shown by	especially
such as	
in particular	

b You are the social programming coordinator for a staff/student social programme which is experiencing problems. Complete these sentences with your own ideas.

1. There has been little uptake of the programme lately. For instance, …
2. Overall participation in the programme in the past year has decreased, as demonstrated by …
3. Activities that involve … are especially …
4. Activities such as … are …

c Write sentences about the English language progress you and your classmates have made. Use linkers for highlighting and giving examples of particular achievements.

The ability of the class is improving, in particular our speaking skills.

d Now go back to p. 89.

8D Using persuasive language

Neutral language	Persuasive language
in the city centre	in the **heart** of the city
a different experience	a **unique** experience
high standards	**exacting** standards
well-trained	**highly** trained
make a dish	**create** a dish
We promise to …	Our **commitment** to you is …
our basic idea	our **core values**

> **Writing Tip**
>
> Many of the texts you read online are for promotion, and their aim is to persuade you to buy something, do something or go somewhere. Notice how they use persuasive language, which makes things seem better, more positive or more important.

a Choose the two words or phrases in *italics* in each sentence that work best as persuasive language.
1. Try one of our *freshly-* / *lovingly-* / *well-* prepared salads.
2. All our staff work to the *most exacting* / *highest* / *required* standards.
3. We *serve* / *offer* / *sell* light meals and snacks throughout the day.
4. Café Colombia is a(n) *nice* / *perfect* / *ideal* place to meet your friends after work.
5. You can have *complete* / *some* / *total* confidence in our specialist products.
6. Why not spend a weekend *away from it all* / *in the countryside* / *far from the bustle of the city*?

b The sentences below promote different products and places. Which are for … ?
- a music venue
- a duty-free shop
- an airport lounge
- a bank
- a language school
- a furniture shop
- a hotel

1. *With good furniture* and each with its own individual character, our rooms offer a *really quiet* atmosphere in which to unwind after a hard day's work.
2. Our beds are *of good quality* and will *be usable for many years*.
3. We have *a lot of* perfumes, and our brands are *known everywhere*.
4. The Basement is *a good place* for parties and live music events.
5. Our *well*-equipped classrooms and *good* teachers will ensure that your course is *different from the usual*.
6. *You're welcome* in our executive suite, where you can *spend* your time between flights in *comfortable* surroundings.
7. *We aim* to provide *a safe place* for your financial investments.

c Replace the words in *italics* in **b** 1–7 with the phrases in the box to make the sentences sound more positive.

tastefully furnished   a unique learning experience
manufactured to the highest standards
an extensive range of   an ideal venue
highly-qualified   truly relaxing   our mission is
globally recognised   a secure home   luxurious
stand the test of time   a warm welcome awaits you
fully   while away

d Choose a place in your town (a shop, a shopping centre, a sports facility, a hotel, a school or university). Write two sentences to promote it. Try to describe it as positively as possible.

e 💬 Read your sentences aloud and listen to other students. What positive features are they promoting?

f ⟫ Now go back to p. 101.

174

Writing Focus

9D Linking: reason and result

Reason	Result
One key factor is … / One of the (main) reasons is …	lead to / result in / cause / mean that …
… because of / due to … owing to (this) …	As a (direct) result / consequence …
… as a (direct) result / consequence of …	Consequently …
	… thus / thereby / hence / therefore …

Writing Tip

There are small differences in use between *thus / therefore* and *thereby*:
The government raised taxes, **thereby**/**thus**/~~**therefore**~~ raising a lot of money. = direct result of action
The government raised taxes. **Therefore,**/**Thus,**/~~**Thereby,**~~ starting a business is a bad idea. = logical conclusion

a Complete the sentences with the reason and result language in the box.

> due to   resulted in   thus   cause
> thereby   one of the main reasons

1 _____ people leave small towns is the lack of a lively cultural life.
2 Climate change has negatively affected rural environments and _____ urban migration.
3 At first, one or two family members move to the city and do well. _____ more family members join them, motivated by the hope to also do well.
4 There is sometimes disharmony in city neighbourhoods _____ the pressure urban migration puts on infrastructure and amenities.
5 Dramatic population decreases can _____ the social fabric of rural communities to disappear altogether.
6 The exodus of inhabitants from small towns leads to less demand for goods and services, and _____ the closure of many businesses.

b Correct the reason and result language in these examples.

1 The recent arrival of large numbers of people from the countryside leads to the current shortage in housing.
2 Increased pressure on city infrastructure often causes that there is a rise in taxes.
3 There are fewer jobs in small towns because the closure of so many businesses.
4 As a result the arrival of rural migrants, city schools have many more children enrolled.
5 Youth unemployment is very high in the town, thereby there's a lot of competition for jobs.

c Write four sentences about present or future changes in your neighbourhood, using reason and result language.

In my neighbourhood, a new sports centre will be built due to the fundraising efforts of the local community. As a consequence, …

d Now go back to p. 113.

10D Film reviews; Concise description

Ways to give information concisely	Examples
1 Add phrases between commas	Daniel Craig, **in a noticeable change from his 007 role**, conveys a menacing charm.
2 Add phrases before noun	**Veteran crime novelist** Harlan Thrombey dies in suspicious circumstances.
3 Use past participle clauses	Knives Out, **the latest film directed by Rian Johnson**, has a stellar cast.
4 Use present participle clauses	**Suspecting foul play**, they're trying to unravel the sudden death of multi-millionaire mystery writer.

a Use one or more of the ways shown in the table to make these sentences more concise.

1 The first *Blade Runner* film, which is directed by Ridley Scott, is a sci-fi classic.
2 When he realises that his father is probably still alive, he decides he must reach him at all costs.
3 Alfonso Cuarón, who is a Mexican director, is planning to make a new film.
4 Because she is determined to solve the crime, she works on the case night and day.
5 Jo March, who is the second oldest sister, is played by Saoirse Ronan.
6 Panem, which is a totalitarian country that is set in the future, is divided into 12 districts.
7 Because they are trapped in the mountains and because they know their food is running out, they send four people off to get help.

b Write about a film you saw recently.

Write some basic information about it (name, director, outline of the story) in only three sentences.
Include at least two of the ways shown in the table to make the information more concise.

c Read your sentences aloud, but don't say the name of the film. Can other students guess the film?

d Now think of a film you did not enjoy. Replace the words in *italics* with your own ideas and continue each sentence concisely.

Rian Johnson's latest film, Knives Out, is the *exciting and absorbing* story of … .
A critical and box office hit, the film has …
Daniel Craig is perfectly cast in the role of …
Chris Evans is also *superb* as …
The film provides a subtle portrayal of …
The plot focuses on …
It's an *original, thought-provoking* film, and *certainly worth seeing*.

e Now go back to p. 125.

175

Verb patterns

When followed by another verb (and object) (and indirect object), individual verbs follow different patterns:

verb + sb/sth + infinitive without *to*
She **makes me wash** the dishes.
I **saw the bus arrive**.

verb + *to* + infinitive
She **agreed to give** a presentation next week.
He **tends not to be** comfortable with new people.

verb + sb/sth + *to* + infinitive
I **asked the guests to wait** outside.
They **want him to come** to the party.

verb (+ sb/sth) + verb + -*ing*
He **admitted cheating** on the test.
He **hates us visiting** unannounced.

verb + preposition (+ sb/sth) + verb + -*ing*
I'm **concentrating on revising** this weekend.
She **insisted on him leaving** at three.

Some verbs have different meanings in different patterns.

admit	verb + verb + -*ing*
admit to	verb + preposition (+ sb/sth) + verb + -*ing*
advise	verb + sb/sth + *to* + infinitive verb + verb + -*ing*
agree	verb + *to* + infinitive
aim	verb + *to* + infinitive
allow	verb + sb/sth + *to* + infinitive verb + verb + -*ing*
anticipate	verb + verb + -*ing*
appear	verb + *to* + infinitive
appreciate	verb (+ sb/sth) + verb + -*ing*
approve of	verb + preposition (+ sb/sth) + verb + -*ing*
argue about	verb + preposition (+ sb/sth) + verb + -*ing*
arrange	verb + *to* + infinitive
ask	verb + (sb/sth) + *to* + infinitive
attempt	verb + *to* + infinitive
avoid	verb (+ sb/sth) + verb + -*ing*
beg	verb + (sb/sth) + *to* + infinitive
begin	verb + *to* + infinitive
believe in	verb + preposition + verb + -*ing*
can afford	verb + *to* + infinitive
can't help	verb + verb + -*ing*
can't stand	verb (+ sb/sth) + verb + -*ing*
care about	verb + preposition + sb/sth + verb + -*ing*
challenge	verb + sb/sth + *to* + infinitive
choose	verb + (sb/sth) + *to* + infinitive
claim	verb + *to* + infinitive
consider	verb + verb + -*ing*
continue	verb + *to* + infinitive verb + verb + -*ing*
*dare	verb + *to* + infinitive (be brave enough) verb + (sb/sth) + *to* + infinitive (challenge sb)
decide	verb + *to* + infinitive

demand	verb + *to* + infinitive
deny	verb + verb + -*ing*
deserve	verb + *to* + infinitive
discuss	verb (+ sb/sth) + verb + -*ing*
dislike	verb (+ sb/sth) + verb + -*ing*
encourage	verb + sb/sth + *to* + infinitive
enjoy	verb (+ sb/sth) + verb + -*ing*
expect	verb (+ sb/sth) + *to* + infinitive
fail	verb + *to* + infinitive
fancy	verb + verb + -*ing*
feel (sense)	verb + sb/sth + infinitive
feel like	verb + preposition + verb + -*ing*
finish	verb + verb + -*ing*
*forget	verb + *to* + infinitive (an obligation) verb + verb + -*ing* (an event)
forget about	verb + preposition (+ sb/sth) + verb + -*ing*
forbid	verb + sb/sth + *to* + infinitive verb + verb + -*ing*
force	verb + sb/sth + *to* + infinitive
get (opportunity)	verb + *to* + infinitive
*go on	verb + *to* + infinitive (do a new activity) verb + verb + -*ing* (continue same activity)
happen	verb + *to* + infinitive
hate	verb (+ sb/sth) + *to* + infinitive verb (+ sb/sth) + verb + -*ing*
hear (noise)	verb + sb/sth + infinitive verb + sb/sth + -*ing*
help	verb (+ sb/sth) (+ *to*) + infinitive
hope	verb + *to* + infinitive
imagine	verb (+ sb/sth) + verb + -*ing*
insist on	verb + preposition (+ sb/sth) + verb + -*ing*
instruct	verb + sb/sth + *to* + infinitive
intend	verb (+ sb/sth) + *to* + infinitive
invite	verb + sb/sth + *to* + infinitive
involve	verb (+ sb/sth) + verb + -*ing*
keep	verb + verb + -*ing*
learn	verb + *to* + infinitive
let	verb + sb/sth + infinitive
like	verb (+ sb/sth) + *to* + infinitive verb (+ sb/sth) + verb + -*ing*
long	verb + *to* + infinitive
love	verb (+ sb/sth) + *to* + infinitive verb (+ sb/sth) + verb + -*ing*
make	verb + sb/sth + infinitive
manage	verb + *to* + infinitive
mention	verb (+ sb/sth) + verb + -*ing*
mind	verb (+ sb/sth) + verb + -*ing*
miss	verb (+ sb/sth) + verb + -*ing*
motivate	verb + sb/sth + *to* + infinitive
need	verb (+ sb/sth) + *to* + infinitive
notice	verb + sb/sth + infinitive verb + sb/sth + -*ing*

object to	verb + preposition (+ sb/sth) + verb + -*ing*
offer	verb + *to* + infinitive
order	verb + sb/sth + *to* + infinitive
pay	verb + sb/sth + *to* + infinitive
permit	verb + sb/sth + *to* + infinitive verb + verb + -*ing*
persuade	verb + sb/sth + *to* + infinitive
plan	verb + *to* + infinitive
plan on	verb + preposition + sb/sth + verb + -*ing*
postpone	verb + verb + -*ing*
practise	verb + verb + -*ing*
prefer	verb (+ sb/sth) + *to* + infinitive
prepare	verb (+ sb/sth) + *to* + infinitive
pretend	verb + *to* + infinitive
proceed	verb + *to* + infinitive
promise	verb + *to* + infinitive verb + sb/sth + *to* + infinitive
propose	verb + *to* + infinitive
recall	verb + verb + -*ing*
recommend	verb + verb + -*ing*
refuse	verb + *to* + infinitive
regret	verb + verb + -*ing*
*remember	verb + *to* + infinitive (an obligation) verb (+ sb/sth) + verb + -*ing* (an event)
remind	verb + sb/sth + *to* + infinitive
require	verb + sb/sth + *to* + infinitive
resent	verb (+ sb/sth) + verb + -*ing*
resist	verb (+ sb/sth) + verb + -*ing*
resume	verb + verb + -*ing*
risk	verb (+ sb/sth) + verb + -*ing*
say	verb + *to* + infinitive (instructions)
see	verb + sb/sth + infinitive verb + sb/sth + -*ing*
seem	verb + *to* + infinitive
start	verb + *to* + infinitive
*stop	verb (+ sb/sth) + *to* + infinitive (purpose of stopping) verb (+ sb/sth) + verb + -*ing* (activity)
succeed in	verb + preposition + verb + -*ing*
suggest	verb + sb + infinitive verb + verb + -*ing*
swear	verb + *to* + infinitive
talk about	verb + preposition (+ sb/sth) + verb + -*ing*
teach	verb + sb/sth + *to* + infinitive
tell	verb + sb/sth + *to* + infinitive (instruction)
tend	verb + *to* + infinitive
think about	verb + preposition (+ sb/sth) + verb + -*ing*
threaten	verb + *to* + infinitive
tolerate	verb (+ sb/sth) + verb + -*ing*

*try	verb + verb + -ing (a new activity)
	verb + to + infinitive (unsure of success)
understand	verb (+ sb/sth) + verb + -ing
urge	verb + sb/sth + to + infinitive

want	verb + sb/sth + to + infinitive
warn	verb + sb/sth + to + infinitive
watch	verb + sb/sth + infinitive
	verb + sb/sth + -ing
worry about	verb + preposition (+ sb/sth) + verb + -ing

would like / love / hate / prefer, etc.	verb (+ sb/sth) + to + infinitive

Phonemic symbols

Vowel sounds

Short

/ə/	/æ/	/ʊ/	/ɒ/
teacher	man	put	got
/ɪ/	/i/	/e/	/ʌ/
chip	happy	men	but

Long

/ɜː/	/ɑː/	/uː/	/ɔː/	/iː/
shirt	part	who	walk	cheap

Diphthongs (two vowel sounds)

/eə/	/ɪə/	/ʊə/	/ɔɪ/	/aɪ/	/eɪ/	/əʊ/	/aʊ/
hair	near	tour	boy	fine	late	coat	now

Consonants

/p/	/b/	/f/	/v/	/t/	/d/	/k/	/g/	/θ/	/ð/	/tʃ/	/dʒ/
pill	book	face	van	time	dog	cold	go	thirty	they	choose	jeans
/s/	/z/	/ʃ/	/ʒ/	/m/	/n/	/ŋ/	/h/	/l/	/r/	/w/	/j/
say	zero	shop	usually	me	now	sing	hot	late	red	went	yes

Irregular verbs

Infinitive	Past simple	Past participle
arise /əˈraɪz/	arose /əˈrəʊz/	arisen /əˈrɪzən/
bear /beə/	bore /bɔː/	born /bɔːn/
beat /biːt/	beat /biːt/	beaten /ˈbiːtən/
bend /bend/	bent /bent/	bent /bent/
bet /bet/	bet /bet/	bet /bet/
bid /bɪd/	bid /bɪd/	bid /bɪd/
bind /baɪnd/	bound /baʊnd/	bound /baʊnd/
blow /bləʊ/	blew /bluː/	blown /bləʊn/
burn /bɜːn/	burned /bɜːnd/	burned /bɜːnd/
	burnt /bɜːnt/	burnt /bɜːnt/
burst /bɜːst/	burst /bɜːst/	burst /bɜːst/
cling /klɪŋ/	clung /klʌŋ/	clung /klʌŋ/
deal /diːl/	dealt /delt/	dealt /delt/
dwell /dwel/	dwelled /dweld/	dwelled /dweld/
	dwelt /dwelt/	dwelt /dwelt/
feed /fiːd/	fed /fed/	fed /fed/
flee /fliː/	fled /fled/	fled /fled/
forbid /fəˈbɪd/	forbade /fəˈbæd/	forbidden /fəˈbɪdən/
foresee /fəˈsiː/	foresaw /fɔːˈsɔː/	foreseen /fɔːˈsiːn/
hang /hæŋ/	hung /hʌŋ/	hung /hʌŋ/
lay /leɪ/	laid /leɪd/	laid /leɪd/
lead /liːd/	led /led/	led /led/
leap /liːp/	leaped /liːpt/	leaped /liːpt/
	leapt /lept/	leapt /lept/
lie /laɪ/	lay /leɪ/	lain /leɪn/
light /laɪt/	lit /lɪt/	lit /lɪt/
offset /ˈɒfset/	offset /ˈɒfset/	offset /ˈɒfset/
overdo /ˌəʊvəˈduː/	overdid /ˌəʊvəˈdɪd/	overdone /ˌəʊvəˈdʌn/

Infinitive	Past simple	Past participle
overhear /ˌəʊvəˈhɪə/	overheard /ˌəʊvəˈhɜːd/	overheard /ˌəʊvəˈhɜːd/
overtake /ˌəʊvəˈteɪk/	overtook /ˌəʊvəˈtʊk/	overtaken /ˌəʊvəˈteɪkən/
rebuild /riːˈbɪld/	rebuilt /riːˈbɪlt/	rebuilt /riːˈbɪlt/
rethink /riːˈθɪŋk/	rethought /riːˈθɔːt/	rethought /riːˈθɔːt/
rise /raɪz/	rose /rəʊz/	risen /ˈrɪzən/
seek /siːk/	sought /sɔːt/	sought /sɔːt/
set /set/	set /set/	set /set/
shake /ʃeɪk/	shook /ʃʊk/	shaken /ˈʃeɪkən/
shine /ʃaɪn/	shone /ʃɒn/	shone /ʃɒn/
shoot /ʃuːt/	shot /ʃɒt/	shot /ʃɒt/
shrink /ʃrɪŋk/	shrank /ʃræŋk/	shrunk /ʃrʌŋk/
shut /ʃʌt/	shut /ʃʌt/	shut /ʃʌt/
sink /sɪŋk/	sank /sæŋk/	sunk /sʌŋk/
smell /smel/	smelled /smeld/	smelled /smeld/
	smelt /smelt/	smelt /smelt/
sow /səʊ/	sowed /səʊd/	sown /səʊn/
spin /spɪn/	spun /spʌn/	spun /spʌn/
split /splɪt/	split /splɪt/	split /splɪt/
spread /spred/	spread /spred/	spread /spred/
swear /sweə/	swore /swɔː/	sworn /swɔːn/
sweep /swiːp/	swept /swept/	swept /swept/
swing /swɪŋ/	swung /swʌŋ/	swung /swʌŋ/
tear /teə/	tore /tɔː/	torn /tɔːn/
undo /ʌnˈduː/	undid /ʌnˈdɪd/	undone /ʌnˈdʌn/
upset /ʌpˈset/	upset /ʌpˈset/	upset /ʌpˈset/
wind /waɪnd/	wound /waʊnd/	wound /waʊnd/

Acknowledgements

The authors and publishers acknowledge the following sources of copyright material and are grateful for the permissions granted. While every effort has been made, it has not always been possible to identify the sources of all the material used, or to trace all copyright holders. If any omissions are brought to our notice, we will be happy to include the appropriate acknowledgements on reprinting and in the next update to the digital edition, as applicable.

Key:
U = Unit, C = Communication Plus, V = Vocabulary, W = Writing

Text:
U2: Solo Syndication for the extract from 'We all crave it, but can you stand the silence? The longest anyone can bear Earth's quietest place is 45 minutes' by Ted Thornhill, *Mail Online*, 03/04/2012. Copyright © 2012 MailOnline. All rights reserved. Distributed by Solo Syndication; Guardian News & Media Ltd for the adapted text from 'Experience: I've been to the quietest place on Earth' by George Michelson Foy, *The Guardian*, 18/05/2012. Copyright © 2012 Guardian News & Media Ltd. Reproduced with permission; Wright's Media, Inc for the adapted text from 'Why Some of Us Are Thrill-Seekers' by Angela Haupt, *U.S. News & World Report L.P*, 06/12/2012. Copyright © 2012 U.S. News & World Report. Distributed by Wright's Media, Inc. Reproduced with permission; **U3:** Adapted text from 'Pod Caribbean Children's Home - Belize - Volunteer Reviews': Linda and Malcolm – 2013 and 'Pod Community Projects - Ghana - Volunteer Reviews': Debbie – Child care, baby weighing and building. Copyright © 2013/2014 Personal Overseas Development Ltd. Reproduced with permission; Excerpt and Listening (Audio Script) from 'The Problem with Volunteering' by Daniela Papi, *BBC Radio 4: Four Thought*, 01/05/2013. Copyright 2013 © BBC Worldwide Limited. Reproduced with permission; Excerpt from 'Surviving malaria on the Mano River', by Will Millard, *BBC News Magazine*, 13/09/2013. Copyright 2013 © BBC Worldwide Limited. Reproduced with kind permission; Excerpt and Listening (Audio Script) from 'Journey of a lifetime, Mum Says 'You're a Long Time Dead'' by Will Millard, *BBC Radio 4*, 13/09/2013. Copyright 2013 © BBC Worldwide Limited. Reproduced with permission; **U4:** Excerpt and Listening (Audio Script) from 'Glucosamine for osteoarthritis; Alcohol addiction; Gut instinct' Dr Mark Porter, BBC Radio 4: Inside Health, 12/02/2014. Copyright 2014 © BBC Worldwide Limited. Reproduced with permission; **U5:** Guardian News & Media Ltd for the adapted text from 'Inside Halden, the most humane prison in the world' by Amelia Gentleman, *The Guardian*, 18/05/2012. Copyright © 2012 Guardian News & Media Ltd. Reproduced with permission; Guardian News & Media Ltd for the adapted text from 'Six surprisingly well-paid jobs' by Donna Ferguson, *The Guardian*, 07/08/2014. Copyright © 2014 Guardian News & Media Ltd. Reproduced with permission; **U7:** Excerpt and Listening (Audio Script) from 'A lie detector on your phone' by Ian Goldin, *Future 60 second idea, BBC World Service*, 16/06/2014. Copyright 2014 © BBC Worldwide Limited. Reproduced with permission; Excerpt and Listening (Audio Script) from 'A remote that can reduce street noises' by Anja Kanngiese, *Future 60 second idea, BBC World Service*, 26/09/2013. Copyright 2013 © BBC Worldwide Limited. Reproduced with permission; Excerpt and Listening (Audio Script) from 'Job candidates must wear masks' by Maurice Fraser, *Future 60 second idea, BBC World Service*, 25/02/2012. Copyright 2012 © BBC Worldwide Limited. Reproduced with permission; Excerpt from 'Rewire: Digital Cosmopolitans in the Age of Connection' by Ethan Zuckerman. Copyright © Ethan Zuckerman. Reproduced with permission of WW.Norton & Company,Inc.; **U8:** Excerpt and Listening (Audio Script) from 'Can extreme calorie counting make you live longer?' by Peter Bowes, *BBC World Service*, 24/03/2013. Copyright 2013 © BBC Worldwide Limited. Reproduced with permission; Excerpt from 'Segmented sleep: Ten strange things people do at night' and The myth of the eight-hour sleep', by Stephanie Hegarty, *BBC News Magazine*, 22/02/2012. Copyright 2012 © BBC Worldwide Limited. Reproduced with kind permission; Guardian News & Media Ltd for the adapted text from 'Aubrey de Grey: We don't have to get sick as we get older' by Caspar Llewellyn Smith, *The Guardian*, 01/08/2010. Copyright © 2010 Guardian News & Media Ltd. Reproduced with permission; **U10:** Text about Scott Berkun. Reproduced with kind permission of Scott Berkun.

Photographs:
The following photographs are sourced from Getty Images.
U1: Barcroft/Barcroft Media; Sam Edwards/OJO Images; Arseniy Rogov/iStock Editorial/Getty Images Plus; Mediaphotos/E+; Richard Drury/Stone; Universal History Archive/Universal Images Group; MCT/Tribune News Service; Image Source; Grant Faint/The Image Bank; Istetiana/Moment; Violet-blue/iStock/Getty Images Plus; Photo and Co/The Image Bank; Tim Kitchen/The Image Bank/Getty Images Plus; Alex Mares-Manton; Westend61; Jaturon Ruaysoongnern/EyeEm; **U2:** CharlieChesvick/E+; Alacatr/iStock/Getty Images Plus; Fabrice LEROUGE/ONOKY; Oliver Furrer/Stone; Yuin Lu Hoo/E+; Dimitri Otis/Stone; Westend61/Getty Images; Mayo5/E+; Steve Bly/The Image Bank/Getty Images Plus; Vuk Ostojic/Moment; Icon Sports Wire/Icon Sportswire; Brazzo/E+; Naumoid/iStock/Getty Images Plus; Westend61; Recep-bg/E+; **U3:** Phil Clarke Hill/Corbis News; Kryssia Campos/Moment; Nick Dolding/Stone; Demerzel21/iStock Editorial/Getty Images Plus; Janet Kimber/The Image Bank/Getty Images Plus; Kike Calvo/Universal Images Group; Paula Bronstein/Getty Images News; Fairfax Media/Getty Images; MikhailSemenov/iStock/Getty Images Plus; Konoplytska/iStock/Getty Images Plus; DaveLongMedia/iStock/Getty Images Plus; Banjongseal324/iStock/Getty Images Plus; Daniilphotos/iStock/Getty Images Plus; Halecr/iStock/Getty Images Plus; Franz Wogerer; Anna Gorin/Moment; Keren Su/Stockbyte Unreleased; Javarman3/iStock/Getty Images Plus; **U4:** Tomohiro Ohsumi/Getty Images News; SelectStock/Vetta; Kate_sept2004/E+; Westend61; Laurence Berger/iStock/Getty Images Plus; Fstop123/E+; Yuri_Arcurs/E+; Greg Blomberg/EyeEm; **U5:** GIUSEPPE CACACE/AFP; Junge, Heiko/AFP; Abzee/E+; Christopher Murray/EyeEm; KARYN NISHIMURA-POUPEE/AFP; Jetta Productions Inc/DigitalVision; GS Visuals/Cultura; LaylaBird/E+; GlobalStock/E+; Burnsboxco/iStock/Getty Images Plus; Wavebreakmedia/iStock/Getty Images Plus; SanneBerg/iStock/Getty Images Plus; Tim Robberts/DigitalVision; SolStock/E+; GCShutter/E+; **U6:** Getty Images/Handout/Getty Images Entertainment; Mireya Acierto/Getty Images Entertainment; Igor Ustynskyy/Moment; Jesus Trillo Lago/iStock/Getty Images Plus; Westend61; Plume Creative/DigitalVision; Simonkr/E+; RUNSTUDIO/Moment; Jose Luis Pelaez Inc/DigitalVision; Authentic Images/iStock/Getty Images Plus; Mixetto/E+; 10'000 Hours/DigitalVision; Kali9/E+; **U7:** Arman Zhenikeyev/Corbis; Colin Anderson Productions pty ltd/DigitalVision; YakobchukOlena/iStock/Getty Images Plus; Scharfsinn86/iStock/Getty Images Plus; William Taufic/The Image Bank; Jacobs Stock Photography Ltd/DigitalVision; Jose Luis Pelaez Inc/DigitalVision; Westend61; Johner Images; Roydee/E+; MarianVejcik/iStock/Getty Images Plus; Creative-Family/iStock/Getty Images Plus; Hinterhaus Productions/DigitalVision; Andresr/E+; Muntz/The Image Bank/Getty Images Plus; Sturti/E+; ColorBlind Images/The Image Bank/Getty Images Plus; Philipp Nemenz/DigitalVision; Jupiterimages/PHOTOS.com>>/Getty Images Plus; Klaus Tiedge; **U8:** Kupicoo/E+; Tara Moore/Stone; Skaman306/Moment; Monkeybusinessimages/iStock/Getty Images Plus; JohnnyGreig/iStock/Getty Images Plus; Westend61; Ajr_images/iStock/Getty Images Plus; BSIP/UIG; Motortion/iStock/Getty Images Plus; Cuiphoto/iStock/Getty Images Plus; GlobalP/iStock/Getty Images Plus; DanielPrudek/iStock/Getty Images Plus; GMint/iStock/Getty Images Plus; Evgeniy1/iStock/Getty Images Plus; Hindustan Times; Malikov Aleksandr/iStock/Getty Images Plus; SergeyChayko/iStock/Getty Images Plus; Fascinadora/iStock/Getty Images Plus; Supamas Ihakjit/iStock/Getty Images Plus; Simonlong/Moment; Jasmin Merdan/Moment; BURCU ATALAY TANKUT/Moment; Thomas Barwick/Photodisc; By_nicholas/E+; Karamba70/iStock/Getty Images Plus; **U9:** VCG/Visual China Group; Barcroft Media; Alastair James/iStock Editorial/Getty Images Plus; Jeff Greenberg/Universal Images Group; Education Images/Universal Images Group; Portland Press Herald; VvoeVale/iStock Editorial/Getty Images Plus; Katatonia82/iStock Editorial/Getty Images Plus; Lukasz Wisniewski/EyeEm; NurPhoto; Domingo Leiva/Moment; S. Greg Panosian/E+; KAZUHIRO NOGI/AFP; Jay Rumph/500px; Terence Lee/Moment; Photofusion/Universal Images Group; David Clapp/Stone; Chameleonseye/iStock/Getty Images Plus; Mihailomilovanovic/E+; Mark Meredith/Moment; iShootPhotosLLC/iStock Unreleased; **U10:** JASON CONNOLLY/AFP; E. Neitzel/WireImage; Paul Bruinooge/Patrick McMullan; Isa Foltin/WireImage; Alberto E. Rodriguez/Getty Images Entertainment; Ned Frisk; Klaus Vedfelt/DigitalVision; SDI Productions/E+; Cmannphoto/E+; Klikk/iStock/Getty Images Plus; Filipefrazao/iStock/Getty Images Plus; YinYang/iStock/Getty Images Plus; Mirrorpix; Simon Stacpoole/Offside; Atsushi Tomura/Getty Images Sport; Julian Finney/Getty Images Sport; Mediaphotos/E+; Axelle/Bauer-Griffin/Contributor/Filmmagic; Amanda Edwards/WireImage; **C:** Teeramet Thanomkiat/EyeEm; Dean Mitchell/E+; Bertram Henry/Stone/Getty Images Plus; Westend61; PhotoAlto/Frederic Cirou/PhotoAlto Agency RF Collections; AndreyPopov/iStock/Getty Images Plus; Njekaterina/The Image Bank/Getty Images Plus;